Language Teaching
A Scientific Approach

Robert Lado

Dean, Institute of Languages and Linguistics

Georgetown University

Language Teaching

A SCIENTIFIC APPROACH

McGraw-Hill, Inc.

New York

San Francisco

Toronto

London

To Alfred Jackson Hanna
historian and teacher
with gratitude

PREFACE

Teaching machines, television, taped courses, and other artifacts are often promoted as ways to solve the teacher shortage, yet their net result is a greater need for better-prepared teachers, since the teacher must use these new gadgets as well as new techniques.

Even as great libraries with all sorts of aids for the reader have not reduced the need for good teachers, so the new gadgets will eventually assume an appropriate role as aids to the learner and to the teacher. It is important at this time that we reemphasize the crucial role of the teacher.

Time was when knowing the grammar of a language from a grammar book was sufficient qualification to teach that language. With recent emphasis on the spoken word, the ability to speak the language has become a dominant requirement, but we should not make the mistake of assuming that any untrained native speaker is qualified to teach his language. Such a limited preparation is inadequate for effective teaching, and it is unworthy of the major role that the language teacher should play in the education of the student.

An educated person must have some understanding of himself and his fellow man and of other cultures as well as his own. No one can cultivate this perspective more effectively than the language teacher, since his subject is a foreign language and its culture. All other influences coming through the curriculum are encoded in the units and patterns of the student's native language and culture, and as a result they tend to be culture-bound.

This book is an introduction to some of the major areas the language teacher should understand in order to follow a scientific approach to his work. Linguistics, the target and source languages, human learning, techniques of teaching, testing, the language laboratory and other technological aids, reading, writing, cultural content and literature, teaching machines, and programmed learning are some of these areas.

A book can only introduce and clarify in part the basic ideas and advances now available or under discussion. The teacher as the central figure in this drama must supply other relevant information and insights in addition to the human qualities that make students want to learn.

Robert Lado

ACKNOWLEDGMENTS

A book such as *Language Teaching* goes through many stages of development. When the final draft nears completion, the author feels keenly the need to have it read and criticized constructively by those who can judge its value and accuracy. I am deeply grateful to those who did that for me and for you, the reader, and I wish to mention their names here so that we shall not forget.

Professors Neil J. Twombly, S.J., Victor A. Oswald, Gerald Dykstra, and Mrs. Bernarda Erwin made suggestions on content and style throughout the entire typescript. Professors James E. LaFollette and Pierre Maubrey contributed French examples. Rev. T. W. Walters, S.J., contributed German examples and other suggestions.

Alfred S. Hayes made suggestions on frequency response of laboratory equipment. Rev. Richard J. O'Brien, S.J., contributed improvements in the grammar and pattern practice parts. William A. Stewart checked the Portuguese phonemic examples.

Eli A. Alvarez, Sr. M. Anna T. Bayhouse, C.S.C., Gabriel Cordova, Jr., Rev. Henry Bedard, S.J., Rev. George R. Graziano, S.J., Mitsuo G. Hashimoto, Sr. Mary I. Hoag, S.S.J., David Korn, Eileen M. Scott, James S. Trichilo, and others contributed critical observations on specific chapters and German and Russian examples.

Sirarpi Ohannessian kindly checked the bibliography and added page numbers to the entries.

To those mentioned, to the authors credited in footnotes and in the bibliography, and to those who taught me in the classroom and through their writing—for example, Theodore Andersson, Noam Chomsky, Charles C. Fries, H. A. Gleason, Jr., Zellig S. Harris, A. A. Hill, Charles F. Hockett, Martin Joos, Tomás Navarro Tomás, Kenneth L. Pike, Henry Lee Smith, Jr., George L. Trager, W. Freeman Twaddel, Leonard Bloomfield, Edward Sapir, H. E. Palmer, Otto Jespersen, and many others—my sincerest thanks.

Robert Lado

CONTENTS

PHONEMIC SYMBOLS FOR ENGLISH, FRENCH, GERMAN, AND SPANISH

[Phonemic symbols, enclosed in / /, represent a range of sounds, or allophones, in any one language. When the same symbol is used for different languages, it may represent quite different ranges of sound. The examples represent single allophones.]

ENGLISH		FRENCH		GERMAN		SPANISH	
/i/	bit	/i/	prix	/i:/	Lied	/i/	piso
/e/	bet	/e/	pré	/i/	litt		
/æ/	bat	/ɛ/	mère	/e:/	Beet	/e/	peso
		/a/	table	/e/	Bett	/a/	paso
/ɨ/	children	/y/	sur	/y:/	kühn		
/ə/	but	/ø/	ceux	/y/	dünn	/u/	puso
/a/	father	/œ/	sœur	/ø:/	löst	/o/	poso
				/ø/	löscht		
/u/	book	/u/	sourd	/a:/	Wahn	/ey/	ley
/o/	/gonə/	/o/	saule				
	going to			/a/	wann	/ay/	hay
		/ɔ/	sole				
/ɔ/	jaw			/u:/	Ruhm		
		/ɑ/	mâle			/oy/	hoy
				/u/	Rum		
/iy/	beet	/œ̃/	brun				
				/o:/	Rotte	/aw/	auto
/ey/	bait	/ɛ̃/	brin				
				/o/	Bock		
/ay/	bite	/õ/	bon				
				/ai/	leite		
/oy/	boy	/ã/	lent				
				/oi/	Leute		
/uw/	boot						
				/au/	Laute		
/ow/	boat						
/aw/	bout						
/p/	pet		pour		Post		pase
/b/	bet		bon		Bett		base
/t/	too		temps		Tasse		teja
/d/	do		dans		dann		deja
/k/	could		car		Kamm		casa
/g/	good		gant		gut		gasa

ENGLISH		FRENCH		GERMAN		SPANISH
/č/	*ch*oke					mu*ch*o
/ǰ/	*j*oke					
/f/	*f*an	*f*aire		*V*ater		*f*ino
/v/	*v*an	*v*a		*w*eg		
/θ/	*th*ink					*c*ero
/ð/	*th*en					
/s/	*s*ink	*c*ent		e*ss*en		*s*eco
/z/	*z*inc	*z*èbre		*S*ohn		
/š/	*sh*ip	*ch*arme		*Sch*iff		
/ž/	vi*s*ion	*J*ean		*G*enie		
/m/	*m*et	*m*oi		*m*ehr		*m*as
/n/	*n*et	*n*ous		*n*ie		*n*o
/ŋ/	si*ng*			si*ng*en		
		/ñ/	ag*n*eau			a*ñ*o
/l/	*l*et	*l*angue		*l*ang		*l*ey
/r/	*r*ead	*r*i		*r*echt		pe*r*o
					/r̃/	pe*rr*o
/y/	*y*et	/j/	*y*acht	/j/	*J*od	/y/	*hi*erro
/w/	*w*et		*oi*seau			*hu*eso
/h/	*h*it	/ɥ/	*hu*ile	/h/	*h*aus	/h/	*j*amás
				/x/	Lo*ch*	

[ƀ] voiced bilabial fricative [an allophone of /b/ in Spanish].

[ ] brackets indicate phonetic notation without reference to phonemic structure.

Language Teaching
A Scientific Approach

Part 1

Language and Language Learning

Chapter 1   *Introduction*

We are witnessing in our time the greatest changes in the history of language learning—changes that reach into every aspect of this time-honored field of study. Formerly known by a few as a mark of education, languages are now studied by people from all walks of life. More languages are studied than ever before, and methods of learning them are changing radically. The goals of the past, usually limited to contact with selected items of literature, have broadened to include spoken communication with and understanding of native speakers on the widest range of human interests.

In attempting to explain this great movement one finds four main forces at work: dramatic advances in linguistic science, new techniques of teaching, invention and mass production of recording and viewing equipment, and an extraordinary interest in learning foreign languages. The significance of linguistic advances to language teaching will become apparent in the first part of the book, which deals with language and language learning. A systematic treatment of new techniques related to the theory of language learning appears in the second part, and a discussion of technological aids constitutes the third part.

BACKGROUND TO THE PRESENT

A brief look at past trends will help the reader to understand the present and possibly future trends. Of the many individual methods advocated in the past, let us consider three main types: grammar-translation, direct, and linguistic.

Grammar-translation Methods   At the end of the nineteenth century, language learning had become grammar recitation and dictionary thumbing.   The students defined the parts of speech; memorized conjugations, declensions, and grammar rules; and translated selections, using a bilingual dictionary or glossary.

With greater interest in modern languages for communication the inadequacy of grammar-translation methods became evident.   Students who devoted years to the study of a foreign language were in most cases unable to use it.   They developed a distaste for the language and an inferiority complex about language learning in general.

These failures are readily understood today.   Translation as a class activity was erroneously equated with understanding, speaking, reading, and writing, which are very different skills and need to be learned as such.   The ability to talk about the grammar of a language, to recite its rules, is also very different from the ability to speak and understand a language or to read and write it.   Often those who can use a language are unable to recite its rules, and those who can recite its rules may be unable to use it.   Translation can be defended as a valuable skill in itself, but not as a substitute for practicing the language without recourse to translation, and the description of the grammar of a language has its value to the linguist and to the student, but not as a substitute for language use.

Direct Methods   As a reaction against grammar-translation methods, there was a movement in Europe that emphasized language learning by direct contact with the foreign language in meaningful situations. This movement resulted in various individual methods with various names, such as new method, reform method, natural method, and even oral method, but they can all be referred to as direct methods or the direct method.   In addition to emphasizing direct contact with the foreign language, the direct method usually deemphasized or eliminated translation and the memorization of conjugations, declensions, and rules, and in some cases it introduced phonetics and phonetic transcription. The statements by some of the leaders of the movement—Viëtor, Jespersen, Palmer, and others—make stimulating reading to this day.[1]

---

[1] "Durch Wörterlisten und Regeln kann man nicht sprechen und verstehen lernen."   W. Viëtor, *Die Methodik des neusprachlichen Unterrichts*.   Leipzig: B. G. Teubner, 1902, p. 30.

"But the disadvantage of dictation, as of all written class work, is that it consumes more time than oral exercises."   Otto Jespersen, *How to Teach a Foreign Language*.   London: George Allen & Unwin Ltd., 1904, p. 96.

The direct method spread rapidly through Europe. It eventually reached the Americas and the Near and Far East. In the United States it did not gain a wide hearing, but it formed part of the discussions about methods that led to the Modern Foreign Language Study.[2]

The direct method overcame the two major faults of the grammar-translation methods by substituting language contact for grammar recitation, and language use for translation. The central idea of the direct method is the association of words and sentences with their meaning through demonstration, dramatization, pointing, etc. This is a valid view insofar as meanings can be dramatized. In supplementing and adapting it to different pupils and situations, the direct methods evolved and changed. Jespersen used reading selections to provide subject matter. Palmer developed a variety of oral drills that are the precursors of pattern practice. When used by competent teachers, the direct methods succeeded with whole classes where grammar-translation had at best helped the exceptional student.

Although direct methods are still widely used today, in the United States the advocates of the direct method, failing to achieve decisive results for a variety of reasons, drifted in the 1930s into the more limited goal of a reading knowledge.[3] This was a purely passive understanding of graded readings with dictionary help on difficult words.

The need for persons who could speak foreign languages during the Second World War showed the inadequacy of this reading knowledge as a first step in learning to speak or even as a first step toward efficient reading. Students taught only to read were bound to the mispronunciations encouraged by spelling and were not able to free themselves from the mistaken idea that pronunciation is a poor expression of the correct written forms, when actually it is writing that constitutes a poor representation of speech. Reading itself tended to remain inefficient because it did not operate through full control of the language.

The direct method assumed that learning a foreign language is the same as learning the mother tongue, that is, that exposing the student directly to the foreign language impresses it perfectly upon his mind. This is true only up to a point, since the psychology of learning a second language differs from that of learning the first. The child is forced to

---

"A certain number of regular sentences should be thoroughly assimilated in the early stages as primary matter in order to serve as model sentences to be developed by the student in the form of substitution tables." H. E. Palmer, *The Scientific Study and Teaching of Languages.* New York: World Book Co., 1917, p. 116.

[2] Robert Herndon Fife, *A Summary of Reports on the Modern Foreign Languages with an Index to the Reports.* New York: The Macmillan Co., 1931.

[3] Algernon Coleman, *Experiments and Studies in Modern Language Teaching.* Chicago: The University of Chicago Press, 1934.

learn the first language because he has no other effective way to express his wants. In learning a second language this compulsion is largely missing, since the student knows that he can communicate through his native language when necessary. Furthermore, with the first language the child's mind can be thought of as a *tabula rasa* where the patterns become impressed, whereas with a second language the habit patterns of the first language are already there, and the second language is perceived through the habit channels of the native tongue.

Linguistic Approach During the Second World War the problem of teaching foreign languages and English as a foreign language[4] for full communication was faced squarely. Linguists insisted on the imitation and memorization of basic conversational sentences as spoken by native speakers. They also provided the descriptions of the distinctive elements of intonation, pronunciation, morphology, and syntax that constituted the structure of the language, which gradually emerged as one mastered the basic sentences and variations. The powerful idea of pattern practice was developed; that is, practice that deliberately sets out to establish as habits the patterns rather than the individual sentences, particularly where transfer from the native language creates learning problems.

After the war the widespread use of tape recorders and other audio devices made it possible to provide authentic spoken models for oral-aural practice as homework. This together with contrastive studies of the target and the native languages written for the language teacher brought the linguistic approach to a high level of effectiveness.

With notable variations among different authors and groups, the methods and materials which today aspire to be up to date usually contain (1) basic conversational sentences for memorization, (2) structural notes to help the student perceive and produce the stream of speech and the sentence patterns of the foreign language, (3) pattern-practice exercises to establish the patterns as habits, (4) laboratory materials for oral-aural practice out of class, and (5) opportunity for use of the language in communication rather than in translation.

WHERE NOW?

If interest in languages should stop at this stage, present methods might well become frozen for generations. The interest in languages is strongly on the increase, however, and we can expect efforts to continue the

[4] C. C. Fries, *Teaching and Learning English as a Foreign Language.* Ann Arbor: The University of Michigan Press, 1945.

changes already in motion. It is important to look ahead to attempt to discover directions in which progress may lie.

Since much of present progress is due to advances in linguistics, it is tempting to look for stricter adherence to its techniques as the road to further progress. This, however, might actually stifle progress, since linguistics as a science describes those phenomena that can be objectively described within the limits of its postulates and leaves undescribed other phenomena that lie beyond. Language teaching, on the other hand, must proceed to teach language in use whether or not every aspect of it has been linguistically described.

In another direction, since electronic devices continue to improve, it is tempting to seek progress by having all teaching done by machines. Great activity, considerable expenditure of money, and a good deal of popular interest center on teaching languages via machines.

One can expect increased aid for the teacher from this direction, but language is more than patterns and words which might be taught by machine. Language is the chief means by which the human personality expresses itself and fulfills its basic need for social interaction with other persons. It is therefore difficult to see how the machine could replace the live, complex human being. In fact, one is repelled by the idea that research with this mistaken philosophy is encouraged or supported. More progress can be expected from research that deliberately sets out to find ways in which the machine can increase the power of the teacher rather than replace him.

There is little promise of progress from the exclusive use of native speakers of the language, small classes, or a particular technique of pattern practice. Neither is there promise of progress in deciding that linguistics, machines, and techniques have had their day and that we must return to the exclusive study of literature. Literary study is not concerned with teaching the basic nonliterary elements of the language, and yet these are precisely the fundamental matters that must be imparted in the language course.

A Scientific View Greatest promise lies in a scientific view of language learning and teaching. Language learning is complex. It ranges from the acquisition of simple automatic skills to an understanding of abstract conceptual and esthetic meanings, all occurring in the same sentences. And this learning must be achieved to an unbelievable degree of facility involving hundreds of articulatory changes and grammatical and lexical selections per minute. For this reason one is no longer justified in expecting any single development to solve all the problems of language learning. It requires scientific training to apply the best that is known to the teaching and learning of a second language.

A glance at the medical profession should be revealing for the scientifically inclined language teacher. The medical doctor knows physiology, anatomy, chemistry, and bacteriology, but in his practice he does not employ any one of these to the exclusion of the others. Armed with knowledge of the medicines that are effective for each disease, he applies them in doses that seem most appropriate for each patient. When a medicine produces undesirable side effects, he suspends it and substitutes another. He must do this in accord with standard scientific knowledge and not according to his whim and fancy. He cannot choose to ignore bacteria as a cause of disease, nor allergies, nor mental disorders. Before he prescribes a drug, he expects information on controlled experiments showing its effectiveness and safety.

Similarly, the language teacher cannot ignore the results of linguistics (the scientific study of language), the psychology of human learning, the age and education of the pupils, or the personality and capacity of the individual student.

A scientific approach to language teaching applies the best that is known to each particular class and its students. When a better way to teach something is reported, the teacher incorporates it into his courses, just as a physician incorporates into his practice new and more effective ways of treating each disease as reported in medical literature.

Professional Qualifications To perform professional duties one must be professionally qualified. The language teacher must be educated, at least to the level of his peers. He must have the general professional preparation of a teacher. And he must have the following special qualifications in the field of the foreign language he teaches.

Language The language teacher must know the target language well enough to be imitated by his students. For the nonnative speaker this means using freely not only the significant sounds, syntactical constructions, and general vocabulary but also many, though not necessarily all, of the details of pronunciation and idiomatic expression of native speech and writing. This level of proficiency for teachers is higher than that needed for purposes other than teaching. The nonnative speaker will have to devote a great deal of effort to the achievement of this level and to maintaining his proficiency once achieved.

The native speaker must be able to use a standard variety of his language in addition to his own dialect if there is a difference. Since students study a foreign language largely to become educated, it is fitting that they should learn educated speech. Not to do so would mislead their listeners into typing them as uneducated. A native speaker of Chinese is expected to teach Mandarin even if his dialect is another.

Proficiency in the target language includes the four skills: understanding, speaking, reading, and writing, but not translation and interpretation, which are separate professional skills essential for the interpreter but not for the language teacher as such.

Although a single standard variety of the language is fully adequate for speaking, the teacher should understand the various major dialects. He should of course be able to adapt his speech to the situations and contacts normally expected of an educated speaker, including changes of form required by social distinctions. These will remain within a single geographic and social dialect for speaking but would include the various major dialects for understanding.

The proficiency levels for reading and writing parallel those of understanding and speaking. The teacher must write in an acceptable style and understand various major forms, including literature generally understood by the educated public. The teacher must be able to write reports and letters and correct those written by his students, but he is not required to write literature in the esthetic sense.

Linguistics It is not enough to speak a language to be qualified to teach it. Even the native speaker cannot model the language or guide the students unless he can isolate and demonstrate its various elements. He must know the description of the structure of the language.

He must also know the linguistic facts of the language of the students in order to understand the particular problems they will have in learning the target language. He must know the chief differences and similarities of the two systems and the major vocabulary facts of the target language. Since dialect and language differences cannot be expected to be fully described for easy reference, the teacher must do partial linguistic analyses for his own information in dealing with the problems of his students.

In order to understand language more fully and to reflect this understanding in teaching, the teacher might familiarize himself with the major changes that the language has undergone in its history. This would explain, for example, why, in English, spelling does not coincide with pronunciation and how the irregular preterites came to be what they are.

Culture The language teacher must understand the intimate relation between a language and its culture. The student cannot go far into the target language without facing differences in cultural meanings, because the meanings expressed in a language are largely culturally determined. One cannot understand a language fully without understanding at least some of the distinct cultural meanings expressed through it.

This involves knowledge of specific facts concerning the culture and some understanding of the major patterns of thought, beliefs, traditions, and values that account for the way the people live and behave and give significance to their accomplishments.

Something of the history, geography, and origins of the peoples who speak the language is necessary for an understanding of the culture and is therefore a qualification for professional competence. For an understanding of the feelings of the people, it is necessary to experience some of their music, their humor, their daily living, and their holidays. An over-all acquaintance with the great achievements of their culture is also necessary, for their memory is part of the present.

Teaching techniques   In addition to the general preparation of a teacher, one needs special preparation to teach a language. The teacher must be familiar with audio-lingual techniques as well as with those that are used to teach reading and writing. He must be skilled in the use of such techniques in class, and he must have some notion of their effectiveness, special strengths, and weaknesses.

He should be familiar with modern theory and practice in the testing of language aptitude, achievement, and proficiency and should be able to prepare tests specifically adapted to his students. He must know something of the statistical interpretation of test results and should be able to read articles on language teaching and testing that contain statistical data.

Language laboratory   The teacher should be familiar with language laboratories and their use. This includes supervision of a laboratory, preparing exercises, and correcting the work of students. It does not include the engineering knowledge to install or maintain a laboratory.

This formidable set of qualifications represents a standard that many good teachers do not fulfill. Insofar as the qualifications are valid, they should encourage teachers to continue their preparation until the standard is met or, in some areas, even surpassed.

MLA Qualifications   The Modern Language Association of America has published a set of qualifications that includes (1) aural comprehension, (2) speaking, (3) reading, (4) writing, (5) language analysis, (6) culture, and (7) professional preparation. Each is described on three different levels of excellence: superior, good, and minimal. These qualifications represent the standards advocated by the largest professional association of language teachers of the United States. They reflect a growing preoccupation with the need for qualified teachers to meet the language needs of the modern world. The MLA Qualifications for Secondary School Teachers are reprinted for the reader on page 230.

Chapter 2

Language and Linguistics

An over-all view of language based on linguistics, as well as on experience in the teaching and learning of languages, will be presented first. This view is independent of any particular science, since language existed with its structure units and patterns before the sciences studied it. Secondly, we shall look at linguistics as the science of the description of language. In subsequent chapters we shall relate language to culture and to the psychology of learning in developing a modern theory of language learning for a scientific approach to language teaching.

LANGUAGE

Language is intimately tied to man's feelings and activity. It is bound up with nationality, religion, and the feeling of self. It is used for work, worship, and play by everyone, be he beggar or banker, savage or civilized.

Because of its pervasiveness, it is the object of study by many branches of learning. Linguistics, psychology, anthropology, education, and geopolitics, to mention a few, deal with language more or less systematically. To the language teacher and the linguist, it is the central subject of study, with the linguist concentrating on its description and the teacher on learning and teaching it.

The Structure of Language When a person speaks, he produces vocal noises that are associated by cultural tradition with meanings. A listener from the same language community hears these noises and understands the meanings.

The vocal noises are not just elementary sounds studied by physicists. These noises are complex structures, themselves made up of smaller units and combining in turn into larger sequences that follow specific patterns.

The meanings of these vocal noises are culturally determined. They are cultural abstractions into which the event eliciting the vocal noise fits. These cultural units of meaning combine in language, forming more complex units of meaning, or messages.

These units and patterns of sound associated with the units and patterns of cultural meanings constitute the system of communication that is language. This system is organized as a structure into which new sounds and experiences are fitted and from which they get their significance.

The Structure of Expression The structure of language has two parallel substructures—expression and content—and a web of associations between the two. *Expression* is the system of sounds, words, phrases, sentences as spoken, heard, felt, or imagined independently of their particular meanings. The expression system is most completely observable in spoken language. *Content* is the system of classified units of cultural meaning and their combinations and relations in a language. *Associations* are ties between expression and content; when units of expression are perceived, they elicit the associated units of content, and when units of content are experienced, they recall the associated units of expression.

The smallest unit of full expression is the sentence, not the word. We talk in sentences. Words are parts of sentences; they do not constitute full expression except when a single word is a sentence, e.g., *Stop! Go! John!* which are single-word sentences.

Each language has a restricted number of patterns of sentences. These patterns of expression are associated with sentence meanings such as "question," "report," "request," and "call."

Sentences are made up of parts such as subject, predicate, objects, complements, and sequence signals (e.g., "however," "and"). These parts are associated with meanings such as "actor," "action," "undergoer," "place," "manner," "time," and "relation."

Words and phrases function as parts of the sentence: nouns and pronouns as subjects and objects, verbs and auxiliaries as predicates, adverbs and adjectives as complements, and conjunctions, adverbs, etc. as sequence signals. These classes of words or parts of speech are associated with class meanings, such as "quality," "thing," "process," or "relation," by cultural tradition. The very same event may be treated as a thing, a process, or a quality according to the class of words into which it is fitted.

Phrases have a *head* (center or nucleus)—the word that stands for the phrase in a larger construction—plus modifiers and determiners, e.g., "a beautifully furnished *room*," or "the continued *vitality* of the program." The italicized word is the head; "a" and "the" are determiners. The grammatical relations between the head and the modifiers and determiners constitute the *structure of modification*.

Parts of speech are primarily classes of *words* that have certain features of form in common and perform certain restricted functions. The words are free units of expression in the sense that they do not have to occur exclusively as part of other words. Words are easily recognized as separable units of language even by speakers whose language has never been written. The fact that there may be some inconsistencies in the isolation of words by speakers cannot eliminate the word as an important unit of expression.

Words are made up of parts of words such as suffixes, prefixes, and stems. These smallest parts of expression associated with some meaning are called *morphemes*. The English word *books* consists of two morphemes, *book* and *–s*. The form *book* is a morpheme as well as a word, since it is the smallest unit of expression that associates with the meaning "book" in English. Since *–s* associates with the meaning "plural," it too is a morpheme. *Book* is a word because it can occur by itself independently of any other word. The suffix *–s* on the other hand is a morpheme but not a word because it must be part of a word.

Languages have a relatively small number of patterns of sentences and of phrases, and even smaller numbers of parts of speech, but they have large numbers of words and morphemes. The dictionaries give testimony to the great number of words that constitute the vocabulary of any language. Dictionaries chiefly list words and define their content.

Words and parts of words are expressed through distinctive sequences of sounds such as those in *kill, pill, bill, hill* which are very imperfectly represented by letters in alphabetic writing. The smallest segment of sound that can change one word into another—for example, *k, p, b,* and *h* in the words above—is called the *phoneme*. A phoneme is a range of sound which is perceived by native speakers as a single unit and functions in the stream of speech as a single distinctive sound unit.

The contrast between two phonemes is heard by the speakers of a language whether or not they know the term or its definition. The words *kill* and *pill* are heard as different words by the contrast between the phonemes /k/ and /p/. This is so even if the speaker cannot explain what he hears. The speakers of a language can usually find other contrasting pairs of words such as *keel:peel, kin:pin, kick:pick* which confirm the contrast. They hear phonemic contrasts whether they are illiterates or whether their language is written in syllabic symbols or word symbols that do not represent phonemes as such.

The definition of a phoneme may vary radically, and some may feel that the idea of a range of sound is not their view, but the phoneme as a minimum contrasting unit of the sound system which can change one word into another cannot be dismissed lightly by the language teacher.

The phoneme does not have a specific meaning. A change of one phoneme to another does not of itself change the meaning; it changes the word and this results in a change of meaning.

Phonemes are units of the sound system. The vocal apparatus can produce thousands of different sounds which can be observed in one language or another. Very few differences of sound, however, constitute phonemic differences in any particular language. English, for example, has hundreds of different sounds in the pronunciation of its single phoneme /k/. This can be observed by getting set to pronounce the word *keel* and feeling the back of the tongue pressed against the hard palate at the dome of the mouth, and the lips spread as in a smile. Getting set then to pronounce the word *cool* and observing the articulation of the first sound, also a /k/, we notice that the back of the tongue is now pressed against the soft palate at the back of the mouth and that the lips are pursed and rounded instead of spread.

Similarly, if one places a thin sheet of paper near the mouth and speaks out loud the word *kill,* the force of the released puff of air after the /k/ will blow the paper forward. Pronouncing the word *skill* the same way will not blow the paper away from the mouth or will do it only slightly. The /k/ of *kill* is quite different from that of *skill:* the first, heavily aspirated, the second unaspirated. Yet in English these different *k*'s are but one phoneme /k/. Their differences do not distinguish words. In some other languages, Arabic and Korean for example, similar differences constitute different phonemes.

Structural Distinctions The most important differences between two languages are not those of words, striking though vocabulary differences may be. The basic differences are in their structures since each language has its own system of sentence patterns, intonation, stress, consonants, and vowels.

Spanish has five simple vowel phonemes: /a e i o u/ as illustrated in the series *paso, peso, piso, poso, puso.* English, in one of its descriptions, has nine simple vowel phonemes: /i e æ ɨ ə a u o ɔ/ as in *bit, bet, bat, children* (in some dialects), *but,* the first vowel of *father, book,* the colloquial pronunciation of the first vowel of *going to* /gonə/, and *jaw* (in some dialects). French has fifteen vowel phonemes of which eleven are oral and four nasal. Of the eleven oral vowels, four are front un-rounded: /i e ɛ a/, *prix, pré, près, là;* three are front rounded: /y ø œ/, *sur, ceux, sœur;* and four are back rounded: /u o ɔ ɑ/, *sourd, saule, sole, bas.* Two of the four nasalized vowels are front: /œ̃ ɛ̃/, *brun, brin;* and two back: /õ ã/, *bon, lent.*

Russian has five vowels: /i e a o u/ in a system similar to though not the same as that of Spanish. German has fourteen vowels: seven short, /i ɛ a ɔ u y œ/, *litt, Bett, wann, sott, Rum, dünn, löscht,* and seven long, /i: e: a: o: u: y: ø:/, *Lied, Beet, Wahn, Sod, Ruhm, Kühn, löst.*

In their consonant systems, Russian stands out for its palatalized set of consonants, and Spanish for its trilled *r* in contrast with its single tap *r.* Also characteristic of the consonant system of Spanish is the use of [s] and [z], voiceless and voiced sibilants, as variants of a single phoneme /s/; [d] and [ð], stop and fricative variants of a single phoneme /d/; and [b] and [ƀ], stop and fricative variants of a single phoneme /b/, as illustrated by the Spanish words *sesgar, dedo,* and *bebo.*

The structure of a language includes not only the phonemes but the permitted sequences in which they may occur. English permits the occurrence of many clusters of consonants at the beginning of words and an even greater number at the end. Words like *street, splendid, scream,* with three consonants initially, or *world, burnt, first,* with three consonants at the end, are commonplace in English. Spanish, on the other hand, permits only a few initial consonant clusters of two consonants as in *plaza, credo,* and no final clusters. French has three initial consonants as in *splendeur, structural,* but only two-consonant clusters at the end.

Similarly, French has a phoneme /ž/ which occurs freely in initial position, e.g., *jour, jouer, jamais, journal.* English has a very smiliar phoneme /ž/, used in *measure, pleasure, leisure,* but it is not permitted in initial position.

Chinese, Thai, and other tone languages use contrastive pitch units as phonemes of pitch or *tonemes.* The words in these languages are expressed by segmental phonemes plus tonemes. In other languages, pitch units are not part of the word but of the sentence and the phrase. When the pitch units are part of the sentence and the phrase rather than of the word, they constitute *intonation.* English has four intonation phonemes and many patterns of intonation.

The patterns of word formation are also part of the structure of the language. English, French, Spanish, German, and Russian permit the use of prefixes, suffixes, stems, and compounds, for example, but the permitted patterns are different for each language. The patterns of formation of the Russian verb are especially difficult to learn, compared with those of English.

In the structure of the noun phrase in English, single word modifiers usually precede the head, and phrase and clause modifiers follow it. In Spanish, a normal position for all such modifiers is after the head. Compare the Spanish *"casa" azul* with the English *blue "house."*

The sentence *¿Es estudiante?* is a question in Spanish. The question is signaled by the intonation, since the subject has been omitted, and no other difference between the question and a statement remains. A comparable question in English, *Is he a student?,* can be expressed with the same falling intonation as a statement. The placing of the verb *is* before the subject *he* is then the contrastive signal for the question.

Relation of Expression to Content Although content and expression are parallel and closely associated, there is not a perfect one-to-one correspondence between the two. Phonemes have the power to change one word into another, but they sometimes produce structurally possible forms that have no unit of content associated with them. For example, changing the /p/ of *pest* to /r/ we get *rest,* which has word content; but changing /p/ to /d/ produces *dest,* which is structurally possible but is not associated with any specific unit of meaning in the content structure of English. Furthermore, the single expression *seal,* in which the phonemes remain unchanged, can relate to two completely distinct units of content: a sea animal or a stamp.

Language Variation Languages spoken by large populations show marked differences among groups of speakers. These variations appear geographically, historically, and socially. Everyone, for example, talks about differences between American and British English, the Spanish of Spain and of Latin America, Canadian French and the French of France. These are oversimplifications that exaggerate the differences between groups and overlook the differences within each group. There are great variations within the regions where English is spoken—England, the United States, Canada, Australia, Scotland, etc. These differences within a region are at times greater than those that might be ascribed to the English of the United States as opposed to the English of England. The same is true of Spanish in Spain and Latin America and of French in Canada and France.

The English of Chaucer and the Spanish of *El Cid* are very different from the English and Spanish of today. The languages have changed and will continue to change with the years. All languages change with time. When the writing system fails to keep up with these changes, it becomes archaic.

Different social and other groups within a language community show differences in their use of the language. In fact, one can even detect family differences and individual differences in the habits of speech. Linguists call the individual way an *idiolect* and the group way a *dialect*.

Furthermore, there are differences appropriate to various occasions, so that a person who does not modify his style to fit the situation will sometimes sound stilted and sometimes sloppy even though he uses the same forms.

We have an uncanny power to associate a particular dialect with the area or social group that speaks it normally. When we hear the dialect, we assume that the speaker comes from that area or that group.

These variations are normal to language. Through the facts of history the speech of a particular area—usually the political or cultural capital—acquires greater prestige than others. This greater prestige makes it a desirable dialect to learn or to adopt. Greater prestige should not be taken for universal appropriateness, however.

Bilingualism Every child learns as his first language that of his parents and his community. Many people learn a second language for purposes of formal education or because of historical situations.

Some individuals become bilingual through necessity, where two different linguistic communities are in contact. Switzerland and Canada are well-known examples. Bilingual situations are much more prevalent than is generally realized. We see them in Wales, the Basque provinces of Spain and France, the Southwest of the United States, Puerto Rico, Turkey, Russia, many African nations, and in fact in practically every country of the world.

The degree of control of the first, second, and even third and fourth languages is not necessarily comparable. The first language may be used only in the home, the second in school, and a third in religious practice, for example.

When each language has a well-defined function and is practiced in connection with that function, there is a more or less stable bilingual situation. When a second language is studied merely as a school subject without a clearly visible function, bilingualism is an unstable linguistic state, and the masses may be expected to revert toward monolingualism. Only a continuing effort to overcome this drift toward what comes naturally will maintain the bilingual-educated state.

Since one's language is so intimately bound up with one's nationality and the self, it is common for emperors—large and small—and empires to try to impose their language on their subjects. Through ignorance of how and why languages are learned, history is full of cases where a struggle between the dominant power to impose its language and the dominated nation to resist it and preserve its own language develops into bitter hatred that flares up intermittently and smolders for centuries. The many attempts to impose a language on a subjugated people by direct pressure have been resisted vigorously and have largely failed. Languages last longer than empires.

Writing Drawings and illustrations are not writing no matter how clearly they convey ideas. There is one essential condition for graphic symbols to become writing; they must represent units of some language. If they represent the phonemes of a language, even though imperfectly, they constitute *alphabetic* writing. English, Spanish, French, and German use the Latin alphabet; Russian uses the Cyrillic alphabet; and Thai uses the Thai alphabet. The symbols are different, but the three alphabets represent, even if imperfectly, the phonemes of the respective languages.

If the symbols represent the syllables of the language, they constitute *syllabic* writing, and the list of written symbols is called a syllabary. If the symbols represent morphemes and words, they are called *logographic* writing.

Writing, then, is the graphic representation of a language. It is usually an imperfect representation. The intonation phonemes are not generally represented in writing. The same letter may represent more than one phoneme, with resulting ambiguity. The letter *i*, for example, may represent /i/ in *to live* or /ay/ in *a live tiger*. Both English /ð/ and /θ/ as in *then* and *think* are represented by the same *th* in spelling. A phoneme may not have a specific symbol to represent it in the alphabet, as is the case of English /ŋ/ as in *thing*.

In the logographic writing of Chinese, the same symbol may represent a number of different words with resulting ambiguity. Good readers supply the missing elements from the context, but this does not alter the fact that the writing system represents the language imperfectly.

LINGUISTICS

What are the intonation, stress, and juncture phonemes of Spanish, French, or English? What are the consonant and vowel phonemes and their sequences in these languages? What morphemes and morpheme sequences are typical of each? What are their sentence patterns? In other words, what is their structure?

Linguistics is the science that describes and classifies languages. The linguist identifies and describes the units and patterns of the sound system, the words and morphemes, and the phrases and sentences, that is, the structure of a language.

The native speakers of a language are not aware of the structure of their language. Through folk traditions handed down to them, they may have the notion that this or that commonly used form is incorrect. They know that words have to be learned, but they forget that sounds, intonation, stress, and sentence patterns have to be learned also.

Linguists observe speech, describe it, classify it, and present its structure as completely, accurately, and economically as possible. Like other scientists, linguists have evolved their own scientific procedures and technical terminology. As in other sciences, there are disagreements among its specialists. They differ as to terminology and procedures, and they differ in detail in the description of particular languages.

The language teacher need not be too concerned with these differences. Some disagreement is a healthy sign of activity. The descriptions will differ in detail, but they are the basic data a person needs as he decides what he must teach.

Linguistic descriptions are divided into *phonology* for the sound system, *morphology* for the patterns and parts of words, and *syntax* for the patterns of phrases and sentences. Allied to linguistics is *lexicography*, which lists and defines the words of a language and presents the results in dictionaries.

Historical linguistics describes earlier forms of a language, while *linguistic ontogeny* describes the development of the language in the individual from childhood. *Contrastive linguistics* describes the differences between the structures of two languages.

Modern linguistics owes much of its impressive advances to the informant technique. A native speaker of the language is interviewed for considerable periods of time by the linguist, who elicits from him sentences and words that gradually reveal the structure of the language.

Phonology   In phonology the phonemes of a language and their variants (*allophones*) are described. The phonemes are represented by phonemic symbols enclosed in slant lines, / /, and variants are placed in brackets, [ ]. For example, a phoneme, /b/, and two variants, [b] and [ḇ], of the same phoneme would be represented by the notation, /b/: [b] [ḇ].

The linguist checks each suspicious sound difference to determine whether it represents two different phonemes or two variants of the same phoneme. If he observes that English has a voiceless sibilant sound [s] in *sip* and a voiced sibilant sound [z] in *easy, lazy,* etc., he has to determine whether the difference is phonemic or not. He does so by the technique of minimal pairs, i.e., he tries to find pairs of words that differ only as to the sounds in question. He soon finds such minimal pairs as *Sue:zoo, sip:zip, sink:zinc, rice:rise, ice:eyes,* in which the difference between each pair of words is [s] versus [z]. This shows that the difference is phonemic: that /s/ and /z/ are two phonemes in English.[1]

In Spanish, the linguist also observes [s] in *misa* and [z] in *misma.*[1] He must decide whether they are separate phonemes or only variants of the same phoneme in Spanish. After long search he comes to the conclusion that there are no minimal pairs for [s] and [z] in Spanish. He then tabulates the occurrences of each in the various phonetic environments in which they occur. If the environments in which [z] occurs are always different from those in which [s] occurs, he concludes that the difference is conditioned by these environments and therefore is not phonemic. [s] and [z] are then classified as variants of a single phoneme /s/.

In some cases the evidence is not conclusive and the linguist must find other data from parallel cases. His conclusions may be difficult to reach even then. The techniques and procedures for deciding such cases are found in the textbooks on linguistics and in specialized articles.

The procedures for determining the stress, intonation, and juncture (border and transition) phonemes are basically the same, but they are more difficult to execute. (See Chapter 8 for discussion of these terms.) Making a careful and detailed *phonetic* transcription of some connected conversational utterances will give pitch points, stresses, and junctures that may be phonemic or subphonemic. The linguist again looks for minimal pairs, i.e., words, phrases, and sentences that differ only as to a single item of pitch, stress, or juncture. He thus determines the minimum number of distinctive points (phonemes) that constitute the system. Having determined the phonemes, he checks the permitted sequences and describes them.

Morphology As stated above, the smallest part of expression associated with a unit of meaning is the morpheme. Thus the word *books* was said to have two morphemes (excluding intonation, stress, and juncture) because no smaller parts are associated with any specific meaning.

Morphemes are represented within braces { }, e.g., {book} {/–s/}. The slant bars inside the braces indicate phonemic script. When the same morpheme, say the plural morpheme {–s}, has more than one shape, e.g., /–s/ in *books,* /–z/ in *cows,* and /–iz/ in *glasses,* the alternation is represented as {/–s/~/–z/~/–iz/}. When two morphemes have the same shape, as do the plural {–s} and the third person {–s}, they are usually distinguished by a subscript, e.g., {–s_1} and {–s_2}.

---

[1] In some dialects this /s/ has an [h] variant in the environment illustrated. The example is valid, however, since the linguist began by observing [z].

The linguist identifies several types of morphemes: (1) bases or roots, which are associated with the core meaning, e.g., *book;* (2) inflectional morphemes that attach to bases without changing the class of words, e.g., *book,* a noun, plus *–s* gives *books,* still a noun; and (3) derivational morphemes that change the core meaning and often the class of the word, e.g., *book,* a noun, plus *–ish,* a derivational morpheme, produces an adjective, *bookish.*

Morphology identifies and classifies the morphemes and describes the types of combinations that build words in the language.

Syntax In syntax the linguist describes the patterns of arrangement of words in phrases and sentences and the matters of agreement among words. The fact that the word order of the sentence *Is he a student?* is that of a question in contrast to the word order of the statement *He is a student* is part of syntax. It is also a matter of syntax that the adjective precedes the noun in *blue house* in English but follows it in Spanish *casa azul.* Similarly, it is a matter of syntax that in French *nez, "nose,"* takes a masculine article, *le nez,* but in Spanish *nariz,* "nose," takes a feminine article, *la nariz.*

Contrastive Linguistics Of special interest to the language teacher is contrastive linguistics, which compares the structures of two languages to determine the points where they differ. These differences are the chief source of difficulty in learning a second language.

The linguist takes up each phoneme in the native language and compares it with the phonetically most similar ones in the second language. He then describes their similarities and differences. He takes up the sequences of phonemes and does likewise. Morpheme and syntax patterns are also compared and the differences described. The results of these contrastive descriptions form the basis for the preparation of language texts and tests, and for the correction of students learning a language.

Lexicography Good dictionaries, monolingual and bilingual, are difficult to compile. They require a good basic linguistic analysis for the proper identification, description, and classification of the words of a language. The task is complicated further by the fact that dictionaries must define the content of the words they list, and the techniques for the description of meanings are still largely subjective. Lexicography is the art and science of dictionary making.

Historical Linguistics Historical linguistics describes earlier forms of a language from documents and other evidence. When no written records can be found, it uses the technique of historical reconstruction by which prehistoric forms of a language are postulated on the basis of correspondences of later languages and dialects derived from it.

Historical linguistics, for example, traces the evolution of the Romance languages—French, Spanish, Italian, Portuguese, etc.—from the original Latin. It reconstructs the general features of Indo-European, the parent language from which came Latin, German, Greek, etc., by the technique of historical reconstruction.

Linguistic Ontogeny The study and description of the development of language from childhood in the individual is the responsibility of linguistic ontogeny. As yet this branch of linguistics has received little attention. Most of the studies of the development of language in the child have been made by psychologists and educationists. As a result they do not report the development of linguistic structure but observations concerning sounds and words without a clear relation to structure.

Linguistic Geography The description of the variations of a language over its geographic area is the subject of linguistic geography. The linguist in this case interviews native informants selected from representative points in an area. He elicits key words and expressions from them and eventually represents their renditions on a map. The dividing line for each difference is called an *isogloss*. When a good many isoglosses cluster at a particular line, they show a *dialect boundary*. A collection of maps showing dialects and isoglosses is a *linguistic atlas*.

Linguistics and the Language Teacher The relevance of linguistic information and training for the language teacher should be self-evident from the fact that linguistics provides the description of the sounds, words, and sentences he must teach and helps him to understand the linguistic problems of his students.

Chapter 3

Language and Culture

Language does not develop in a vacuum. A language is part of the culture of a people and the chief means by which the members of a society communicate. A language, therefore, is both a component of culture and a central network through which the other components are expressed.

Differences in cultural meanings across languages are a problem in learning a second language. The Eskimos of the cold Arctic regions have many different words for snow. These words express differences which are not normally implied or observed by the English speaker but are necessarily expressed in Eskimoan. An English speaker learning that language must learn what those words mean.

As the chief instrument of communication, language attaches specific words and phrases to the most frequent and most important cultural meanings. Since snow is important in Eskimo life, it becomes differentiated into more specific cultural meanings than the general one called snow in English, and specific words and phrases take on the function of representing those meanings in the language of the Eskimos.

A very comprehensive dictionary collecting these words and phrases and including also idioms, proverbs, names of heroes, well-known legends and stories, heroic deeds, beliefs, etc., would be in fact an excellent index to a culture. Such a collection coupled with a systematic analysis of the structure of a culture would constitute a most complete codification of its content.

CULTURE AND ANTHROPOLOGY

Culture From the beginning, man has been a social being and has lived in societies. In so doing, he has developed patterned ways of doing things and talking about them that facilitate the communication and interaction necessary for social living. When these patterned ways of acting, talking, thinking, and feeling become sufficiently uniform in a society and sufficiently different from those of other societies, they constitute a culture.

When a person comes into contact with people of another culture, he may notice that they speak a different language, dress differently, and have some characteristics of behavior that identify them as members of a different society. This superficial recognition of cultural groups different from one's own is essentially well founded, as there are indeed very different cultures within the unity of the human race. Japanese society, for example, has evolved a Japanese culture, which though similar in many ways to other cultures is sufficiently different to be identified both by simple observation and by more careful study as a distinctly Japanese way of life.

Japanese culture, being more specifically compartmentalized socially than that of the United States, shows patterns of behavior that reflect the social categories. Since age groups are highly differentiated, one expects and finds different patterns of behavior for each.

The average observer, however, misses the subtle differences between cultures that are less striking than those of language, clothing, and food, and he tends to assume that these differences do not exist. Unless he has had special training or has special insight, he will not understand that the differences are not merely matters of specific items, such as a particular way to prepare rice or bury the dead, but that those items are shaped into different patterns in an over-all system. Whether or not drinking wine at mealtime has any special significance or what that significance might be cannot be determined in the abstract without reference to the particular culture in which it occurs.

Cultural Anthropology Cultural anthropology is a branch of anthropology which seeks to describe the structure of a culture as completely and neatly as possible. To perform its task, anthropology, like linguistics, works within certain postulates and uses certain techniques of description for the collection and testing of cultural data and the identification of the units and patterns that constitute the structure of the culture. Cultural anthropology seeks not merely to portray a culture by recording it in greater or less detail but, more importantly, to identify its structure.

Cultural Anthropology and the Language Teacher Since the language teacher does in fact teach culture when he teaches a language and since in teaching a language he must touch upon the cultural content that language serves to communicate, he should welcome the information and understanding that cultural anthropology supplies.

This does not mean that the language teacher must teach anthropology or that he is or has to be a cultural anthropologist. Culture is not anthropology any more than language is linguistics. The language teacher teaches a language and the cultural content that is necessary if one is to know and use the language.

Cultural anthropology is useful to the language teacher in determining the cultural content of what he teaches. He must decide in addition how the cultural content is to be learned, the order of presentation, and what content beyond the scope of anthropology must be learned in a language course in order to contribute effectively toward the development of educated individuals in a society.

CULTURAL CONTENT IN FOREIGN LANGUAGE LEARNING

Goal: Expression and Understanding We define the goal in learning a foreign language as the ability to use it, understanding its meanings and connotations in terms of the target language and culture, and the ability to understand the speech and writing of natives of the target culture in terms of their meanings as well as their great ideas and achievements. This definition excludes the necessity of learning to act like a native but includes the need to understand what a native means when he says he acted in a particular way, and it includes the need to know what interpretation the native will make when he is told that someone acted in a particular way.

On the way to the attainment of this goal there are three streams of influence that affect the cultural content involved in language learning: (1) the romantic clichés and prejudicial distortions that often constitute the students' image of the target culture, (2) the literature and great achievements of the target culture, and (3) the study of a culture as a structured system of patterned behavior, that is, as the characteristic ways of a people.

False Clichés　Merely to confirm the false clichés, or stereotypes, of one culture regarding another is obviously not learning a foreign language and culture. It is enculturation of an undesirable kind, the very same kind that the learning of a foreign language is best suited to counter. Yet this type of cultural content is often found in textbooks and in the teaching of language in the schools. Such for example is the type of lesson that in a Spanish language class depicts Mexicans as always wearing gay sombreros, uttering romantic nonsense to señoritas, and endlessly dancing the Mexican hat dance.

This sort of romantic concept may counteract the distrust that one culture fosters when it pictures the members of another as lazy, deceitful, superstitious, and ignorant, but it substitutes the equally false notion that the other culture is always having fiestas and little else. When students taught these clichés have to use the language, they turn out to be both ignorant and unaware of the fact that they are ignorant. Learning Spanish with these notions will not contribute to understanding between the speakers of English and Spanish. There will not be adequate communication even when the student has mastered the sounds and the constructions of Spanish.

It is important not only to reject false clichés but to learn instead cultural content that is authentic. For this purpose it is necessary to understand the structure of cross-cultural communication so that the misconceptions involved in the false clichés may be exploded by pointing out the facts in their setting, that is, in the framework of the target culture, and not as they might be interpreted from the outside.

The understanding of the structure of the target culture and of cross-cultural communication is important also because we lack full descriptions of the major cultures of the world. The language teacher is in the predicament of having either to omit much of the target culture or to do some analysis and interpretation on his own in filling essential areas of content.

Literature and Great Achievements　So long as foreign language study was valued primarily as a means of gaining access, for educational purposes, to the literary classics of the target culture, it was sufficient and proper to consider these classics the only cultural material of interest to the language student. The term "culture," in fact, was used largely to denote the possession of the speech, knowledge, and manners of those who studied the classics.

The twentieth century, through its revolutionary advances in transportation and communication, has brought all but the most isolated of men in contact with other cultures and other languages. The purpose of studying a foreign language has changed from the narrow one of coming in contact with great literature only, to the broader one of coming in contact with the members of other cultures as well as with their literature, art, science, technology, and language. The cultural stream of the classics of literature has expanded to include great achievements in other fields, but it has refused to admit the relevance of the ways of a people in the cultural content of the language course.

On the surface, then, there seems to be a conflict between the study of language for its literature and great achievements on one hand and the anthropological view of culture on the other. The anthropological side argues that its view is necessary to understand literature and great achievements. The literary side contends that literature has universal validity.

In actual fact, if our goal is to understand and to express the target language and culture, both points of view complement each other. Contact with at least some of the great literary and other achievements of the target culture must remain an important objective in language learning because of the many references that the language makes to them in totally unrelated discourse and because of the educational values of such an experience in freeing the spirit for the development of its own talents and destiny.

It is assumed in this discussion that the target language is being taught as part of the general development of an educated person and not just as part of the technical training of an anthropologist or a literary critic. Earlier in the chapter, the limit of responsibility as to cultural anthropological meaning was set as that necessary to speak with understanding and to understand native speech. Further definition of this limit and a clearer definition of how far it is necessary to go into great achievements in a culture is, however, also necessary.

A distinction must be made between technical and nontechnical information. Technical information is defined as that which is necessary for the performance of one's job or professional work. Thus, a literary critic must know a great deal about literature and criticism that is not generally known by educated persons other than literary critics. Such information is technical. On the other hand, an appreciation of the major works of literature of a people might be considered desirable nontechnical information for educated persons in that culture. To demand that a person learning a second language acquire the technical knowledge of a literary critic is unwarranted, but to demand a degree of appreciation of major literary works is justified.

Linguistic-Cultural View   It is essential to our goal that we understand the cultural units of meaning attached to units of expression such as words, idioms, and proverbs, as well as literary masterpieces. These units of meaning are *elementary meaning units* (EMUs) in the culture and differ from culture to culture and therefore from language to language. Spanish, for example, makes a semantic distinction between some parts of the human anatomy and parallel parts of animals. "Leg" is *pata* for an animal and *pierna* for a person. "Back" is *lomo* for an animal and *espalda* for a person. "Neck" is *pescuezo* for an animal and *cuello* for a person. If a Spanish child says at table that he wants the *pierna* of the chicken, he is promptly corrected and told that chickens do not have *piernas;* they have *patas.* German makes a similar distinction for *mouth,* using *Mund* for the mouth of a person and *Maul* for that of an animal.

The various words that Eskimoan has for snow represent different EMUs in that culture. When Japanese borrowed the word *milk* as *miruku,* it stood for canned milk, a new EMU different from ordinary milk, which continued to be associated with the regular Japanese word. The word *wine* in English and *du vin* in French stand for fermented grape juice, but the function and connotation of wine are very different in the two cultures. Understanding these EMUs is necessary for full communication with natives, to understand their reports on great achievements, and to read their classics.

These EMUs also point to the need for understanding a foreign culture through its own language rather than through translations, which, because they render everything in the EMUs of the native language of the student, color or obscure the EMUs of the target language and its culture. No translator could render *pierna* and *pata* as *human leg* and *animal leg* and have his work accepted.

The members of a culture do things in certain patterned ways for certain culturally shared and generally understood purposes or meanings. When they observe other members of the culture doing the same things in the same situations, they grasp the same meanings. The patterns of action are considered form; their generally understood significance is their meaning; and the restrictions as to where and under what conditions both form and meaning may occur constitute their distribution.

When a person of one culture observes another culture, he unwittingly tends to interpret what he observes as having the same purposes and significance as in his native patterns of behavior. When the two cultures differ in manner or in the significance of actions, the outsider misunderstands. Furthermore, since his patterns of action and their association with particular significances are mostly matters of habit that operate below the threshold of awareness, he is apt to persist in his misunderstanding of the target culture.

In recognizing the importance of cultural meanings and patterns, it is necessary to distinguish two types of variations within a culture: subcultural and individual.

Subcultural Variations and Individual Freedom Subcultural variations in the English-speaking world are, for example, the regional cultural differences represented by the United States, England, Scotland, Ireland, Australia, New Zealand. If we limit ourselves to the United States, regional variations pertain to the Middle West, the Far West, the South, etc. Social and educational differences within any given area also constitute subcultural variations. Major cultural variations cannot be ignored when learning English as a foreign language. The same is true for Spanish, French, Arabic, Chinese, Russian, or any of the other major cultures of the world.

In addition to group variations, individuals within a culture may follow, approve, and support some or all of its patterns, or may not follow, may disapprove, and even resist them. The fact that individuals may do this does not deny the existence of the patterns; on the contrary, it tends to confirm them by the fact that the individual must go against them if he wishes to assert his individuality. The patterns themselves may in many instances allow for more than one position within the culture. Such is normally the case, for example, in elections, where the voters are given a choice.

Cultural Relativity and Ethical Values In describing a culture scientifically, one avoids value judgments from without because of the danger of calling bad what is merely different, or calling good what is merely pleasing to the outside observer. In Great Britain automobiles are driven on the left side of the road although in most other countries they are driven on the right. It would be naïve to say that the British drive on the wrong side of the road or that driving on the right is better. One says that driving on the left is proper or right in Great Britain, and that it is improper in France and Spain. The principle that the ways of different cultures are valid within the cultures themselves has a limitation based on the unity of the human race and the ethical nature of man. Without this limitation it would follow that the action of a tribe of cannibals whose members invite their enemies to a peaceful banquet and after feasting them kill and eat them would be as acceptable culturally as any other action just because cannibalism happens to be their pattern of behavior.

Most of us reject this extreme relativistic position. Cultures, like individuals, are subject to restrictions stemming from the ethical nature of man. If we must judge the individual of another culture, this must be done within the framework of that culture, which in turn is subject to the broader ethical framework of the human race. This broader framework is recognized in international law and international courts of justice, and has been referred to by great men of many faiths as the natural law.

LEARNING CULTURAL CONTENT

Influence of Native Culture The student learns the target culture not from scratch as he learned his native one, but with the experience, meanings, and habits of his native culture influencing him at every step. The native-culture experience will facilitate learning those patterns that are sufficiently similar to function satisfactorily when transferred. The native-culture experiences will interfere with those cultural patterns and meanings that are not equatable with similar ones or that are partly similar but function differently in the target culture.

Target Language Versus Native Language An initial over-all view of the target culture can probably be glimpsed more rapidly through the language of the student than through the target language, which for some time will be an imperfect instrument of communication for him. However, since the EMUs of the native language are different from those of the target language, the study of the cultural content of the target language through the native language of the student gives him no experience in understanding the EMUs of the target culture. He merely learns about the target culture in terms of the cultural categories of his native culture. Furthermore, information about the target culture given in native-language publications tends to be presented from the point of view of the native culture of the student, since members of this culture are the ones who will buy and read such publications. As a result the materials are usually slanted in their direction. Learning cultural content through the target language will not only identify the EMUs of the target culture but will give the student freedom to extend his understanding of the target culture independently, according to his interests.

Motion Pictures and Other Visual Aids Motion pictures made in the setting of the target culture provide a powerful medium for giving the student experience in cultural meanings within his control of the language. Many are unsatisfactory because of their point of view, however, and because they depict the unusual, the atypical, whereas the student has to learn the typical, the usual, the central cultural meanings. Some commercial motion pictures can be found that would be satisfactory. They are precisely the ones that deal with everyday living. When the original dialogue of the film is inappropriate, a new one specifically written for language learning can be substituted.

Color slides are another good tool for learning cultural content. Pictures and recordings of a variety of types have added to the resources available to the language student today. The teacher is responsible for guiding him into genuine experience in the foreign culture patterns and meanings. Pictures may do harm rather than good when they merely illustrate the false clichés that are current in the student's native culture or when they naïvely illustrate the target culture in the units and patterns of his native culture.

Two Stages in Learning Cultural Content The student's control of the target language is obviously inadequate in the early stages for any attempt at systematic treatment of cultural content through it. At this stage, one attempts to clarify specific cultural items and patterns as they occur in learning the basic structure of the language.

Once some control of the language has been achieved, cultural content may be learned through the target language in systematic and more comprehensive assignments. The degree of control of the language required for shifting to this second stage is admittedly a matter of opinion. This need not weaken the position taken here, since the shift should be gradual rather than abrupt and since the areas of cultural content can be selected to present the easier ones first.

A Modern Theory of Language Learning

Chapter 4

LANGUAGE IN USE

Learning a second language is more than learning a description of it. The process of speaking and listening is involved, and this process combines linguistic and psychological as well as other elements. To formulate a theory of second-language learning we must know what is involved in the process of speaking and listening, so that we may account for learning that process.

The Process of Speaking and Listening When a person speaks, we assume that the following takes place: Through some motivation the person decides to speak, and some content is brought under attention. Through association of this content with expression in the language, sentences are constructed with words, intonation, phonemes, etc. This happens at the conversational speed of some 500 sounds per minute. To achieve this requires great facility in using the language and an adequate memory span to complete sentences and sequences of sentences within the structure of the language.

In listening, the process is partly reversed, starting with expression as heard in context, followed by recall of content through associations between expression and content. Great facility is required also for listening at conversational speed, as is an adequate memory span with attention on the content of what is heard.

Reading and writing are parallel processes to listening and speaking, with the writing system associated with units of expression and the matter of fluency measured in different terms.

Each one of these factors—memory, facility, fluency, units and patterns, etc.—can be described and sometimes measured separately, but when a person is speaking or listening, they are all involved simultaneously. For example, through some personal motivation you decide to send greetings to a friend whose brother is taking leave of you. You say the sentence, *Give John my regards.* You use a request sentence pattern, the words *give, John, my, regards,* a falling intonation at the end, some sixteen consonant and vowel phonemes, three word junctures separating the four words, etc., and you do all this in less than two seconds! Expression begins while the content is still under attention; memory span holds the length of the sentence with ease.

Your listener probably began grasping the content of the sentence before you finished expressing it, and the context thus provided made it easier for him to perceive the rest.

To account for this process we must assume a memory store within the nervous system of the speaker-listener where each unit and pattern of expression and content is retained for instant use. These units and patterns are not observable directly in the store but are assumed from the speaker's ability to produce them and to react to them in normal use of the language.

We assume further that these units and patterns parallel the units and patterns that the linguist describes in speech. Thus each phoneme, word, and sentence pattern, and each permitted sequence of sounds has a counterpart in the memory store.

The units and patterns are available to the speaker under a speaking-listening attitude or attention posture that we shall call *speech set.* The phonemes are available as part of words and morphemes, not in isolation, except when there has been special phonetic training. For example, the /g/ /i/ /v/ phonemes of *give* are expressed automatically in a habit bundle as the word is elicited. Phonemic variants are available automatically in their usual phonetic environments and not in others. For example, the /g/ of *give* is exploded as an initial stop; the /i/ is automatically rather long before the voiced continuant /v/, etc.

The expression is available in association with content, and the content in association with the expression; one elicits the other. Typical sequences are recalled when part of the sequence is experienced. If I say "To be or not . . ." to a group of English-speaking students, they will probably finish the famous quotation from Shakespeare for me.

Attention and facility   Under a normal speech set the speaker has his attention chiefly on the content, and he manipulates the mechanics of expression largely through bundles of habits below the threshold of awareness. Attention, however, can be shifted to a particular word, sound, or other element of expression. The shifting of attention is controlled partly at will and partly by habits, attitudes, and such external factors as intensity of the sound, size of the letters, duration, repetition, relative movement, change, and contrast. Attention cannot be directed to all the elements in the process of speech since there is a definite limit to the number of items that can be held under attention at any one time.

The facility necessary to use a language ranges from habit for the phonemes and variants to less automatic selection of inflections, words, phrases, and sentence types to the least automatic selection or minimal facility when new arrangements of words are expressed.

Recall and memory span   To bring into use something after it has slipped out of attention or use is *recall*. To hold something under prolonged attention or to reproduce it immediately involves *memory span*.

The speaker of a language recalls the words and sentence patterns he needs as he speaks. This represents complete recall. He must keep under attention or under immediate recall a length of sentence in order to be able to complete it properly.

Psychologists have studied memory span with series of digits to be repeated in sets of increasing length. This ability to repeat series of numbers is weaker in a language that is not well known.

Motivation and will   The need and urge to communicate through language to fulfill the complex needs of a human being are a constant stimulus to use language. Urges, desires, wants, needs, ideals, and values result in conflicting motivations from which the will selects some to act upon and combats others through inhibition of practice.

Fluency and monitor function   "Language in use" means speaking at normal conversational speed under a speech set. At normal speed the speakers have the capacity to notice errors in expression even though correct use proceeds below the level of awareness. The errors noticed are distortions of the speech of the speaker rather than variations from a standard that may not be the speaker's own speech. This capacity is labeled monitor function.

Definition of Knowing a Language in Use   We can now define completely for our purposes what it is to know how to use a language. A person knows how to use a language when he can use its structure accurately for communication at will, with attention focused on the content, recalling automatically the units and patterns as needed, and holding them for a normal memory span at conversational speed, noticing any errors that occur.

Psycholinguistics The combined approaches of psychology and linguistics have been discussed at interdisciplinary seminars in an attempt to understand language better. Although the problems that are considered in psycholinguistics include many that are not of direct concern to the language teacher, this combined approach is well suited to the study of language in use and language learning. The theory developed in this chapter is based on a psycholinguistic frame of reference.

THE PSYCHOLOGY OF LEARNING

Psychologists have made three major contributions to our understanding of learning which are of interest to the language teacher: learning theories, experimental research on learning, and laws of learning. We will discuss them briefly from the point of view of their applicability to a theory of second-language learning.

Learning Theories There are at least eight psychological theories of learning which differ in terminology, content, and sometimes in the definition of learning. These theories, based on experiments performed chiefly on animals, tend to account for some part of the learning process over the entire animal kingdom.

When E. L. Thorndike explained learning as trial-and-error activity with successful attempts reinforced by satisfying consequences, and when he attempted to relate this to brain and nerve activity, he succeeded in finding a focus that might apply to all animal life but does not account for much of what is characteristic of human learning.

When W. Köhler and K. Koffka explained through the gestalt theory that we grasp total configurations rather than separate parts, they again dealt with only part of the learning process.

Language learning cannot be understood through trial and error, association, gestalt, or overt behavior alone. It requires a more comprehensive explanation because it involves simultaneously the widest range of human activity.

Experimental Research on Learning Experimental research on learning has been extensive and, in general, carefully controlled. It should be applicable to second-language learning, but for our purposes it suffers from too narrow a view of the problem of learning.

The experimental research that interests us has been channeled into three main streams: (1) conditioning, (2) verbal learning, and (3) motor learning, skills, and trial and error. Research on conditioned reflexes was made famous by Pavlov's experiments on dogs. He demonstrated that a reflex such as salivation, which is normally elicited by food without direct control from the will, can be induced by an artificial stimulus such as the sounding of a bell by simply sounding the bell regularly when food is supplied. The conditioning was demonstrated by finally inducing salivation with the sounding of the bell alone.

Although the experiments were performed on dogs, it is assumed that the process applies to man as well. And the principle of conditioning is generally taken to apply to learning beyond that of reflexes. Nevertheless, a theory of learning cannot be built on conditioning alone. Only some parts of language learning might be explained by conditioning, e.g., the arbitrary connection between a word and its meaning.

Research on verbal learning, from the classical experiments of Ebbinghaus,[1] has dealt chiefly with the memorization of syllables in a particular order (serial learning) or of one syllable or word with another in a pair (paired associates). In both cases, the material learned tends to be from the researcher's native language, and the learning tasks are only remotely relevant to learning a foreign language.

Experiments on motor learning, skills, and trial-and-error learning, though suggestive for some aspects of language learning, do not deal with language-learning tasks or specific units and patterns of language structure.

The fact is that language-learning research to be fully relevant must deal with language structure in use or with tasks which are clearly relatable to language structure in use. New units and patterns of expression must be produced or perceived in association with new units and patterns of content, and this involves the whole range of learning from skills and motor learning to association of units of expression with units of content, and gestalt perception of pattern in a field. Language-learning research must encompass the simplest phoneme as well as the most abstract cultural or individual value.

Laws of Learning The empirical laws of learning apply to a limited part of the process of language learning, and their relevance will have

---

[1] H. Ebbinghaus, *Das Gedächtnis: Untersuchungen zur experimentellen Psychologie.* Leipzig: 1885. Trans. by H. A. Ruger and C. E. Bussenius as *Memory: A Contribution to Experimental Psychology.* New York: Teachers College, Columbia University, 1913.

to be demonstrated with language materials under language-learning conditions. Since the laws are stated in general terms, their interpretation for language learning can lead to ambiguities and contradictions. The following are some of the more generally mentioned laws of learning.

The fundamental law of contiguity When two experiences have occurred together, the return of one will recall or reinstate the other.

Law of exercise Other things being equal, the more frequently a response is practiced, the better it is learned and the longer it is remembered. Contrariwise, when a response is not practiced, it tends to be forgotten.

Law of intensity Other things being equal, the more intensely a response is practiced, the better it is learned and the longer it will be remembered.

Law of assimilation Each new stimulating condition tends to elicit the response which has been connected with similar stimulating conditions in the past.

Law of effect Other things being equal, when a response is accompanied or followed by a satisfying state of affairs, that response is reinforced. When a response is accompanied or followed by an annoying state of affairs, it is avoided.

A THEORY OF SECOND–LANGUAGE LEARNING

Because of its complexity, language-learning theory needs special treatment. It is discussed here under three aspects: theory proper, experimental research, and laws of language learning.

The theory of foreign-language learning presented here is intended to account for the major differences in performance in using a second language as it is learned, and not to conflict with well-attested observations. The theory does not deal with learning the first language, which would raise the additional problems of growth. The learning of a second language by young children is dealt with, however, insofar as it does not go beyond the level of mastery of the first language, as at that level it would become the first language.

The theory is in the nature of a proposed explanation whose status is still partly conjectural. If its major propositions and outline are confirmed, it will bring greater understanding and system into foreign-language learning and teaching and will make possible various experiments intended to identify more effective approaches to learning and improve present successful ones. The theory must be internally consistent and permit the statement of inferences that can be tested.

Definition of second-language learning Learning a second language is defined as acquiring the ability to use its structure within a general vocabulary under essentially the conditions of normal communication among native speakers at conversational speed. More specifically, it means the acquisition of the ability to use, in speaking, the units and patterns of expression of the second language associated with the units and patterns of content that together constitute the language. And it means the acquisition of the ability to grasp the units and patterns of content when listening to the second language. It means, in other words, learning the expression, the content, and their association for rapid use in the proper positions within the system of the target language.

Schematically, the task can be symbolized as follows:

$$C \rightarrow E \quad \text{in speaking}$$
$$E \rightarrow C \quad \text{in listening}$$

E represents the unit or pattern of expression in its proper environment, C the unit or pattern of content in its proper environment, and $\rightarrow$ the association of a particular E with a particular C in the sequence indicated by the arrow.

Autonomy of expression, content, and their association Learning the three elements of a unit or pattern—expression, content, and their association—proceeds at different rates and in no set sequence. Sometimes one learns the form of a word without grasping its content, and later in some other context or situation the content becomes clear. At other times one learns a meaning but fails to learn the expression at the same time. Finally, one may know a meaning and its expression separately without having fully learned to associate the two in speaking or listening. Various degrees of these three cases can be observed, for example, in the situations in which one remembers the expression in part or the content imperfectly, or one can remember the content when hearing the expression but not the expression when the content is in mind.

Learning expression and content Learning the E's and the C's can be facilitated by indirect props[2] such as articulatory description, phonetic transcription, synonyms, but the final identification of units and patterns of expression and content is in the nature of a gestalt. It is ultimately an insight that permits us to identify a unique occurrence of a form or a meaning as the occurrence of a class of sounds, words, sentences, etc., different from all other classes but internally the same for all the unique occurrences of the units that make up the class.

---

[2] This is an extended use of the term in the meaning of a crutch or an aid to speaking and listening.

Learning associations The arbitrary association of E's with C's in pairs such that when an E is experienced, it recalls its C, and when the C is experienced, it recalls its E constitutes associationist learning. The association is learned through exercise and is not completely reversible; it must be experienced in both directions if it is to be learned in both directions. This irreversibility is evident from the difference in the ability of students to speak and understand and to read and write.

Learning through experiences All language learning occurs through experience, except for analogic creations which may combine previous experiences into new sequences. This is confirmed by the fact that children learn the language that is spoken around them. A Japanese child raised in an English-speaking environment will learn English rather than Japanese, and an English child raised in a Japanese environment will learn Japanese.

Trace, habit, and facility Each new experience is assumed to leave a *trace* in the memory store of the individual. The trace itself is not directly observable but is inferred from such observable phenomena as availability of response, memory span, etc.

Ease in using a language unit or pattern is a *facility*. Habits which permit the rapid use of language are also facilities. Facilities, then, include not only habits but also ease short of habit, thus ranging from habits at one end of a scale to the minimum facilitation resulting from a single experience, i.e., a trace. A trace is assumed to exist even if no facility can be overtly detected.

Learning a second language then involves acquiring varying degrees of facility for each phoneme and sequence of phonemes; for each word, part of word, and pattern of words; for the parts of speech, modification structures, and parts of sentences; and for each sentence type and sequence of sentences. These facilities must be learned so that they can operate when attention is on the content and the thread of the argument and not on the expression items.

Facilities in the use of the phonemes involve eliciting the phonemes as part of a word, a phrase, or a sentence, and not necessarily as sounds in isolation, except through linguistic training.

The facilities must be developed to such a degree that they can be elicited or experienced even though the speaker's attention is busy scanning ahead of the items in use or keeping the sense of the argument properly in line with his intended message.

Previous experience as a factor Since all experiences leave a trace in the memory store, it may be assumed that all previous experiences are a factor in learning a new language. In practical terms, however, only repeated experiences that have left a facility of the force of habit will potentially influence new language learning.

Facilitation and interference   When the native-language facility involves language units or patterns similar to the new ones to be learned, there will be either facilitation or interference in learning depending on the degree of functional similarity.   If the expression, content, and association are functionally the same in the native and the new languages, there is maximum facilitation.   Actually, no learning takes place since the student already knows the unit or pattern and merely transfers it.

If the unit or pattern is not the same and will not function as the same in the new language without structural retraining, there will be interference with the new language both because new forms have to be learned as facilities and because the field that elicits the new facility is similar to that which elicited the old, thus activating the native language facility and distorting the new one.

Total and partial experience and set   Each occurrence of speaking or listening under a normal communication set, that is, with attention to the thread of the content at conversational speed, is a total language experience.   In the process of learning a foreign language such total experiences are not readily possible even when the learner is fully exposed to the language.   When he is forced to adopt a normal language set, he falls back on the responses which are available to him—those of the native language.   The experience thus is imperfect and the desired trace and facility are not made or strengthened.   This is the same as saying that if he speaks the target-language structures imperfectly or hears them imperfectly or inaccurately, then he does not learn the foreign language.

When total experiences are not readily possible, learning takes place by partial experiences.   Learning the expression, the content, and the association separately is learning through partial experiences.   Another well-known partial experience is mimicry, in which the learner repeats an utterance after a model with primary attention to the form.

When the learner does not succeed in producing the whole utterance by direct imitation, he further reduces the learning task by attempting a part of it or by a slower rendition, or he uses props to help him succeed. A common partial experience in learning is mimicry of each phrase separately, or of the words separately, or even of a part of a word or phoneme that is giving trouble.   This splitting into small portions permits the learner to focus attention on the trouble spots.   Once success is achieved in this partial experience, the facility achieved permits a new attempt in a higher partial set or a full experience.   Slowing down the model and the response operates on the same principle, that of permitting attention temporarily to be focused on the trouble spots to permit accurate partial experiences.

Common props used by learners are conscious control of articulation, conscious modification of a similar response available in the native language or some other previous experience, and conscious attempts to interpolate an articulation somewhere between two previously available ones, as for example the English phoneme /æ/, which is somewhere between /e/ and /a/.

Another example of learning by partial experiences is the silent rehearsal of a response. Children keep repeating to themselves silently the message they are asked to convey to someone. If one gives an utterance in a foreign language for imitation by a class and asks them to be silent for ten seconds before repeating it, most students will keep repeating it silently to themselves so as not to forget. This silent repetition is clearly a partial learning experience.

These and other partial experiences contribute to the total learning experience, but they are not a substitute for it. For example, although successful imitation of the phrases of an utterance separately makes it easier to imitate the total utterance, it does not constitute experience in speaking the total utterance.

Attention and awareness Attention and awareness, which are the capacity to perceive certain things, events, qualities, and effects, more clearly and consciously than others in a field, are important in language learning. Knowing a language is defined as the power to use its complex mechanism through bundles of habits while only the thread of the argument and some matters of selection and agreement are under attention. This power is achieved gradually by strengthening the facilities for partial use through repeated experiences so that attention is freed from the mechanics of language use.

In other words, before learning, attention must control every minor element of speaking or listening expression, content, and association. Since attention is limited in the number of items that can be held simultaneously under it, learning occurs when attention can be shifted to larger units and patterns and eventually to the total utterance by increased facility with the smaller units and patterns.

When new facilities are difficult to learn because of conflicts with previous facilities that operate under similar attention sets, learning requires that attention be focused on the new facility directly—partial experience—to reinforce it to a point where it can be operated accurately in the set.

Volition and learning The student's will power is of major importance in the learning of language. It partly controls his attention and largely controls his practice exercises. Practice exercises undertaken with the will to learn result in more learning than similar exercises without the will to learn. Deliberate shifting of attention from the mechanics of language in partial experiences to the thread of content by an act of the will increases learning. Cooperation of the learner is an essential factor in learning. Cooperation of the learner means his willingness to do the things that will result in learning, chiefly practice with the will to learn.

Motivation Human motivation is infinitely more complex than animal motivation. Thus a wealthy person having all his apparent needs fully satisfied may by an act of his will choose to leave all his comforts and wealth and go to some remote and primitive society to work for his fellow man under unbelievable hardships. And in the process he may learn a strange language in short order when earlier in school he did poorly in foreign languages.

Language learning is related to human motivation moderated and partly controlled by the will. High motivation increases learning. For example, when dull practice is shown to contribute to language learning which in turn contributes to the fulfillment of some future spiritual goal, the learner wills to continue the dull practice and wills to learn instead of yielding to the superficially more pleasurable activity of sleeping or watching a movie.

Motivation and will can be manipulated in part by external controls so that a person who is not motivated to learn a particular foreign language can be induced to practice it by lures that are opposed to his longer-range motives. The result can be practice without the will to learn and less learning than when the learner is personally motivated to learn and wills to practice for learning.

When a person is shown that language learning is relevant to his motivation, the result will be more learning. When a person understands the relevance of language learning to his long-range motivation but has not the will to control his immediate pleasure seeking, outside forcing of his will results in increased learning and, by diverting attention away from immediate pleasure seeking, may result in continued learning practice from personal will.

The urge to communicate, since man is social, is a force that increases language learning. The urge for fulfillment is a powerful force if language learning is shown to be a means.

Memory span and monitor function After a unit or pattern becomes available by some partial exercise such as mimicry, learning still continues through exercise. This learning is shown both in the increased time that the unit can be held under attention and repeated and in the length of the utterance that can be held under immediate memory. Each experience increases this memory span, until the student reaches the range considered normal for native speakers. This memory span permits scanning ahead in order to select the proper form of the immediate unit, remembering the restrictions imposed by what was expressed before. However, that there is a limit to a memory span can be shown by the example of a speaker who in dictating correspondence to a stenographer forgets the beginning of his sentence and cannot go on until the secretary reads it back to him.

Learning also occurs in the ability to notice that some error has been made even though the error is in a unit which normally operates below the level of awareness. This is the monitor function, which enables the person who knows a language to detect his own errors even though he is not listening for them. The person who has not yet fully learned a foreign language fails to notice his own mistakes. For example, a person learning Spanish, French, German, or any language that has gender agreement will not detect his own mistake in using a masculine article with a feminine noun in the early stages even though he may be able to recite rules concerning this agreement.

Availability of response and recall time   Once an expression, its content, and their association are available in partial exercises such as mimicry, or in total experience immediately preceded by specific exercise, they will fade from attention and be stored in the memory store. When these stored facilities are needed for communication, the time required to recall them for use will still be more than the normal time required by those who already know the language.

Learning occurs in the form of decreased reaction time between a stimulus and overt speech and between exposure to an utterance and perception of it and its content. This reaction time decreases with exercise. Learning in the form of shorter reaction time is important in recall, which is the ability to bring forth from the memory store at will the units and patterns of the language for use in communication. As a result of learning, each fresh experience will tend to reduce the recall time.

Individual differences   Language learning proceeds at different rates for different persons under seemingly the same conditions. These differences are related to different capacities which are the results of genetic potential plus total past experience. Although these differences are not all of a single dimension but vary as to the number of units that can be learned, memory span, recall time, ability to imitate sounds, etc., they are grouped for the present discussion as a general factor of language-learning aptitude. Future research and understanding will surely force a recognition of different dimensions of language-learning aptitude, without eliminating the factor of individual differences as to capacity for language learning.

Language learning and order of skills   More fundamental than whether the correct order of teaching the skills is listening, speaking, reading, and writing is the fact that reading and writing are partial skills and exercising them constitutes partial language experiences, whereas speaking and listening are total language experiences. The person that learns the total skills can more easily learn the partial ones than vice versa.

Some Suggested Experiments   Illustration of some of the points in our discussion may be obtained by conducting the following experiments.

1. The purpose of this experiment is to identify conditions under which the great human power to associate expressions with specific objects or situations operates.   On the assumption that memorizing examples of each of the basic patterns of a language facilitates learning the patterns, prepare 100 simple drawings partially illustrating 100 basic sentences in the target language.   Mimic each sentence, looking at its corresponding drawing until rendition is phonemically correct.   Attempt recall by looking at the pictures the following day and a month later.   Compare the results—numbers of correct responses, reaction time, and accuracy of rendition—with the results of control groups using the native language. The experiment may be varied by using 25 pictures with four sentences associated with each picture, etc.

2. To check the rate of increase in the permanence of a response when exercise is spaced at increasing intervals: (a) double the time between subsequent recalls; (b) triple the time interval between subsequent recalls; (c) quadruple the time between subsequent recalls.   The optimum increase in time is the highest one which will maintain as constant the amount and accuracy of recall.

3. Compare the relative effectiveness of pattern-substitution exercises (see Chapters 10 and 11) with straight memorization of sentences. Compare an experimental group which has memorized a basic sentence and devoted thirty minutes to pattern-substitution drills with a control group which has memorized the same basic sentence but devoted thirty minutes to memorizing other examples of the same pattern.   Test the two groups on handling new sentences as well as on the sentences used in the learning exercises.   Repeat the tests a week later.

Hypothetical Laws of Language Learning   The following laws of language learning, although based on experience and inferences from learning research, are nevertheless entirely hypothetical.   If they are not convincing in the light of the theory stated or on the basis of observed facts, the laws will have to be tested experimentally if this is possible.   They should then be accepted, rejected, or modified, but not before then.

They are presented as quantitative laws when possible.   When no quantity relationships are postulated, they become descriptive matters and may belong under the heading of theory.

Law of exercise, contiguity, and intent Other things being equal, learning of E, C, or → occurs in relation to the number of times a unit or pattern is exercised correctly with the intent to learn. E's and C's that are exercised contiguously (close in time and/or space) develop associations so that the recall of one tends to elicit the other. Thus one E will become associated with its C and will also develop associations with contiguous E's.

The amount of learning increases rapidly with each repetition through the third under the same circumstances. Additional repetitions produce less increase in learning, and eventually the increment stops if the repetitions continue without rest or variation.

Law of familiarity of response Other things being equal, it is easier to associate a familiar C stimulus with a familiar E response than with an unfamiliar E response. It is easier to associate an unfamiliar C stimulus with a familiar E response than to associate a familiar C stimulus with an unfamiliar E response.

For example, exercising the response by partial exercise to make it familiar produces more learning than exercising the association before the response is familiar. The law, if confirmed, would mean that translation as a language-learning exercise occurring before the student is familiar with the E response in the target language is not the most effective type of exercise.

Law of geometric increase of permanence Other things being equal, the length of time that a response may be remembered, i.e., recalled at will, increases by a ratio of two or three times the length of time preceding its previous correct exercise with intent to learn. Sleep counts as zero in the computation of time in the ratio.

Law of recall under similar set Other things being equal, partial experiences produce learning under partial speech set (see page 33 for a description of set). Recall under total speech set for communication is not exercised with partial experiences.

Similarly, experiences involving exercise of serial recall of lists such as paradigms do not of themselves constitute experiences in total language learning. They may increase the familiarity with the forms, but the serial learning of the list is all but useless in itself.

Law of motivation through urge to communicate The exclusive use of the foreign language as the vehicle of all communication during the learning period increases learning by increased motivation through the urge and need to communicate.

Part 2

Language
Teaching

Chapter 5

Principles of Language Teaching

"Scientific" does not mean perfect or omniscient. A scientific approach to language teaching uses scientific information; it is based on theory and a set of principles which are internally consistent. It measures results. It is impersonal, so that it can be discussed on objective evidence. And it is open, permitting cumulative improvement on the basis of new facts and experience.

The approach presented in this book is based on the science of linguistics, the psychology of learning, the theory stated in Chapter 4, the principles given in this chapter, hypotheses made from the theory or from linguistic experience, and objective evidence of results. It is a conscious attempt to arrive at a scientific approach.

Because scientific information should not be applied without reference to conditions and goals, some of the typical variables that operate in language teaching are discussed in addition to the principles that characterize this scientific approach.

PRINCIPLES

The following principles are necessary and sufficient to define the scientific approach. Stated briefly here, they are developed into practical teaching programs in succeeding chapters. The principles are subject to change or elimination as new scientific facts are added to our knowledge.

Principle 1. Speech before Writing   Teach listening and speaking first, reading and writing next. This principle is the basis for the audio-lingual approach.

From linguistics we know that language is most completely expressed in speech. Writing does not represent intonation, rhythm, stress, and junctures (see Chapter 8).

This principle does not mean that we should teach only audio-lingual mastery. It implies that deciphering written material without knowing the language patterns as speech is incomplete, imperfect, or inefficient.

The principle applies even when the goal is only to read. Having mastered the basic constructions of the language orally, the student can expand his reading capacity to a higher level of achievement than if he sticks to deciphering script. Although more experimental evidence is needed to prove or disprove this claim, a tactical advantage supports this teaching principle. Students who have mastered the language orally can learn to read more or less readily by themselves or with limited help. Students who have learned to decipher script cannot as a rule learn to speak by themselves.

The principle can be defended also on the basis of attitudes toward further learning, as students who learn the written forms first tend to feel that speech is a distortion of what they imagined the pronunciation to be. This attitude interferes with further learning.

A recent psychological experiment seems to support the principle by having shown greater transfer from audio to visual learning than the reverse.[1]

Corollary   Speech cannot be invented by the student; it has to be imitated. Poor models produce poor imitations. Good models do not guarantee good imitations, but they are necessary to permit good responses.

In the light of this corollary, native speakers who possess an acceptable variety of speech are desirable models, as are those who, though not native speakers, have achieved a high level of mastery. Tape or disc recordings can now be used by any teacher, native or not, to provide good models and a variety of authentic native speakers.

Principle 2. Basic Sentences   Have the students memorize basic conversational sentences as accurately as possible. This practice, advocated

---

[1] Paul Pimsleur and Robert J. Bonkowski, "Transfer of Verbal Material Across Sense Modalities." *Journal of Educational Psychology,* vol. 52, no. 2, pp. 104–107, 1961.

by linguists, has a strong psychological justification not dealt with in published experiments but tested repeatedly otherwise. Give the students a series of six or seven digits in the native language as models to be repeated after one hearing and then do the same with a similar series in the target language; you will find that the students fail many more series in the target language even though they can say the digits individually. Similarly, students can repeat much longer utterances by imitation in their native language than in a foreign one.

Students have a much shorter memory span in a foreign language than in their native one. When examples or models are given in the foreign language, they may not be heard correctly, or even if they are, they may be forgotten in seconds. The student cannot use the examples to understand the grammar or to create other sentences by analogy because he does not remember them. The extra effort needed to memorize dialogues in a foreign language enables the student to use them as models and to proceed with further learning.

Linguistics supports the use of conversations because they present words in sentence structures and in context. Conversational dialogues are preferable to poetry or formal prose because conversations show a greater range of the basic constructions of the language in matter-of-fact context. Poetry uses more of the unusual constructions and the less typical variants of common constructions. Prose makes little use of questions, requests, and answers; it is characterized by longer statement patterns.

Principle 3. Patterns as Habits Establish the patterns as habits through pattern practice. Knowing words, individual sentences, and/or rules of grammar does not constitute knowing the language. Talking *about* the language is not knowing it. The linguist, the grammarian, and the critic talk and write about the language; the student must learn to *use* it.

To know the language is to use its patterns of construction with appropriate vocabulary at normal speed for communication. Understanding or even verbalizing a pattern may help a student to learn it but will never take the place of practicing the patterns through analogy, variation, and transformation to establish them as habits. This is pattern practice.

Principle 4. Sound System for Use Teach the sound system structurally for use by demonstration, imitation, props, contrast, and practice. Observation repeatedly shows that merely listening to good models does not produce good pronunciation after childhood. Partial attempts, props in the form of articulatory clues, and minimal contrasts to focus sharply on the phonemic differences eventually result in satisfactory responses, but to increase facility and fluency, practice becomes indispensable.

Principle 5. Vocabulary Control   Keep the vocabulary load to a minimum while the students are mastering the sound system and the grammatical patterns.   The attempt of many students to concentrate on learning vocabulary at the beginning is misguided.   Linguistics shows that words, no matter how many, do not constitute a language.   The most strategic part of a language for use is the system of basic patterns and significant sound contrasts and sequences.   Every effort should go into teaching these elements; hold the vocabulary load at first to the words needed to manipulate the patterns or illustrate the sounds and contrasts.

Corollary   Expand the vocabulary to adequate levels and teach specialized vocabularies when the basic structure has been mastered.

Principle 6. Teaching the Problems   Problems are those units and patterns that show structural differences between the first language and the second.   They will be illustrated in later chapters.   The disparity between the difficulty of such problems and the units and patterns that are not problems because they function satisfactorily when transferred to the second language is much greater than we suspect.   The problems often require conscious understanding and massive practice, while the structurally analogous units between languages need not be taught: mere presentation in meaningful situations will suffice.

Corollary   Since the problems differ according to each native language, different emphases in teaching are required for the different language backgrounds.

Principle 7. Writing as Representation of Speech   Teach reading and writing as manipulations of graphic representation of language units and patterns that the student already knows.   When standard spoken utterances differ from their graphic representation, it is due to inadequacy of the writing system.   This principle implies that teaching the graphic symbols and the association of these symbols with the language units they represent are separate tasks.   It also implies that teaching reading and writing are distinct from teaching speech and should not be confused with it.

The distinction is obvious in teaching Chinese, for example, where the writing system is logographic and therefore basically different from alphabetic writing.   The distinction between speech and writing is still basic in learning French, Spanish, or German when the first language is English, even though they use the same alphabet.

Principle 8. Graded Patterns   Teach the patterns gradually, in cumulative graded steps.   To teach a language is to impart a new system of complex habits, and habits are acquired slowly. This observation, together with the linguistic view of language as a structure, is the basis for this principle. There are strategically advantageous places to begin and sequences to follow in teaching the structure. The following supplementary statements will help to interpret the principle.

Supplement 8.1 Begin with sentences, not words, and order the sequence of materials on the basis of sentence patterns. This represents a radical change from the usual practice of beginning with the parts of speech and leaving the construction of sentences to the end of the book or not dealing with it at all. Early in teaching any materials, there should be graded questions and responses, requests and greetings, as well as statements.

Supplement 8.2 Introduce subsentence elements, such as parts of speech, structure words, and modification structures, in connection with full sentence patterns. Linguistically, these subsentence elements are not free and are not fully taught unless placed in a sentence frame.

Supplement 8.3 Add each new element or pattern to previous ones. This is the sense of "cumulative steps." There is, for example, a tactical advantage in teaching questions with *do* (*Do you understand?*) before teaching questions with the interrogative words *what, when,* etc. (*What do you understand?*) Once the *do* pattern has been taught, the *what, when, where* questions are more easily presented and understood.

Supplement 8.4 Adapt the learning difficulty to the capacity of the students. This is the meaning of "graded steps," which require a more sophisticated interpretation than that applied in linear programmed learning, where everything is broken down to minimal steps so that the poorest students will not make mistakes.

Supplement 8.5 There is a conflict between having students memorize dialogues that are contextually natural, on the one hand, and introducing structural patterns in graded steps, on the other. If the dialogues are natural, they will include patterns not yet taught in the early lessons. If the grading is perfect, the dialogues will be artificial for some time. The proposed solution is to keep to a minimum the patterns that are introduced in the dialogues before they appear in graded steps. This can be made easier by selecting contextual areas that permit such restriction within normal conversational style and by carefully editing the resulting dialogues. The nongraded patterns that have to be introduced are memorized as if they were unanalyzable lexical units.

Principle 9. Language Practice versus Translation Translation is not a substitute for language practice. Arguments supporting this principle are (1) that few words if any are fully equivalent in any two languages,

(2) that the student, thinking that words are equivalent, erroneously assumes that his translation can be extended to the same situations as the original and as a result makes mistakes, and (3) that word-for-word translations produce incorrect constructions.

Psychologically, the process of translation is more complex than, different from, and unnecessary for speaking, listening, reading, or writing. Furthermore, good translation cannot be achieved without mastery of the second language. We, therefore, teach the language first, and then we may teach translation as a separate skill, if that is considered desirable.

Bilinguals who achieve full use of both languages do not translate when using either. They are said to have acquired two coordinate systems. Translation, on the contrary, develops a subordinate, overly complex functional organization of the second language.

There is insufficient evidence for or against the use of translation to convey the meaning of what is taught or as a means to check comprehension. The use of full sentences in the first language to give the meaning of the dialogues for memorization, however, is a common device which many linguists accept and use.

Principle 10. Authentic Language Standards Teach the language as it is, not as it ought to be. Often the speakers of a language have a notion that they speak incorrectly and that some imagined earlier form or a form spoken elsewhere is the correct one. Yet linguistics tells us that the forms used by educated native speakers and not any imagined artificial standard are the guide to what is correct and acceptable as educated native speech. This principle means that the language style to be taught is that of educated native speakers.

The principle does not mean that only one style is correct. On the contrary, if contractions are the accepted standard in informal conversation, then they should be taught for informal conversation by the students, but they should be taught without prejudice against teaching the full noncontracted forms for more formal speech or writing.

A language is a structure of communication. Communication engineers call noise any disturbance in the communication channel. Using an inappropriate dialect or style interferes with full communication and constitutes "noise" of a sort.

The principle does not make allowances explicitly for geographic dialect differences, yet these can often become a problem. In some languages, such as Chinese, a standard geographic dialect, Mandarin, is recognized as the national standard. In other languages, no single dialect can be said to be the accepted standard. A strategic decision is necessary in such cases, taking into account the use to be made of the language and the people with whom the student expects to communicate.

Principle 11. Practice The student must be engaged in practice most of the learning time. This principle has a psychological justification, since, other things being equal, the quantity and permanence of learning are in direct proportion to the amount of practice.

Linguists have demonstrated the importance of practice through mimicry-memorization and pattern practice (see Chapter 6 for mimicry-memorization and Chapters 10 and 11 for pattern practice). Fries, for example, recommended devoting 85 per cent of class time to practice and no more than 15 per cent to explanation and commentary. The strongest support for this principle is in the success of the intensive courses in English developed under Fries's direction and the success of the intensive language programs under linguistic auspices during the Second World War. Although these did not include controlled experiments, the evidence was convincing.

Principle 12. Shaping of Responses When a response is not in the repertory of the student, shape it through partial experiences and props. In language learning, the student is often unable to produce or to hear elements and patterns which differ from those of his first language. The principle, therefore, recommends two treatments: (1) Partial practice: break up the response into smaller parts, practice these, then attempt the full response. (2) Props: give articulatory or other hints to help the student approximate the response.

Principle 13. Speed and Style Linguistically, a distorted rendition is not justified as the end product of practice. Psychologically, partial experiences and props are necessary as intermediate steps to a full experience. The principle makes sure that the practice ends in a linguistically acceptable and psychologically full experience.

Principle 14. Immediate Reinforcement Let the student know immediately when his response has been successful. Thorndike proved experimentally that blindfolded subjects did not learn to draw 4-inch lines even if they drew thousands of lines if they did not find out when they had succeeded.[2] Skinner proved that experimental animals learned better when correct responses or successively closer approximations were reinforced with food or some other reinforcer.[3] Principle 14 implements the obvious applicability of this psychological evidence to language teaching.

[2] E. L. Thorndike, *Human Learning.* New York: The Century Company, 1931, pp. 8ff.
[3] B. F. Skinner, *The Behavior of Organisms.* New York: Appleton-Century-Crofts, Inc., 1938.
C. B. Ferster and B. F. Skinner, *Schedules of Reinforcement.* New York: Appleton-Century-Crofts, Inc., 1957.

Principle 15. Attitude toward Target Culture Except in cases of incompatibility, as in wartime, impart an attitude of identification with or sympathetic understanding of the people who speak the second language rather than merely a utilitarian attitude toward the language or a disinterested or negative attitude toward the people or the language. This principle is based on the belief of many teachers and has been partly confirmed by the research of Wallace Lambert and his associates, who used attitude questionnaires and correlated their results with achievement in French.[4]

Principle 16. Content Teach the meaning content of the second language as it has developed in the culture where the language is spoken natively. A language is the most complete index to a culture. This principle applies with less force or does not apply when the language is taught for scientific reading only or as a national language (for example, English in Nigeria) where the meaning content is largely that of the country where it is being used for communication.

Principle 17. Learning as the Crucial Outcome Teach primarily to produce learning rather than to please or entertain. This principle is based on the observation that classes that are the most entertaining are not always the most effective. It is also based on the analogy with medical science. In developing a new drug, for example, no thought is given to whether it has a pleasant taste. Results and absence of side effects are the decisive criteria of goodness. Once the drug is found effective, it is put into palatable form, but effectiveness comes first.

In language teaching we have not yet reached this stage of scientific precision. It is common to discuss materials and techniques on the basis of whether or not the student or the teacher finds them interesting, without sufficient regard for effectiveness. In a scientific approach, the amount of learning outweighs interest. Once the effectiveness of a technique is demonstrated, working to make it more palatable, more absorbing, more interesting, is in order, but not before, and certainly not as a substitute for effectiveness in terms of learning.

CONDITIONS AND VARIABLES

Although principles remain constant in all language teaching, specific conditions and variables must be considered when programming any teaching. The chief conditions and variables that must be faced are

---

[4] Wallace E. Lambert, *et al.*, *Attitudinal and Cognitive Aspects of Intensive Study of a Second Language.* (Mimeographed.) Montreal: McGill University, 1961.

related to (1) the student, (2) the materials and equipment, (3) the teacher, and (4) the setting.

The Student Age, educational level, capacity, handicaps, level of proficiency, goals, and linguistic and cultural background are significant variables with regard to the student.

Age is a major variable. Children and adults must be taught differently. The teacher must recognize the learning characteristics of at least four age groups: (1) preschool, (2) primary school, (3) secondary school, and (4) college, university, and other adult groups.

Preschool children can learn a second language by exposure in much the same way that they learned their first. They can learn it to the degree of accuracy of native speakers. No special technique is necessary to teach this age group other than to bring the children in contact with appropriate situations in which the second language is used as the medium of communication.

Primary school children require special techniques. They learn by play and memorization. They can achieve superior pronunciation by dint of their power to mimic sounds accurately. Children are driven to activity and to learning by play rather than by any work motive or other sophisticated motive that drives adults.

Secondary school pupils can study for the sake of a grade or other indirect reward. They can still achieve a good pronunciation and can study grammatical patterns deliberately. Work must be made palatable at this stage, however.

Adults learn more effectively by systems and by systematic cataloguing than do children, and they respond favorably to the work motive, i.e., to putting forth sustained effort for some goal other than the immediate enjoyment of the activity itself. They are poor mimics of the sounds of a foreign language and must be helped with props, partials, and successive approximations to the desired pronunciation. They can also be influenced by inhibitions and prejudices to a significant degree. The capacity to learn a foreign language diminishes somewhat with age after adulthood, but it is not lost. Those who are in the top third in language-learning capacity among all adults at age twenty-one may still remain in the top half at age forty-one. This age factor can be counterbalanced by knowledge of other languages and of linguistics and language-learning theory and practice, with the result that an adult may achieve greater capacity to learn another foreign language at forty-one than he had at twenty-one.

Educational level Language teaching must obviously differ for literate and illiterate students. It must also differ for various levels of education, with the college or university level and the primary education level sharply distinguished.

It is not clear that distinctions must necessarily be made for different professional groups and disciplines, but specialized vocabularies are of course necessary at the advanced level for these different groups. There is also a strong motivational factor involved in professional differentiation of vocabulary at an earlier level, and this factor may affect learning. In other words, a group of dentists learning a foreign language will feel especially motivated if the vocabulary refers to dentists and their work even though linguistically this is not necessary.

Capacity There is a verbal aptitude distinct from general intelligence.[5] Individuals differ in their ability to learn a second language. Some individuals learn more by memorizing connected sentences, others by analogy, still others by rules and systems. Individual differences in amount of learning and quality of achievement are surprisingly great. Some individuals, for example, may learn three times as much as some of their classmates in eight weeks of intensive study of a second language.[6] In view of these differences, students should not be forced to follow exactly the same steps in the class or in programmed learning.

Handicaps The principles have to be modified or suspended in cases when students have some physical or mental handicap. Blind students, for example, cannot use an ordinary textbook or visual aids. They cannot use the phonemic alphabet. They may, on the other hand, have greater acuity in listening and a longer memory span for speech than those who depend on their sight for much of their learning.

Stutterers cannot be expected to be free of stuttering in the second language. Students with a hearing impediment will need special props or a hearing aid.

Level of proficiency The rate of learning is in inverse relation to the level of proficiency that has been achieved in the language, i.e., the higher the level of proficiency, the slower the rate of learning.[7] The principles of language teaching provide in part for differences in learning according to level of proficiency by putting speech first, limiting vocabulary at the beginning, etc.

Habit is of greatest weight in the early stages, when the sound system must be learned. Habit becomes less dominant though equally strong where changes must be learned at higher levels. Vocabulary expansion and cultural information become more important then.

Memory span is greater at the advanced levels, and the need to memorize conversations is accordingly less.

[5] J. B. Carroll, "A Factor Analysis of Two Foreign Language Aptitude Batteries." *Journal of General Psychology,* vol. 59, pp. 3–19, 1958.
[6] R. Lado, "Measurement in English as a Foreign Language." Doctoral dissertation, Ann Arbor: The University of Michigan, 1950.
[7] R. Lado, "The Relation of Entrance Level to Rate of Progress in Aural Comprehension." *Language Learning,* vol. 2, no. 4, pp. 105–112, 1949.

Goals Although the principle of teaching speech first applies in all cases, it applies with greater force when the goal is to teach the language than when it is to use the language as a tool in reading or in travel. Perfection in pronunciation is most important for the teacher and least important for the one who wants to read for content only. Memorization of conversations is most important for the future teacher and the tourist, though for different reasons.

The principle of teaching identification with or sympathetic understanding of the people who speak the language natively applies with greater force when the goal is to educate than when it is to teach a communication tool. It may not apply or might have to be suspended when the language is taught as a national instrument of communication, as English is taught in the Philippines.

Materials The equipment and aids available to the student and the teacher vary from bare walls, hard benches, and noisy surroundings to fully equipped electronic laboratories and closed-circuit television. Great hopes and expectations rose with the advent of the language laboratory, television, and, most recently, teaching machines and programmed learning. After the first enthusiasm it was realized that these aids are no better than the materials fed through them and the teachers who guide the students. The principles of the scientific approach apply with full force in the preparation and use of all the materials.

The Teacher There are great variations among language teachers with regard to their qualifications and the time they may devote to the teaching of language. The teacher may speak the language natively, or he may have studied it as a second language himself. His speech may be some standard or substandard variety. He may be a trained and experienced teacher, or he may not have any teaching experience or training at all. Different provisions are necessary to compensate for these differences, but the principles apply in all cases.

They apply also in foreign languages in the elementary school (FLES), where languages may be taught by one who does not know the foreign language and yet directs the class (a situation we cannot endorse) or, at the other extreme, all language classes may be handled by a fully qualified language specialist.

Linguistic and Cultural Setting The setting influences what can be taught and what needs to be taught. In the country where the language is spoken, the students will need to use it for ordinary communication in addition to whatever goals have been set up. When teaching in a setting where the second language is not spoken, all experiences and practice will have to be provided by the class and the teacher.

The ideal setting for teaching a language is, of course, the country where it is spoken natively. By residing in that community and being forced to use the language for communication, the full impact of a language as the chief means of communication in a culture is brought out.

Lacking this setting, the next best thing is to create the atmosphere of the second culture through proper decoration of a classroom, a lounge, and/or, when possible, a house. Agreements to speak only the second language and to be active in language clubs can be realized with varying degrees of success.

Although the principles of language teaching may be more difficult to apply in some settings than others, they do apply regardless of setting.

Establishing
a
Linguistic
Beachhead

Chapter 6

The beginning student does not hear the target language. He controls none of its grammar, none of its vocabulary. He has no memory in it; as soon as the model stops, he forgets. It will take a long time if the teacher waits until the student knows these things before using the language. The student must break into the language. He must establish a linguistic beachhead.

Speaking is knowing Teachers and students have tried reading, translating, and analysis as ways to enter a language. These are partial experiences. *The student does not know a sentence until he can speak it.* When a student reads a sentence aloud, he has to manipulate only part of the language, and the memory and attention factors are bypassed or minimized. Translation adds complexity but is still less than using the language as language. Analysis is quite removed from language use.

Memorizing dialogues in the ASTP[1] Materials prepared by linguists during the Second World War contained useful dialogues which the students had to memorize as perfectly as possible. The students were

[1] Army Specialized Training Program. More specifically, the spoken language materials prepared by linguists for the armed services during the Second World War.

drilled until they could rattle off the dialogues with ease. This gave them the power to hear, recall, understand, and speak the material. They had broken into the language. They had established a linguistic beachhead.

What utterances? Linguistics offers help in choosing utterances for memorization. Poetry uses unusual sentences and special vocabulary. Reading selections have long statements of a few types of sentences but few, if any, questions and requests. Conversational material in a standard dialect exemplifies most naturally the questions, requests, answers, statements, and vocabulary that constitute the language. So dialogues are chosen for memorization.

Young children can also memorize nursery rhymes, songs, and prayers, and adults will do well to memorize songs, proverbs, well-known poems, and quotations, but selected and carefully graded dialogues are the most useful for memorization.

Dialogues versus isolated sentences The chief value in memorizing is that it gives the student authentic sentences that he can vary and expand and eventually use in many situations. Basic sentences are memorized as units as if they were single words or brief proverbs. Isolated basic sentences illustrate the major patterns without contextual relation to one another. A connected dialogue makes contextual sense, but it introduces material that would otherwise be unnecessary at a given point for a systematic progression in the language.

The possibility of dramatizing the dialogues and the added motivation of speaking the language from the beginning tip the scale in favor of memorizing dialogues as against isolated basic sentences. The dialogues should be graded, without violating normal usage, to keep to a minimum the material outside the basic sentences that will have to be memorized. They should also be short in order to keep within reason the effort required to remember the fixed series of sentences.

How much to memorize? If our students could memorize large amounts of the language, say ten plays or a full-length novel, they might be pretty advanced in the language. The difficulty is that to memorize material in a foreign language is much more difficult than memorizing it in the native one. In the native language we know everything except the particular string in which the sentences and words appear. And memorizing this takes enormous effort and time. In the target language everything has to be memorized as if it were a series of nonsense syllables in strange sounds. The task is hopeless.

We could benefit from selected experiments to determine when sheer memorization becomes uneconomical. Meanwhile, the general experience of teachers seems to be that the long dialogues of the spoken-language materials developed during the war and after required too much time and effort with regard to the sequence of utterances.

Closer to optimum use of memorization would be to begin with a short dialogue that includes the patterns to be taught in the lesson. To employ shorter dialogues and more of them is more efficient. Here is an example for English as a foreign language:

Is Victor home?
Yes, he is.
May I see him?
Yes, you may.

This dialogue illustrates short answers. It does not show all the possible variations, but it anchors two good examples in context: *Yes, he is. Yes, you may.*

A similar example in Spanish might be,

¿Está Victor?
Sí, está.
¿Puedo hablar con él?
Puedes. ¡Victor! Aquí está Juan.

This is not a direct translation of the English dialogue, nor should it be. Each language has its own structure and the dialogue should illustrate it rather than be a word-for-word translation of the native language of the student. *¿Está Victor?* is a full sentence in Spanish even though the translation of the words, *está,* "is," and *Victor,* "Victor," does not constitute a sentence in English. *¿Está Victor?* means something like "Is Victor here?" One can also say, *¿Está Victor aquí?* with the word *aquí* expressing the meaning "here," but this would hide rather than reveal the difference. One may avoid such problems temporarily to keep the principle of grading, but the purpose of the dialogues is to teach examples of the problems. Thus the short answers in these dialogues illustrate the structural differences between English, Spanish, French, German, and Russian. The differences will remain unexplained at this stage.

FRENCH EXAMPLE:
C'est vous Jean Levet?
Oui, c'est moi.
Vous êtes étudiant?
Oui, je le suis.
Vous avez des frères?
Oui, j'en ai.

GERMAN EXAMPLE:
Ist Peter zu Hause?
Ja.
Kann ich ihn bitte sprechen?
Ja, einen Augenblick, bitte.

RUSSIAN EXAMPLE:

Иван дома?

Дома.

Можно его видеть?

Конечно, можно.

Although a bit of humor or suspense might add interest to the dialogue, this is a marginal matter when we remember that the student has to repeat the dialogue many times to the same audience; suspense and humor soon turn flat in such circumstances. Interest in the dialogue is best maintained with useful material that is seen to contribute toward mastery of the language.

Supplementary memorization: motivation and fun In addition to memorizing graded dialogues to penetrate the language, all the memorization that can be made amusing and fun will help. Nursery rhymes may not exemplify the basic sentences, but for generations they have been enjoyed by small children. Let the children memorize some nursery rhymes for the pleasure of it, and they will add to their beachhead in the language.

> Humpty Dumpty sat on a wall,
> Humpty Dumpty had a great fall;
> All the King's horses and all the King's men
> Couldn't put Humpty together again.

> A dillar, a dollar
> A ten o'clock scholar,
> What makes you come so soon?
> You used to come at ten o'clock
> But now you come at noon.

> One, two, buckle my shoe;
> Three, four, knock at the door;
> Five, six, pick up sticks;
> Seven, eight, lay them straight;
> Nine, ten, a good fat hen.

If there is a language club, interest the students in presenting a play. Memorization of the parts will then be justified, and the amount of language they will learn will be considerable. Folk songs are learned and sung with gusto; take advantage of the factor of motivation and have them sing from memory.

Teaching the Dialogues Teaching a dialogue involves (1) making the form of each sentence available as a response, (2) putting across the meaning, and (3) practicing the association of form and meaning so that when the meaning is recalled, the form is also recalled and produced with ease, and when the form is heard, the meaning is instantly remembered.

The students do not learn a dialogue by merely hearing it in a meaningful situation. The task is a difficult one, and the teacher has to break it down into partial tasks. These partial tasks are taught by imitation and with the aid of props.

Making the form available Getting the students to speak the sentences with ease is more difficult than attaching the meaning to the form. Traditionally, too much effort was put on attaching the meaning to a form that the students could not speak, and not enough effort was put on learning to speak the form. Psychological research shows that it is more effective to practice the form until it is familiar and then to attach a familiar meaning to it than to practice attaching a familiar meaning to an unavailable form.

Imitation The first step is to let the students hear a sentence from the dialogue and to ask them to repeat it as soon as they can. It is usually necessary to let the students hear the sentence several times. This is the mimicry part of the mimicry-memorization technique.

Say the sentence three times and then motion to the class to repeat after you. If the sentence is long, break it up into phrases and say each phrase two or three times before motioning to the class to repeat. Begin with the last phrase and go back.

When the students fail to imitate well the complete phrases because the ability to do so is not within their initial capacity, break up the difficult phrases into words, syllables, or individual sounds until the class can imitate successfully. This is, of course, much less than full use of the language. Imitating the form alone is a partial experience. Breaking a sentence into phrases, words, syllables, and individual sounds further reduces the task so that the attention of the student, which would normally be on the meaning, is on an individual sound, or sequence of sounds. When the students succeed in imitating the parts, combine these into a larger stretch until the class can imitate the entire sentence readily.

Imitation of parts of the sentence is often not enough to elicit good pronunciation from the class. You can further reduce the task by slowing down the model. This must be done without artificially distorting the sounds. For example, intervocalic Spanish /d/ is a fricative [ð], as in *todo* [toðo]. You can slow down the pronunciation of this word, but if you break it up into two phrases, /to/ and /do/, the stop variant of /d/ will become the appropriate one. The same is true in the German word *sehen,* in which the *h* is either pronounced or not according to whether the word is broken into syllables or not. When you slow down the model even without distortion, you should repeat it at normal speed before leaving the exercise, since slow pronunciation is not full pronunciation.

Props When imitation is not enough, try props. The most effective prop is an articulatory hint, not a full description of the sound. The student has already made an attempt, based on his native language habit, and has produced a distortion. The articulatory hint should then be a minimal comment directed at the specific distortion introduced by the student.

Since the teacher knows ahead of time what the difficult items will be, a facial diagram can be ready at hand to show the proper articulation of these items.

Group recitation before individual recitation Begin with group or choral recitation, and when the class has made some successful repetitions, that is, when you cannot detect any gross dissonances in the group response, move to individual recitations. Group recitation offers clear advantages at the beginning of a drill. The student is less inhibited in a group response; he recites more readily, and everyone has a chance to practice every sentence.

Both individual and group recitation, like all other class drill, must be lively in pace and varied in speed, volume, attitude, and order for best results. No matter how carefully prepared the dialogue and drill, a slow, uninterested pace and tone on the part of the teacher will kill the interest of any class. A lively pace and an interested tone by the teacher will enliven even poor material.

With a small class you may use a fixed order for individual recitations. You are within conversational distance of all the students, and all can be kept fully attentive to each recitation. Long individual responses, fashioned while the class sits passively, do not constitute an effective way to teach.

A refinement that you may use occasionally to keep a whole class alert during individual recitation is to give a stimulus to the entire group and wait a moment before designating who is to respond. You may designate the student by looking at him and nodding slightly, by pointing, or by addressing him by name. There is no special merit in one style over another.

This stage of learning does not usually include the complete recitation of the dialogue from memory. It merely involves repeating each utterance easily and well.

A phonemic alphabet? Preschool and primary school children can imitate sounds better than they can read or write the symbols that represent them. Mimicry-memorization needs no written props for these age groups. Secondary school and university students are helped by special written symbols that call their attention to the distinctions required in the target language. A special alphabet having one symbol for each phoneme is a guide to listening and imitating. The student should not be asked to transcribe whole utterances or even to read them without having heard and imitated them. The phonemic writing of the dialogue merely helps the student concentrate more fully on learning the phonemes he cannot distinguish by hearing.

In theory any set of graphic symbols that represents all the phonemes unambiguously should be acceptable. In practice we ought to weigh the difficulty of learning the symbols and whether or not familiar graphemes are known by the students. If the phonemic alphabet will cause more trouble than the imperfections of ordinary spelling, one may decide to use normal spelling with a few special marks at the trouble spots. This might be the case in teaching Spanish. In teaching Chinese there is really no choice but to teach a special alphabet.

Then too, the learning of a standardized and widely accepted set of symbols such as the International Phonetic Alphabet (IPA) or some widely used adaptation may be so valuable as a tool for future study of languages that it can be justified even if the normal alphabet is regular in its representation of the sounds.

Specific research in the teaching of Spanish, French, English, etc., would help in deciding when to use and when not to use a phonemic or special alphabet.

Putting the meaning across In most cases putting the meaning across is a minor part of teaching a dialogue. Most linguists simply supply a roughly equivalent utterance in the native language. This is often printed side by side with the dialogue in the target language. The student can read this meaning to himself, and the class is still conducted in the target language.

Another way to provide the meaning is to work with a composite picture or a series of pictures. The dialogue or the picture is explained in the native language beforehand. The target dialogue is then learned and associated with the pictures.

Since it is desirable that the student associate the target language with the teacher as well as with particular meanings, we favor giving the meaning in writing, not on the same page but perhaps in an appendix where it will not be associated sentence by sentence with the target language. Further, we would not practice the dialogue with the native language as the stimulus but would use instead a composite picture or series of pictures or a key word or phrase to indicate which dialogue is to be practiced.

Context and dramatization can be trusted to supply a good deal of the meaning. No harm will result if the student does not grasp every detail of the meaning of the dialogue as long as he can say it with ease and accuracy. The meaning will be brought out by repeated use of the dialogue.

After the first few dialogues, the student may know enough of the language to understand new dialogues with the explanation of a few new words in the target language itself. If every time that real communication is needed the teacher turns to the native language, the target language will not be taken seriously as an instrument of communication. The learning drive that the urge to communicate instills will be lost.

Practicing recall Pictures with numbers to indicate the sequence of sentences in the dialogue or series of pictures tied to the utterances are a powerful aid to recall of basic sentences in the dialogues. The human brain seems to have an extraordinary capacity to recall utterances associated with particular objects, persons, or drawings. Once the picture has been labeled, it will elicit the label even if there is only a remote resemblance between the meaning of the utterance and the subject of the drawing.

Ultimately, the dialogue exercise closest to a total experience is a recitation between two students completely from memory. When the dialogues consist of a reasonable number of lines, this is not a forbidding task.

Applying the laws of learning Insofar as the laws of language learning are known and relevant, they should be used for the improvement of language teaching in a scientific approach and in the memorization of dialogues and other material.

If the law of geometric increase in permanence [2] is valid (see page 45), and if we assume that the permanence after each successful recall is three times as long as the rest period that preceded the recall, the following review schedule might be possible: A dialogue is brought to a satisfactory level of mastery the first day. It is reviewed the following class day. It is then reviewed after rest periods of 3, 9, and 27 class days following each successive review (actually 3, 12, and 36 class days after the first review) and so forth. This schedule of review would permit the teacher to introduce a new dialogue each class day for a semester at three classes a week (about 40 dialogues) and to review them with no more than four dialogues (three for review and one new) in any class day.

As to memorizing of long utterances and the use of the dialogues themselves, much could be learned by a few carefully controlled experiments to explore the best use of the learning power of the students.

[2] Period during which the response can be recalled at will.

Cultural notes It is difficult to present much of a dialogue without getting into matters of cultural content. If these matters are not clarified at the time, the student will assume that they are the same as in his own culture and may, as a result, misunderstand what is said and done. Matters of cultural content can be handled by brief cultural notes in the simplest of terms, preferably in the target language. When clarification is not possible through the target language, a written note in the student's language might be read silently by him without using the language aloud in class. These notes would be prepared *ad hoc* to fit the dialogues.

Systematic treatment of cultural traits will have to wait until the intermediate level when the student may discuss them in the target language. A more comprehensive treatment of the culture requires advanced knowledge of the language.

Chapter 7

Phonemes Across Languages

Pronunciation is the use of a sound system in speaking and listening. Our goal, obviously, is not to have the students talk about the sounds of the language but to use them in utterances for communication. All language teaching involves pronunciation.

The pronunciation of a language is made up of consonants, vowels, intonation, stress, rhythm, junctures, and their sequences. Included in pronunciation, then, are the phonemes, their allophones, and their phonemic features. Also included are the syllable patterns, sound clusters, and phrase patterns permitted in the language.

The use of the pronunciation system of a language is a matter of habit or a system of habits. This set of habits operates below the threshold of awareness for the most part. When an individual listens efficiently, he is not aware of the sound system that reaches his ears; yet everything he understands via the language passes through that sound system. Similarly, when he speaks efficiently, he is not aware that he encodes everything into the sound system, yet he does.

The use of the sound system of the native language is learned early. One- and two-year-old children use complex intonation patterns before they speak many words or sentences.

Uniqueness of Each Language System Each language has its own pronunciation system, which is different from all others. Even two languages as closely related as Spanish and Portuguese have very different sound systems.

Spanish has five vowel phonemes; Brazilian Portuguese has seven. Spanish: /i e a o u/, *piso, peso, paso, poso, puso.* Portuguese: /i e ɛ a ɔ o u/, *aquí, você, café, lá, avô, avó, tatú.* All Spanish vowels are oral. Portuguese has very prominent nasal allophones for its vowels or a separate nasalized phoneme that can be superimposed on the seven vowels. The vowel systems of Japanese and Spanish are more alike than those of Portuguese and Spanish, since Japanese has five vowels.

Sound systems may differ as to the sequences of phonemes permitted. English has many postvocalic consonant clusters of three and even four consecutive consonants: *ants, bursts, glimpsed.* Spanish permits only postvocalic clusters of two consonants, and not many of these.

Phonemes may have different restrictions on where they may occur. English has /ŋ/, as in *sing* and *singing,* in final or medial positions in words but never initially. Burmese, on the other hand, has this sound initially as a phoneme.

Sound systems differ drastically at times in intonation, stress, and rhythm. French has syllable-timed rhythm and no phonemic stress. English has stress-timed or phrase-timed rhythm and four phonemic stresses. Spanish has syllable-timed rhythm and three phonemic stresses. Chinese has a minor intonation system but an elaborate system of phonemic tones that identify words much as consonants and vowels identify words in English. In such greetings as *Guten Morgen, Herr Meier,* German very frequently uses a perfectly level intonation, which signals acute boredom to an American listener, but it is of course perfectly ordinary German with no overtones of boredom at all.

WHY TEACH PRONUNCIATION?

Children learn the pronunciation of the language around them without being taught pronunciation formally. Why teach pronunciation at all? Because except during preschool age the student will not learn it or will not learn it well otherwise. Merely hearing a foreign language does not result automatically in good pronunciation.

We are all familiar with persons who have spent a lifetime in a foreign-language environment and have not learned to pronounce the language well. Foreign students often continue some mispronunciations for years even though the language is spoken natively all around them.

Transfer   The learner transfers the sound system of his native language and uses it instead of that of the foreign language without fully realizing it.   An English speaker learning Chinese will use English intonation instead of Chinese tones.   A Spanish speaker learning English will use Spanish /i/ as in *ir* for both English /iy/ and /i/ as in *eat* and *it*.   The Japanese speaker learning Portuguese will substitute his five vowels for the Portuguese seven and will not use the nasal allophones.

This transfer occurs even when the learner consciously attempts to avoid it.   Force of habit influences his hearing as well as his speaking.   He does not hear through the sound system of the target language but filters what reaches his ear through his own sound system.   A three-syllable word produced with equal stress on all three syllables will be perceived differently by a French speaker, who will hear it as stressed on the last syllable; a speaker of Persian, who will assign a stress to the first syllable; and a Spanish speaker, who will hear a stress on the middle syllable.   Each hears the word in accordance with the dominant stress pattern of his own language.   The transfer of the native sound system occurs in the phonemes, allophones, and their distribution.

Noise   In communication terms, the substitution of another sound system produces noise that cuts down the intelligibility of what is transmitted.

In linguistic terms, the phonemic distinctions that serve to identify the words and sentences of the target language may be lost, with resulting ambiguity; a different phoneme or pattern may be substituted, with resulting misunderstanding; or nonpermitted sequences or units may be introduced, with failure of communication.

Since language has considerable redundancy (signals may be repeated several times, e.g., the plural is given three times in the Spanish phrase, *los amigos buenos*), the total message may still be transmitted, but the chances of misunderstanding or loss of information increase with every linguistic signal that is not differentiated.

Secondary and Tertiary Reactions   In addition to the message intended in communication, there are secondary individual reactions based on one's personal experience, likes, beliefs, and culture.   There is further an association of particular dialects with particular groups of people, socially, regionally, culturally, and professionally.

When a student uses his native sound system in the target language, the listeners will have tertiary reactions to his accent.   These tertiary responses will vary according to the listener, his cultural image of foreign accents and of that particular foreign accent, the use being made of the language by the speaker, etc.   For example, it is said that as a young man, Charles Boyer, the film star, became interested in speech lessons to overcome his French accent in English, upon which he was told that if he lost his French accent, he would lose his job. On the other hand, a teacher of English with a strong French accent cannot easily get a job. An accent associated with an uneducated group would hinder a speaker by tertiary association.

Interference with Memory Imperfect hearing of the sound system results in weaker memory of utterances and messages. Other factors are involved in this type of memory, but improvement of pronunciation in hearing and speaking results in improved memory.

HOW PERFECT A PRONUNCIATION?

More than one level of accuracy in pronunciation may be satisfactory, depending on the goals, the age of the pupils, and whether the language will be a second or a foreign language. Three levels are identifiable immediately: (1) for full communication, (2) as a model by a language teacher, and (3) as a national language without regard for international use.

For full communication the standard might well be the phonemic distinctions of the language. Subphonemic variations do not change the words. Subphonemic distortions can therefore be tolerated even though the goal is full communication.

This level would permit a Spanish speaker learning English to use unaspirated Spanish [p] for both unaspirated and aspirated /p/ in English. It would permit English speakers learning Spanish to use English /d/ as both the stop and fricative allophones, [d] and [ð], of Spanish /d/. Such substitutions would be noticed as a foreign accent but would not result in ambiguity or misinterpretation.

If the goal of the student is to teach the language or to use it in radio broadcasts, for example, both phonemic and subphonemic accuracy and authenticity should be sought, even if such accuracy is not easily secured.

In India, the Philippines, Nigeria, and other countries where English is taught as a second language for national communication, arguments are strong for accepting the type of mutation English which exists in each of these countries and which has been influenced by the local languages. The argument can become purely rhetorical if no other English can be taught, but if there is a choice, then a more widely acceptable pronunciation might be preferable since the language will also be used in international communication.

For reading purposes only, the phonemic distinctions should still be taught, or they will not be used for efficient silent reading. Latin and Greek can be, and have been, studied with the sounds of a modern language, and Latin has been pronounced as English and as French, to mention two instances. But there are arguments to justify an effort to produce the sounds of Latin as nearly as possible as the ancient Romans produced them, and classical scholars in general make this effort. There are also arguments, practical and linguistic, to justify the use of the so-called ecclesiastical pronunciation of Latin, which uses the sounds of a modern Italian dialect.

What Dialect? How shall we decide what dialect to teach? Should we teach British or American English, the Spanish of Spain or that of Latin America, Mandarin Chinese or Cantonese, Brazilian Portuguese or that of Portugal?

Sometimes it is immaterial. When two varieties are acceptable as the speech of educated speakers, either can be taught. The choice might be made on the basis of the speech of the teacher or that of those with whom the students will communicate. This decreases the "noise" in communication. The present-day situation in English, Spanish, and Portuguese permits such a choice.

When one variety has more prestige or wider acceptability, it may be necessary to teach it. Mandarin Chinese is usually selected on this basis. Within the major national varieties of English, Spanish, Portuguese, French, German, etc., there is greater acceptability and prestige for the speech of the educated. This should be taken into account.

The reasoning is simple. The students usually study a language as part of their general education. If we teach them a variety that is associated with the educated, the interpretation of those who hear them will be correct. If, on the contrary, we teach them a variety associated with uneducated groups, those who hear them will take them erroneously as uneducated.

To this should be added that linguistically it is better to follow the speech of one model in learning to speak, and to hear a variety of speakers and dialects in learning to understand.

STRATEGY

Teaching pronunciation is difficult. It does not take care of itself, except with preschool children. Pronunciation must be taught.

Presenting the pronunciation of a language in an introductory lesson, or lessons, is not enough. Students do not acquire the habits of pronunciation of a second language all at once. It is more effective to present an introductory lesson or lessons and follow them up with a pronunciation section in succeeding lessons until the desired level of mastery is achieved. This requires an extended program.

When the goal is full mastery of the language, a separate class and set of lessons will eventually be required. These are usually known as phonetics or pronunciation courses, and they are particularly important for language teachers.

Teaching the Problems   One does not teach everything about the sound system of the language. This would be pedantic and would hinder more than it would help.

The learner transfers the sound system of his first language to the second. Some elements and patterns will function well and do not have to be taught. The moment the student observes them, he can use them. A Spanish speaker learning Japanese does not have to be taught the five vowels of Japanese; he knows them because he has a similar five-vowel system in Spanish. He will have to be taught the voiceless variants, which differ from Spanish.

Other pronunciation matters will need minor attention from the teacher. An English speaker learning Spanish learns easily the one Spanish /i/ vowel, as compared to his /iy/ and /i/ in *eat* and *it*. No elaborate lesson is necessary. Even if this phoneme were never taught, it would be handled well by mere exposure to Spanish. Simple reference to the Spanish vowels with examples will suffice.

Still other pronunciation matters are hard to master. They must be taught thoroughly, or they will not be learned. Those elements and patterns that differ structurally from the first language and represent a more complex system are the real problems. Spanish, Portuguese, Tagalog, and other speakers learning English have tremendous difficulty with English /iy/ and /i/. Hearing English for years is not enough. A detailed phonetic explanation with examples is not enough. Hard teaching with practice for an hour or two on this one problem is not enough. A simple test using minimal pairs such as *eat:it* will show many errors on the part of Spanish, Portuguese, Tagalog, Japanese, and other teachers of English who have studied English for years. Even those who have spent a year in an English-speaking country may still have trouble with this sound contrast.

With such problems, strategy requires that they be brought to consciousness, understood, practiced consciously, and then practiced extensively with attention on communication.

Problem features   Even in teaching the problems, it is confusing and pedantic to describe everything as if the student were starting from scratch. Emphasize and practice the features that constitute the problems. Spanish speakers have trouble pronouncing English initial /sp/, /sk/, /st/, as in *speak, school, study.* They intrude an initial /e/ and produce non-English *espeak, eschool, estudy.* It would be confusing to teach this problem by describing the phonemes /s/, /p/, /k/, /t/ and the clusters /sp/, /sk/, and /st/. The students know this from Spanish, which has these phonemes and these sequences, as in *español, escuela, estudiar.* The problem is their occurrence initially without a preceding vowel. This is what the students cannot pronounce and probably do not hear.

By contrasting a description of the sound system of the target language with that of the first language, we anticipate the problems that need to be taught and the particular features that are difficult. An increasing number of such comparisons is becoming available in print, and they should be studied by the teacher and materials writer. But the teacher must nevertheless understand contrastive problems because dialect and individual differences among students will produce differences in learning.

Problems as habits Do not expect the class to overcome a problem once and for all because you have explained and practiced it. New pronunciation habits must be learned to a high degree of automaticity with attention on the message, on communication, and not on the sounds themselves. This is not easy to achieve. Some problems must be understood, practiced, and practiced again and again with attention shifting to the message. In some cases as many as a hundred separate practice periods may be required to master the problem. Scientifically spaced practices may reduce the number of experiences necessary, but they will still be many.

Order of Presentation Although there is no one scientific order of presentation of the sound-system of a language, there are guidelines that will show the advantages of one choice over another. The target language and the native language make a difference. The age of the students may also be a factor in determining the order.

You cannot teach the sound system all at once, as we noted above. The over-all system should probably be presented at first for general orientation and set but not for mastery. One cannot learn a complex sound system such as that of a language at one sweep.

The question is then in what order to teach the intonation, stress, rhythm, tone if any, juncture, consonants, vowels, and sequences.

Traditionally, the consonants and vowels have been taught first; stress, rhythm, and intonation were not taught until later, or were not taught at all.

Since intonation, stress, rhythm, and juncture affect consonants and vowels more or less heavily, they should also be taught from the beginning if they constitute learning problems. Do not begin teaching the entire intonation system. Select a problem and teach it. Use other intonations that do not constitute learning problems.

Do not distort the system in the attempt to simplify it. Grade the material by selection rather than by distortion. In teaching English, for example, begin with the common intonation pattern represented by /2 3' 1 ↓/ as in

^{2}I need a $^{3'}$map^1 ↓

where 2 = mid, 3 = high, 1 = low, ↓ = fade-out juncture, and the stress mark on 3 represents the center of prominence or stress. (See Chapter 8 for a description of intonation patterns and their notation.)

The stress and rhythm system of French is simple but constitutes a problem for English speakers, who substitute their English rhythm and stress contrasts. In the early lessons in French, nasal vowels must perhaps also be begun, because of their difficulty and high frequency. Gradually, other vowel problems must be taught and practiced. The consonants can be interspersed or held for later.

In teaching English, intonation, stress, and rhythm are complex and constitute major problems for many language backgrounds. With intonation and rhythm, the vowels need to be taught gradually, because of their difficulty and frequency. Semivowels such as /r/, /y/, and /w/ should come at the stage when vowels are being taught. Systematic drill on consonants and consonant clusters may be withheld long enough to permit basic work on intonation, rhythm, and the vowels.

In any language teach one problem at a time. Withhold other problems until one solution is made available as a response. Progress cumulatively, using insofar as possible what has been taught previously.

Withhold vocabulary problems when concentrating on a pronunciation problem. This rule does not apply when an unusual word is needed to illustrate a minimal contrast between phonemes. In such cases, however, teach the word as a form only, not necessarily its meaning. Withhold also grammatical problems not yet taught when teaching a pronunciation problem.

So far, the order of teaching pronunciation problems has been considered only from the point of view of what is best for pronunciation. In teaching a language, we must consider also the order of teaching vocabulary and grammar. This will cause problems of coordination. Here are two main guidelines.

When a grammatical problem that needs to be taught involves a pronunciation problem as well, teach the pronunciation problem even if it does not fit the order of presentation of the sound system. For example, the automatic alternation of the plural, $\{/s/\sim/z/\sim/iz/\}$, in English as in *books, eggs, boxes* should be taught early enough to facilitate the grammar problem even if it does not fit neatly into the order of presentation of the consonants and vowels.

When a vocabulary item is necessary to operate a grammatical pattern, and that vocabulary item contains a pronunciation problem, teach the pronunciation problem for that word. The personal pronouns in English have to be taught early. This will involve pronunciation problems, such as /š/ in *she* or /z/ in *his*. The verb *be* has to be taught early. This introduces the problem of /z/ as in *is*.

Chapter 8

Intonation and Rhythm

The first formal exercise in pronunciation should deal with intonation and rhythm. Rhythm includes stress, time, and junctures. It is probably more effective to teach consonants and vowels within appropriate intonation and rhythm units than to teach the consonants and vowels in detail by themselves, later attempting to fit them into authentic intonation and rhythm.

All pronunciation involves the use of features of sound, including intonation and rhythm, that constitute the sound system of a language. It also involves disregarding, or separating, nonlanguage features of sound, such as the timbre of male versus female voices, etc. Use of the sound system is basically the use of units and patterns, some of which are recurrences of the same unit or pattern and others are occurrences of different units or patterns. There is functionally no middle ground between the same units and different units. All occurrences of the high phoneme of intonation in English function as if they were identical in every occurrence, even though they vary within a given range. And all occurrences of this high intonation phoneme function as completely different from and in contrast with every occurrence of any other intonation phoneme in English.

Although listening and speaking are intimately related, they are different operations. Our goal is to teach the students to hear and speak through a foreign sound system. In this endeavor, perception is the first step. The teaching of intonation begins with a model for perception.

Perception is more than mere identification of an utterance as an occurrence of a unit or pattern of a sound system. Perception is the ability to identify that utterance as the same as all other like occurrences of that unit or pattern and as different from all others that are in contrast with it.

Perceiving Intonation, Stress, and Juncture Sounds have no meaning in themselves; they merely serve to express or identify a unit or pattern which in turn has meaning. As a result, teaching perception precedes teaching the meaning. The student is asked to identify the sound or pattern which he hears. This can best be done by comparing one sound or pattern with another.

In teaching the English intonation pattern illustrated by the example, "²I need a ³′map¹ ↓" (see page 77), begin by giving this example orally to the class some three times. Then add other examples of the same and of other patterns. Ask the students after each example whether it is the same as or different from the first. Ask the class as a whole so that everyone will respond. At first some will be confused and will say it is different when it is the same. With a little practice the responses become uniform, indicating that the class can identify the pattern.

Models for Perception: Props and Partials If the student has trouble identifying the examples, draw his attention to the element or feature that he is missing. Use any means at your command. Various props have been developed and tried with success. Compare the following.

Description A verbal description of the feature might help. For a Spanish speaker learning English, one might say, "Notice the high pitch and the drop in the last word of '²I need a ³′map¹ ↓.'" For a French speaker learning English, one might say, "Notice the stress on '³′map¹.'" And again it may be necessary to say, "Notice the high point and length in '³′map¹.'" For a Thai speaker, it may be better to say, "Notice the drop in '³′map¹.'"

It is usually good to repeat the examples two or three times, or more, depending on difficulty.

Lines A line through the written sentence often helps:

I need a│map.

The height of the line above or below the printed words indicates the phonemic levels of English intonation:

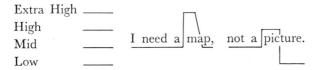

Extra High ——
High   ——
Mid   ——   I need a map, not a picture.
Low   ——

This basic line notation, developed by K. L. Pike for the Michigan English Language Institute materials, has been modified in various ways and used by many. The straight line and angular changes do not imply fixed levels. They represent normal fluctuation within each phonemic level.

In the following modification the tail indicates a final fade-out juncture:

I need a map.

Stress is often indicated in addition to the intonation and juncture. Accent marks prevail in marking stress:

I need a road map.

' indicates primary stress, ˆ secondary, ` tertiary, and ˘ weak. The weak stress is usually left unmarked.

Because of the problem and expense of printing lines through the text, the line is sometimes drawn above the text:

I need a map.

Dots on a scale A pseudo musical notation has been developed[1] to represent intonation, stress, and juncture for teaching. This notation is learned quickly by students and is easily read.

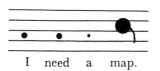

I   need   a   map.

The size of the dots represents stress. Four sizes are needed for the

[1] By Kenneth L. Croft.

four-stress system of English. Three sizes, or stresses, would suffice for Spanish.

⬤ indicates primary stress, ● secondary, • tertiary, and · weak.

Intonation level is represented by the height of the dot on the scale:

Extra high
High
Mid
Low

Juncture is represented by the direction of the tail attached to the last dot:

Sustain •—   Rise ⌣   Fall ⌐

Numbers For printing purposes the use of raised numbers is the simplest complete notation. It takes a little longer for the students to master this number system to represent intonation, but once learned, it is effective. Low intonation is usually represented by 1, mid by 2, high by 3, and extra high by 4:

^{2}Ì nèed ă ^{4}róad mâp^2, nòt ă ^{3}píctŭre^1.

Capital letters, italic type, etc. Special typographical devices such as boldface or italic type, capital letters, different letter sizes, or colors are sometimes used. These methods may help informally, but they do not represent the intonation and stress systems completely and are therefore imperfect.

Partials Giving the example in parts or giving it more slowly as a partial experience is another approach:

^{3}máp^1 ↓
^{2}ă ^{3}máp^1 ↓
^{2}nèed ă ^{3}máp^1 ↓
^{2}Ì nèed ă ^{3}máp^1 ↓

Avoid further distortions when giving examples more slowly. These are partial experiences that should not be left as such but should be restored to the full utterance at normal speed before leaving the exercise.

Imitation Perception usually runs ahead of pronunciation. After perception comes imitation, the simplest form of pronunciation. Imitation is the most direct road to full pronunciation. When imitation works, go to the next stage: repetition without an immediate model.

Props and Partials for Pronunciation When imitation does not work, use such props as lines, dots on a scale, etc. Sometimes, however, the meaning is so closely associated with the intonation in the native language that the student cannot imitate what he hears in the target language as long as he thinks of the meaning. A Spanish-speaking student uses a rising intonation on tag questions such as, "It's a good day, isn't it?" when he thinks of them as questions. Imitation has been attempted in some cases as many as 12 consecutive times without success. Partial exercises are in order in such cases.

Slowing down the model without otherwise distorting it may help. Echoing the intonation and rhythm with the nonsense syllable *la* also helps. This is a partial experience since it eliminates meaning temporarily.

^{2}là la lâ ^{3}lá^1 | ^{3}lá la^1 ↓

Since it is the meaning "question" that triggers the rise at the end, you can remind the student that he is telling you, not asking.

An often effective shock treatment is to put the intonation on a phrase in the native language where it does not belong. Students will hear it then.

Verbal hints are an obvious help; for example, such hints as, "High on 'isn't,' low on 'it,' " may be all the student needs.

Pointing out a similar intonation in the native language will work in some instances if there is one similar enough.

Giving several other examples in the same intonation pattern is a powerful help:

^{2}It's a good ^{3}day^1, | ^{3}isn't it?^{1} ↓
^{2}They're coming ^{3}home^1, | ^{3}aren't they?^{1} ↓
^{2}We'll rent a ^{3}boat^1, | ^{3}won't we?^{1} ↓

The force of parallel rhythm and intonation can also be used to advantage in choral recitation to practice good rhythm in general.

Variation Once the student is able to imitate and remember the examples, he should learn to vary the sentences to suit other situations. This variation can be done by substitution, transformation, expansion, reduction, combination, etc. An example of simple substitution is the following:

[The teacher gives the cues and the responses]
^{2}It's a good ^{3}day,^{1} | ^{3}isn't it?^{1} ↓
^{3}Morning^1 ↓
^{2}It's a good ^{3}morning,^{1} | ^{3}isn't it?^{1} ↓
^{3}Summer^1 ↓
^{2}It's a good ^{3}summer,^{1} | ^{3}isn't it?^{1} ↓

[The teacher gives the cues and the class gives the responses]
³Day¹ ↓
²*It's a good* ³*day,*¹ | ³*isn't it?*¹ ↓
³Winter¹ ↓
²*It's a good* ³*winter,*¹ | ³*isn't it?*¹ ↓

[Continue with *spring, year,* etc.]

These pattern-practice exercises require the student to concentrate on the changes while continuing to use the desired rhythm and intonation pattern. Other pattern-practice exercises are presented in Chapter 11 devoted to this subject.

Selection The last stage in teaching intonation and rhythm is that of selection, which is essentially full communication use of the language. The student is given a topic, a picture or set of pictures, a story, or some combination of these as stimulus for his speaking exercise. He may be asked questions to elicit desired sample responses. If the pattern practice has been done well, this last exercise will show the results and reap the benefit. If not, it will bog down. The usual mistake is to skimp on pattern practice and to go into selection before the problem patterns are handled with ease. The argument is that the students want to learn to speak. They may not realize that they are learning to speak when they are doing pattern practice, but they are.

The Consonant and Vowel Network

Chapter 9

The stages in teaching consonants and vowels are similar to those in teaching intonation and rhythm. Any differences lie chiefly in the props to be used, which are articulatory for the most part.

Perception Give the problem sound in a word. Direct the students' attention to it by saying something like, "Notice the vowel (or consonant)." "Notice the first (or second or last) vowel (or consonant)." It may be necessary to give the sound in isolation once or twice to draw attention to it. Give other examples—three or more as needed.

The students will attempt to pronounce the examples quietly first. There is no harm in this, and there may be some advantage in it. We do not know how much of a difference attempting to pronounce a sound from the beginning makes in learning to hear it. We suspect it does make a difference, but controlled experiments are needed before we can state this as a fact.

When you sense that the students are beginning to hear the sound, go on to a perception exercise. There are many good exercises to practice perception. Here are a few.

Comparing sound with sound Give pairs of words or phrases containing the sound problems. In some of the pairs the two members are the same; in others they are different. Ask the students to say "same" or "different" accordingly. When the two sounds in the pairs that are different constitute a perception problem, some of the students will say they are the same, because they do not hear the difference. Props and partials are needed at this point. These will be discussed after we illustrate other perception exercises.

A variation of this technique consists of sets of three words or phrases, some of which contain the problem sound while others have the sound that is confused with it. Ask the students to identify by number the words that contain the problem sound. Make the responses uniform to avoid confusion. For example, have the students say simply, "One and two," "One and three," or "One, two, and three," to indicate the numbers of the phrases that contain the problem sound.

The response can be expressed in different ways. Saying the numbers out loud works quickly as a starter. Writing the numbers on a piece of paper and checking them is more accurate. Writing the numbers down works well as a quick review exercise the next class period or later.

Identifying sounds by number Give the sound and call it number one. Give the sound that is confused with it and call it number two. Then give a series of words or phrases and ask the students to say "one" if they hear the first sound and "two" if they hear the other. The students can be asked to show one finger or two instead of saying the numbers. Or they can write down the numbers.

Sounds to phonetic symbols or letters If phonetic symbols are used, you can ask the students to write the symbol for the vowel or consonant being taught. Writing the entire word or phrase in phonetics or ordinary spelling (dictation) is slow and less effective than concentrating on the problem itself.

It must be remembered that using the writing system introduces an additional learning problem. In teaching Chinese, the problem is so obvious that no one can miss it or confuse learning writing with learning the sound system. In Russian with its Cyrillic alphabet, it is not usually overlooked. The problem, however, is present in French and Spanish as well, though less heavily. It should not be overlooked in teaching any language.

Props and Partials As a rule, listening alone is not fully effective in teaching perception of the problem sounds. Props and partials increase effectiveness in presenting a problem and in practicing its perception.

Isolate the sound as a first partial. Slow down the pronunciation of the word as a second partial. In both cases the sound should then be restored to normal speed in an utterance.

Articulatory description The most powerful prop is an articulatory description or hint. The teacher should know the full phonological description of the sound, including distinctive features such as voicing, point and manner of articulation, etc. As a rule the full description should not be given to the students, because they do not need it and may actually be confused by it. The teacher should know what the usual mispronunciation is and thus be able to limit the articulatory comment to that feature only.

For example, a Spanish speaker learning English will tend to unvoice the /z/ in *easy,* saying /iysi/ instead of /iyzi/. He transfers his one *s*-like phoneme from Spanish with its voiceless allophone between vowels. It is wasteful and pedantic to go into a full description of English /z/ when what the student needs to do is to voice his [s].

Shift of position It is sometimes possible to find the desired sound as an allophone of another phoneme in the native language. For example, Spanish speakers learning English have trouble pronouncing final /n/ and /ŋ/, as in *sin:sing, ban:bang.* They can pronounce /n/ in medial position as in *sinner,* then prolong it as in *sin-n-n-ner,* prolong it again, and stop in the middle of it. After several repetitions they can shorten the /n/ to normal length at normal speed in final position.

Mirror When the sounds are articulated with the lips or teeth so that the articulation can be seen, as, for example, with the English phonemes /b/, /v/, /θ/, /ð/, /f/, /m/, /p/, a small mirror can be used by the student to watch his own articulation, which at first has to be set deliberately under full attention. English /b/ and /v/ as in *boat* and *vote* can be taught with the help of a mirror when imitation alone has failed.

Facial diagrams A side interior view of a face as shown in the figure below is very effective in showing graphically the articulation of a sound without using the native language.

Facial diagrams for [a] and [iy].

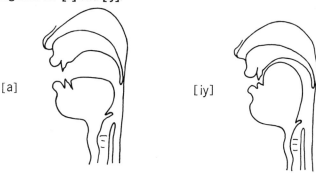

[a]   [iy]

The teacher should learn to draw quickly the position of the articulators for the sounds to be taught. Flash cards with the facial diagrams already prepared beforehand are also very effective.

Front views of the mouth are sometimes useful to show rounding of the lips and slit or grooved position and articulation of the tongue.

The foreign sound in the native language Sometimes, when everything else has failed, it helps to place the new sound in a word or phrase in the student's own language. This brings into sharper focus the articulation of the new sound. Placing a Spanish trilled /r̄/ in an English word makes the trill more prominent to an English speaker. Putting the English phoneme /æ/ as in *hat* in place of the Spanish phoneme /a/ of *mano* may do what imitation, articulatory description, and modification of a Spanish sound failed to accomplish.

Interpolation The English /æ/ of *hat* is a problem for Spanish speakers. They can pronounce /e/, with higher tongue position, and /a/, with lower tongue position, but not /æ/, which is somewhere between the two. To teach /æ/, pronounce and have the class imitate /e/ and /a/ several times; then pronounce and have them imitate the /æ/ between them in the series /e/, /æ/, /a/. This will usually help.

Repetition Once the students succeed in producing the problem sound by imitation with props as needed, go into practice without an immediate model. This can be accomplished by repeating a memorized phrase or dialogue, speaking the words associated with a set of pictures, reading aloud, answering questions, or finishing incomplete sentences.

Variation through Pattern Practice From repetition of known examples go to pattern practice using the sound in a variety of words with attention on vocabulary, type of construction, or meaning. Substitution, transformation, expansion, synthesis, completion, etc., are easily applied, making the changes in various elements, not necessarily the one containing the problem sound.

Selection Ultimate free use of the sound system requires selection of full utterances to fit the communication situation. The situations can be controlled by questions, suggested topics, pictures, stories, etc., so that the student is forced to use the problem sounds even though he is speaking freely.

Clusters and Sequences Many pronunciation problems involve consonant and vowel clusters and sequences. This is so even when all the phonemes involved are found in the native language but not in that position or that order.

Spanish has the sequences [st], [sk], [sp], but they never occur without a preceding vowel. As a result, Spanish speakers learning English have trouble with these sounds as initial clusters. They pronounce non-English *espeak, estudy, eschool* instead of *speak, study, school.*

The steps in teaching clusters are the same as in teaching individual consonants and vowels. The props will depend on the facts of the case. Initial [sp], [st], [sk] can be elicited by telling the students to pronounce a long [sss], which they can do well, and then to add [piyk]. The process is repeated with shorter and shorter [s] until a deliberate but satisfactory [spiyk] finally emerges.

Authentic Models Teachers can now provide authentic pronunciation models easily for their students by means of a tape recorder or a phonograph. A portable tape recorder is almost indispensable for the language teacher. With a tape recorder the resourceful teacher can not only present the models supplied by the course material but can prepare special exercises to meet the needs of the particular class taught.

Visitors and professional speakers can be recorded for the benefit of the students, thus bringing to the class a variety of good native speakers even when the teacher does not happen to be a native speaker of the target language.

Chapter 10

From Sentences to Patterns

What does "grammar" mean? Grammar as the memorization of rules, the use of terminology, or the analysis of sentences by the students has been challenged by many and relegated by linguistics to a minor role in teaching languages. On the other hand, grammar as the patterns of form and arrangement, including intonation, stress, and juncture—the structure by which the speakers of a language communicate—cannot be so relegated. Anyone using a language must use its grammar; mere words without grammar do not constitute a language.

Even children who have never studied the rules of grammar make use of the grammar of the language. This is seen in the mistakes they make. When a child says, *He goed,* he is forming a "regular" preterite on the pattern: *showed, weighed, served: "goed."* His error reveals the fact that he has been applying the pattern even though he is not able to describe it.

Patterns and Sentences A grammatical pattern is an arrangement of parts having linguistic significance beyond the sum of its parts. The parts of a pattern are expressed by words or classes of words so that different sentences often express the same pattern. All the sentences of a language are cast in its patterns. *John telephoned, The boy studied, We understood* are different sentences expressing the same statement pattern in English. *Llamó, Estudió, Entendimos* express a simple state-ment pattern in Spanish, one that would not be permitted in English.

Such a pattern is not a conjugation or declension. Patterns are sequences of parts as used in speech or writing; conjugations are inven-tories of the various forms of a word or class of words. *Amo, amas, ama, amamos, amáis, aman* never occurs as an utterance except in a classroom. No one speaks in conjugations, but everyone speaks in patterns.

A pattern is not a sentence, however. Sentences express patterns. Each sentence illustrates a pattern. To memorize a sentence does not imply that a pattern has been memorized. There can be countless sentences, each unique, yet all constructed on the same pattern.

Patterns and Grammar   Children learn the grammatical patterns of their language before they study grammar in school. When a child says *goed* instead of *went* or *knowed* instead of *knew,* he is applying the regular preterite pattern on the analogy,

open : opened = go: *goed*

Similarly, when a Spanish-speaking child says *sabo* instead of *sé* or *cabo* instead of *quepo,* he too is applying a regular pattern where it is not allowed:

comer : como = saber : *sabo*

One does not notice the countless times that children apply a pattern and it fits.

This application of patterns has been demonstrated further with children by showing them a picture of some strange creature, giving it a name, and then showing them a picture of two or more of these creatures and asking them what they are called. Children change the strange name to a regular plural with ease. A circle with stick legs and an eye is labeled a *clug,* for example. When confronted with two circles with legs and eyes, the child says they are *clugs.*

Patterns are learned in childhood. Adults no longer have to learn new patterns; they learn new words that are used in old patterns. That the old patterns are alive is shown by putting unknown words and phrases into them.

Native Language Factor   The most important factor determining ease and difficulty in learning the patterns of a foreign language is their similarity to or difference from the patterns of the native language. When the pattern in the target language is parallel to one in the native language, the student merely learns new words which he puts into what amounts to an extended use of his native pattern. Since his word learning capacity is not lost, he makes rapid progress. When, however, the native language pattern does not parallel that of the target language, the student tends to revert to his native language patterns through habit.

Grading the Patterns   There is no single grading scale for teaching the patterns of a foreign language. Any systematic cumulative progression, taking into account the structures that are difficult, would be satisfactory from a linguistic point of view.

TEACHING GRAMMATICAL PATTERNS

Three approaches to the teaching of grammar will be discussed: the older and discredited one of the grammar-translation methods, the newer one of the mimicry-memorization method, and the still newer one of pattern drills and pattern practice. The grammar-translation approach is not recommended. The mimicry-memorization method is offered as a successful approach to be used for part of the teaching task or in the absence of more refined patterned and graded materials. The pattern-practice approach is presented as most effective at its appropriate stage.

Grammar-translation Methods   In the grammar-translation mode, the books begin with definitions of the parts of speech, declensions, conjugations, rules to be memorized, examples illustrating the rules, and exceptions. Often each unit has a paragraph to be translated into the target language and one to be translated into the native one. These paragraphs illustrate the grammar rules studied in the unit. The student is expected to apply the rules on his own. This involves a complicated mental manipulation of the conjugations and declensions in the order memorized, down to the form that might fit the translation. As a result, students are unable to use the language, and they sometimes develop an inferiority complex about languages in general. Exceptionally bright and diligent students do learn languages by this method, or in spite of it, but they would learn with any method. The grammar-translation method is largely discredited today.

Mimicry-memorization Method   Mimicry-memorization was the method developed in the Intensive Language Program of the American Council of Learned Societies and used by the United States Armed Forces during the Second World War to teach foreign languages intensively to military personnel. It was successful because of high motivation, intensive practice, small classes, and good models, in addition to linguistically sophisticated descriptions of the foreign language and its grammar.

Grammar is taught essentially as follows: Some basic sentences are memorized by imitation. Their meaning is given in normal expressions in the native language, and the students are not expected to translate word for word. When the basic sentences have been *overlearned* (completely memorized so that the student can rattle them off without effort), the student reads fairly extensive descriptive grammar statements in his native language, with examples in the target language and native language equivalents. He then listens to further conversational sentences which recombine the basic sentences for practice in listening. Finally, he practices the dialogues using the basic sentences and combinations of their parts. When he can, he varies the dialogues within the material he has already learned.

This approach was developed for use when linguistically trained teachers were not available, and when materials had to be prepared with utmost speed. It was successful, especially when the students had the benefit of a full nine months or a year of intensive concentration in the language. The problem of motivation was also a special one, since the urgency of the situation justified intensive mimicry-memorization practice without sufficient variation or challenge.

Pattern-practice Approach The mimicry-memorization exercise tends to give the same amount of practice to easy as well as difficult problems. It also concentrates unduly on the memorization of specific sentences, and not enough on the manipulation of the patterns of sentences in a variety of content situations. For those patterns that are functionally parallel to the native language, very little work needs to be done, and very little or no explanation is necessary. On the other hand, for those patterns that are not parallel in the two languages, more specific understanding of the grammatical structure points at issue is needed *while* the sentences are learned and not before or after. And more practice with the pattern is necessary before it is learned, that is, used without attention to its structure. When the teachers and the materials provide for these differences in difficulty through a pattern-practice approach, better results may be expected. For these reasons the pattern approach is described in some detail.

Basic sentences The memorization of sample sentences that contain the grammatical problems to be mastered is common to both pattern practice and mimicry-memorization. For this practice there is ample justification in linguistics and in psychology. The utterances have to become readily available if the student is to use them in the rapid sequence of conversation. Leonard Bloomfield, who set the stage for the mimicry-memorization approach, puts it this way:

> The command of a language is not a matter of knowledge: the speakers are quite unable to describe the habits which make up their language. The command of a language is a matter of practice. One might memorize the notes and chords which make up a certain piece of music, but one would then still be utterly unable to play the piece until one had practiced it over and over again for many hours. The same thing is true of a language. It is helpful to know how it works, but this knowledge is of no avail until one has practiced the forms over and over again until one can rattle them off without effort. To understand the forms is only the first step. Copy the forms, read them out loud, get them by heart, and then *practice them over and over again day after day,* until they become entirely natural and familiar. *Language learning is overlearning; anything less is of no use.*[1]

Teaching the patterns A sentence can be learned as a single unstructured unit like a word, but this is only the beginning. The student must acquire the habit of constructing sentences in the patterns of the target language. For this he must be able to put words almost automatically into a pattern without changing it, or to change it by making the necessary adjustments. This idea of learning the pattern rather than just sentences is clearly stated by C. C. Fries.

> The fundamental matters of the language that must be mastered on a production level should, as soon as possible, be made unconscious habits. For this purpose many whole sentences, questions and responses, demand repetition and more repetition and these will become automatic reactions early. But besides such specific formulas, useful phrases and sentences, there are many "patterns" that must eventually become the customary molds into which the productive expression must fit without conscious thought. . . . These, in the early stage of language learning, remain for considerable time on the level of *production with conscious choice* rather than of *production as an automatic unconscious habit.* Only after much practice of the same "patterns" with diverse content do the patterns themselves become productively automatic. When the student has reached this level of achievement, within a satisfactorily useful but definitely limited range of vocabulary items, he has "learned the language."[2]

[1] *Outline Guide for the Practical Study of Foreign Languages.* Baltimore: Linguistic Society of America, 1942, p. 12.
[2] *Teaching and Learning English as a Foreign Language.* Ann Arbor: The University of Michigan Press, 1945, pp. 8–9.

Teaching a problem pattern begins with teaching the specific structure points where a formal change in the pattern is crucial and where the student is not able to manipulate the required changes. The steps in teaching problem patterns are (1) *attention pointer,* usually a single sentence calling the students' attention to the point at issue; (2) *examples,* usually minimally contrastive examples showing a pair of sentences that differ only on the point or points being made; (3) *repetition* by the class and presentation of *additional examples* of the same contrast; (4) *comments* or *generalization* elicited inductively from the students and confirmed by the teacher; (5) *practice,* with attention on the problem being taught.

These steps are intended to clarify the crucial point of contrast at the time when sentences are being learned. They should take only a small portion of the class time—no more than 15 per cent.

Types of Exercises Many teachers make the mistake of trying to explain everything at length while the class listens passively. Long explanations without active practice are a waste of time, and even with practice they are inefficient. Most of the class should be devoted to practice. The following are brief descriptions of some of the more effective types of exercises.

Listening It is understood that the student does not invent the target language. He must listen to good models. Random listening helps, but selective listening following instructions is more effective. Listening is assumed to be most effective when it is in preparation for speaking.

Listening can be combined with other activities. If these include a verbal response, the exercise becomes one of speaking. Nonverbal responses intended to show comprehension produce good listening exercises.

Action responses to show understanding of commands or statements in the target language are a useful variation. These responses are either fully acted out; and the students actually get up, sit down, go to the door, or shake hands; or the responses are only pantomimed, and the students pretend to go to sleep, wash their hands, swim, etc. In another type of exercise, they mark pictures that correspond to what they hear.

A different type of listening exercise is useful at the beginning of a pattern-contrast drill. The teacher presents a minimal pair of sentences illustrating a contrast. The sentences are repeated by the class and written on the board for all to see. The teacher then gives a series of additional examples, which are like one or the other of the contrasting pair on the board. The class is asked to indicate after each example whether it is like the first or the second of the original pair.

Oral repetition In this practice the student repeats the pattern sentences provided orally by the model. This is the most basic and important of all exercises. It begins with the presentation of the very first sentence of the pattern, the basic sentence, and continues through all other examples of the pattern taught for speaking.

Repetition is not dull as long as the student is learning something in repeating. Ideally, repetition should never be asked of the student immediately after he has succeeded in a perfect response. If additional experiences with the same sentence are necessary, they should always involve some variation in speed, volume, audience, environment, intent, tone, etc.

Repetition should not only be used to learn the basic sentences; it should be used when examples are presented to demonstrate a grammar point: the teacher speaks the minimal contrast and the class repeats. New examples are given to show the patterns more precisely, and the class repeats each example as it is offered. Repeating the examples provides the experience to permit the student to work with what he has said. Discovery of the pattern is experienced more fully through examples the student has repeated than through those merely heard. Furthermore, examples that are repeated can be retained longer by the student than those that have not been repeated.

Oral substitution Once the student can speak the basic sentence by repetition, oral substitution becomes the most useful and powerful drill available to practice the pattern. It is fast, flexible, and versatile, and it approximates conversational use of the language. Several variations are described for the reader: simple substitution, substitution in variable position, substitution that forces a change, substitution requiring a change, and multiple substitution.

Simple substitution The model sentence is presented orally and repeated by the class until production is satisfactory. If the problem is, for example, the placing of adjectives after the noun in Spanish, whereas in English they would precede the noun, the substitutions might be adjectives, as in the following:

STIMULUS: Me gusta la casa blanca. [I like the white house]
RESPONSE: *Me gusta la casa blanca.*
STIMULUS: Verde. [green]
RESPONSE: *Me gusta la casa verde.*
STIMULUS: Nueva. [new]
RESPONSE: *Me gusta la casa nueva.*
STIMULUS: Grande. [big]
RESPONSE: *Me gusta la casa grande.*

(The meanings are given in square brackets for the reader, not for use in the exercise.) The exercise is conducted completely in the target language. The meaning of the words is assumed to be known since this is a grammar drill, not a vocabulary lesson. The teaching of vocabulary is discussed in Chapter 12.

The pace of the exercise is kept lively. Substitutions occur only in adjective position. If a student misses the response, it is given to him without holding up the class or embarrassing him unduly. The first few examples are executed solely by the teacher to illustrate the exercise for the students. After these, the teacher signals the class or individual students to respond.

Simple substitution in variable position A variation of the simple substitution in fixed position introduces substitutions that sometimes fit one spot, sometimes another. In the above example the substitutions might be broadened to include nouns as well as adjectives. Nouns would be placed in the position of *casa,* and adjectives in that of *blanca.*

s: Me gusta la casa blanca.
R: *Me gusta la casa blanca.*
s: Torre.   [tower]
R: *Me gusta la torre blanca.*
s: Verde.
R: *Me gusta la torre verde.*
s: Silla.   [chair]
R: *Me gusta la silla verde.*
s: Nueva.
R: *Me gusta la silla nueva.*

The student has to react to *torre* as a noun and place it in the noun position. He has to recognize and use *verde* as an adjective and place it in the adjective position. No complications involving gender and number are introduced at this stage. The substitutions are carefully selected to fit the pattern. These exercises can be led orally by the teacher, by a tape or other recording, through radio or television, or even through programmed machine instruction.

Substitutions that force a change If the problem includes changes in the form of the adjective and the article to agree with the noun, the exercise would be as follows:

s: Me gusta la silla nueva.
R: *Me gusta la silla nueva.*
s: Libro.   [book]
R: *Me gusta el libro nuevo.*
s: Mesa.   [table]
R: *Me gusta la mesa nueva.*

s: Blanca.
r: *Me gusta la mesa blanca.*
s: Vestido. [dress]
r: *Me gusta el vestido blanco.*

There are many varieties of substitutions that force a change. Changing the person of the subject will force an agreement change in the form of the verb in some languages. A time substitution from *now* to *yesterday* would force a change in the tense of the verb. Most languages have systems of agreement through which the introduction of one item can force adjustments in other parts of the sentence.

Substitutions that must be changed If the model sentence requires the plural and the substitutions are given in singular, the substitutions themselves are changed to agree with the context.

s: The books are coming.
r: *The books are coming.*
s: Boy.
r: *The boys are coming.*
s: Child.
r: *The children are coming.*
s: Goose.
r: *The geese are coming.*

Example showing adjustment of verb form in Spanish:

s: Los niños llegaron ayer. [The children arrived yesterday.]
r: *Los niños llegaron ayer.*
s: Salir. [Went out]
r: *Los niños salieron ayer.*
s: Escribir. [Wrote]
r: *Los niños escribieron ayer.*
s: Jugar. [Played]
r: *Los niños jugaron ayer.*
s: Trabajar. [Worked]
r: *Los niños trabajaron ayer.*

Multiple substitutions This type of drill involves simultaneous substitution of more than one element per response.

s: Juan llegó ayer. [John arrived yesterday.]
r: *Juan llegó ayer.*
s: María. Mañana. [Tomorrow]
r: *María llegará mañana.*
s: Pedro y Juan. Ayer.
r: *Pedro y Juan llegaron ayer.*

s : Yo. Mañana. [I]

R : *Yo llegaré mañana.*

s : Nosotros. Ayer. [We]

R : *Nosotros llegamos ayer.*

Transformation   Transformation practice, as the name implies, takes one pattern as stimulus and transforms it into another pattern in the response. The best way to start a transformation exercise is to demonstrate it by doing several examples. The students are then signaled to continue the transformations according to the examples.

s : Columbus discovered America in 1492.

R : *America was discovered by Columbus in 1492.*

s : Edison invented the electric light.

R : *The electric light was invented by Edison.*

s : Alexander Graham Bell invented the telephone.

R : *The telephone was invented by Alexander Graham Bell.*

s : Hernán Cortés conquered Mexico.

R : *Mexico was conquered by Hernán Cortés.*

s : Shakespeare wrote *Romeo and Juliet.*

R : Romeo and Juliet *was written by Shakespeare.*

These examples happen to make some sort of contextual sense, which adds interest to the exercise, but transformations do not depend on context. The examples illustrate the transformation desired, and the student proceeds with the same grammatical transformation by analogy:

s : The students are busy.

R : *Are the students busy?*

s : The teacher is reading papers.

R : *Is the teacher reading papers?*

s : The class can go faster.

R : *Can the class go faster?*

s : We should remember the lesson.

R : *Should we remember the lesson?*

s : John is a senior this year.

R : *Is John a senior this year?*

This is not a conversation even though it involves questions and answers. Nobody speaks in this order. The exercise is merely a way to practice the production of questions by supplying answers as controlling stimuli.

Exercises that depend on the context would be of the conversational type or the situation type, which may in addition involve some grammatical transformation.

Conversation practice Conversation practice has been used in many different ways by teachers, but it usually means exchanging information more or less freely without any special control of the patterns practiced. Conversation practice as used here means strictly controlled pattern drill which approximates ordinary conversation.

Transformation and other exercises can easily be changed to conversation exercises. Take for example the transformation of statements into questions. By changing the subject in the transformed questions a conversation practice is achieved.

s: The students are busy.
r: *Are the teachers busy?*
   Yes, they are.

s: The class can go faster.
r: *Can the teacher go faster?*
   Yes, he [or *she*] *can.*

s: We should remember the lesson.
r: *Should the teacher remember the lesson?*
   Yes, he [or *she*] *should.*

These are essentially conversations, and the pattern is strictly controlled. There is, however, a minimum of information requested and received.

Question-and-answer exercise The question-and-answer exercise may be only a special case of the conversation exercise, or it may be basically different. In the question-and-answer exercise the responses or answers are governed by the form of the question and by some situation or information that is known to the student.

s: How many brothers and sisters do you have?
r: *Five* [or whatever the number].

s: Where do you live?
r: *At 5404 New York Avenue* [or whatever the address].

s: When did you visit New York?
r: *Last year* [or whatever the time].

s: How far is your home from here?
r: *Five blocks* [or whatever the distance].

Questions and answers should be graded and designed to practice the pattern being taught. The above exercise would be too complex if it were not a review drill which assumes that the patterns have been studied before.

Completion exercise Completion exercises have been widely used in workbooks and in tests. They are incomplete sentences or phrases with enough context to determine the material that is required to complete them. When the missing word or phrase is at the end of the incomplete sentence, these exercises can be offered orally with speed and effectiveness. When the missing element is in the middle of the sentence, it is necessary to tap, say "blank," or pause at the point where the student is to supply the completion. This tends to make the drill more artificial. As written exercises, they have been used effectively for some time.

Completion from a list is a variation of this exercise. The completion elements are listed for the student to choose from. Without such a list, it is sometimes difficult to prepare a context that will allow only one correct answer. When three or four choices are given for each item, we have the multiple-choice item so generally used in testing.

Addition exercise In the addition exercise, the stimulus is added to the basic sentence rather than substituted for any part of it. The place where the stimulus word or phrase is to be added depends on the structure involved. Since these are cumulative additions, the utterance soon becomes quite long, and a new basic sentence has to be introduced to begin the process again. The following French example involves a rather complex phrase structure:

s: J'ai lu un chapitre.   [I read one chapter.]
r: *J'ai lu un chapitre.*
s: Long.   [long]
r: *J'ai lu un long chapitre.*
s: Du livre.   [of the book]
r: *J'ai lu un long chapitre du livre.*
s: Que j'ai acheté.   [which I bought]
r: *J'ai lu un long chapitre du livre que j'ai acheté.*
s: Français.   [French]
r: *J'ai lu un long chapitre du livre français que j'ai acheté.*

Synthesis From two simple sentences which supply the lexical information in a given order, a complex sentence pattern is constructed and practiced. The examples show the students the desired pattern.

s: We went to the zoo. I remember when.
r: *I remember when we went to the zoo.*
s: John needed ten cents. I know why.
r: *I know why John needed ten cents.*

s: He bought peanuts. I don't know where.

r: *I don't know where he bought peanuts.*

s: He went to see the monkeys. I asked him why.

r: *I asked him why he went to see the monkeys.*

s: They ate the peanuts. I don't know who.

r: *I don't know who ate the peanuts.*

s: He came back. I don't remember when.

r: *I don't remember when he came back.*

Composition As commonly used, composition exercises consist of a more or less free essay on some assigned topic. This is an effective exercise, but it does not provide sufficient controls for intensive practice of a particular problem. In fact, it is often possible for students to write a composition and avoid using the patterns that trouble them.

A composition exercise as defined here is more controlled and may refer to the "composition" of single sentences from a list of words. There is an element of creativity in this exercise, but the student must work with a word or on a model that forces him to use the problem pattern.

An example would be to have the students produce an affirmative statement about something in the past with each of these words, *go, sleep, study, think, run, stop, want.*

This type of exercise tends to be slow and to allow the student to introduce problems that he cannot handle yet. These difficulties are sometimes overcome by having the composition exercise center around some common experience such as a field trip, an excursion, a motion picture seen by everyone, a story known to all, or some well-known personality.

Chapter 11

Pattern Practice

You have seen a student reading aloud in class. He makes a mistake. The teacher corrects him; he nods and goes on reading. Or you have seen a student translating a passage into the native language—a translation prepared the night before. Notes between the lines refresh his memory and make sure he does not forget at the critical moment. He makes a mistake in translation. The teacher corrects. He nods or repeats in the native language and goes on to the next sentence.

Or you may remember this from your own experience: You prepared the translation of the passage assigned, looking up the words in the glossary, footnotes, or a dictionary. Some words did not stick to your memory so you wrote them down between the lines. When the word appeared again later in another sentence, you could not remember what it meant.

In an informal experiment the author memorized the English equivalents of 50 difficult German words. He read the German-English pairs, covered the English column, and tried to recall the English word by looking at the German. When a word was missed, he looked at the English equivalent, made a tally beside it, and went on. This process was repeated for the whole list until all the English equivalents were recalled once through. Surprisingly, the first reading was enough to remember some of the words, while others required as many as 16 readings. And in a few cases the words checked 16 times were missed the following day in class.

Certainly it is true that some things in a foreign language are easy to learn and to remember, while others can be unbelievably difficult. Books that presume to be scientific by repeating each new word at least three times in short succession are a step in the right direction but still remain far from language realities. For some of the words three repetitions are too many; for others, not enough.

Or do you recall this? You learned that initial *s* in German represented a voiced sibilant [z]. When reciting in class, however, you pronounced it voiceless, [s]. By the time the teacher corrected you, you already knew what to do; you did not remember soon enough. A sarcastic teacher once told a student to skip his first try and give the second.

Some teachers expect the student to apply in use everything mentioned in class, as if explaining something were enough to establish a habit. It is actually normal to forget difficult patterns, not once but many times. Rare individuals might learn a language under such conditions, but they would learn it without a class or a method, and we do not know but that they might not learn it faster that way. For the usual student, including the brilliant one, this kind of teaching is ineffective and leads to many frustrations.

These examples show a misconception of the nature of language learning: that a language is a scheme of so many words and rules to be put into the student's head whence they will flow as needed if the student is intelligent enough to remember them at the right time and tempo.

Just how impossible of realization this scheme is can be seen when we recognize that in this very sentence you are reading there are scores of grammatical rules and lexical contrasts in effect and consequent choices to be made. Here are some choices: *Just* means "exactly" in this context, not "fair" or "only." *How* does not signal a question here because of the word order of the subject *scheme* and the verb *be*. *This scheme is* indicates a statement in contrast to the question *is this scheme*. *Realization* modifies *impossible* by the function of the preposition *of*. *Impossible* means "not possible"; *possible* means "it can exist or occur"; hence *impossible* means "it can not exist or occur." *Just* is invariable in form, i.e., it does not change for gender, number, or case. *How* is invariable in form. *How* means "to what degree" in this context, not "in what manner." *Of* as a preposition connects a noun object to a noun head. *Realization* is singular; the plural ends in *s*. *Realization* is a noun; words ending in *–tion* are usually nouns. *Of* is invariable in form; prepositions are not inflected in English. *This* is singular; *these* is plural. *This* and *these* agree in number with the noun they determine. And so on and on. Eight words—and more than fifteen rules and contrasts.

Habit ignored or held in contempt The fact that language operates largely on the basis of habit should be obvious to everyone. It is only through habit that the thousand-and-one rules of grammar, pronunciation, and vocabulary are used by every fluent speaker of the language at normal speed. We do most of the choosing of words and patterns through habit. Our attention is on the thread of the meaning and only secondarily on some aspects of style and selection of forms.

Correcting a student's mistake and having him nod by way of response is almost useless. We can assume that his mistake is a habitual one. What he needs is habit-forming practice. A nod does not affect his speaking habit. Without practice there can be little language learning.

Many teachers and students even today hold language drill as drudgery and prefer the mental gymnastics of laboriously analyzing parts of language without regard for total speech or for the establishment of habits. They use the highest power of reason to manipulate the mechanics of the language which the speakers of it handle habitually without awareness. They should render to habit what is normally habitual and thus free the intellect for its proper role.

Repetition and drill on problems are not enough. To repeat basic sentences in a dialogue is a good way to begin, but it is not enough. After the third correct repetition without variation, very little learning occurs.

Drill on problems with attention on the problems is good too, but only up to a point. Yet most language teaching tends to stop here. The problem is understood. The exercise based on the problem is handled successfully when the students know they are drilling that problem. But when later they try to communicate in the language, their attention necessarily shifts to the message, while the mechanics of the language falls back upon the habit system, and the native language takes over.

Need for pattern practice What is needed is practice that will gradually force the students' attention away from the linguistic problem while forcing them to use language examples that contain the problem. This will engage the habit mechanism and more quickly establish the new habits.

Definition of Pattern Practice There are many types of pattern practice, but simple repetition and conscious-choice drill on linguistic problems are not pattern practice in this technical sense. These are preceding stages of practice. Pattern practice is rapid oral drill on problem patterns with attention on something other than the problem itself.

Rapid oral drill In pattern practice, the student produces a sentence after each cue at normal conversational speed. A class may produce

20 to 30 different sentences per minute following as many cues supplied by the teacher. This represents 1,000 to 1,500 recitations in a fifty-minute class. Compare this with a grammar-translation class where each student takes one minute to give his part of the translation. This gives only 50 recitations compared with 1,000. If learning increases with the number of recitations when the same utterance is not repeated more than three times, pattern practice must be far superior. With group recitation in pattern practice, the number of student responses in a class of 10 students would be 10 times 1,000, or 10,000.

Concentrating on problems   Each pattern practice drills one problem or set of problems. A conversational class is not a pattern-practice class because the students are not forced to practice a specific problem with every recitation.

Structuring habit responses   To force the students to use the problem pattern while thinking of something else, e.g., the message, (1) the class is not told what the practice is about—it is shown how to proceed with the practice through several examples, and (2) the cues that control the changes in each succeeding response are chiefly *not* at the problem point of the pattern. This may seem paradoxical, but it is in effect a highly important feature of pattern practice. When the student expects a change at the crucial point, his attention will be on it, and his habit system is not involved. By fixing the changes elsewhere, the teacher forces the student to focus his attention away from the crucial point, and to carry the pattern increasingly through habit responses.

Types of Pattern Practices   Many of the exercises described in preceding chapters can be made into pattern practices. A number of them will be illustrated. Many others can be invented as needed.

Simple oral substitution   A new word or phrase is substituted in the same position with each response. The teacher gives the substitution orally, and the student or class incorporates it in the preceding response.

For example, questions with *do* are a problem in English as a second language for persons of certain linguistic backgrounds. The class has memorized a basic sentence: *Do you understand?* They know that *do* must be used in this type of question and that it must precede the subject. They cannot handle this automatically as a habit yet.

> [Cues and responses by the teacher]
>> Do you understand?
>> Hear.
>> Do you hear?
>>
>> See.
>> Do you see?

[Cues by the teacher, responses by the class]

s: Understand.

r: *Do you understand?*

s: Hear.

r: *Do you hear?*

s: See.

r: *Do you see?*

s: Believe.

r: *Do you believe?*

s: Approve.

r: *Do you approve?*

s: Try.

r: *Do you try?*

The student must listen to each substitution given orally by the teacher. He gradually turns attention away from *do* and onto the substitutions.

Without additional complications the practice would soon become mechanical, since the student can put the substitution in place without having to make any choice. Supplying some less familiar substitutions and insisting on good pronunciation, intonation, and rhythm are enough of a load for a few good experiences in using *do you* automatically.

Simple substitution: pictures The cues can be provided by a series of pictures. Beautiful pictures will help but are not really necessary. Simple line drawings identified once for the class will do quite well. Take for example the figure below. The pictures should be identified once for the class: train, ship, plane, bus, bird, fish, elephant, camel, moon, star, sun, cloud.

Next, take the basic sentence, "Do you see the train?" and then give examples orally, pointing to the appropriate pictures.

TEACHER: Do you see the train?
Do you see the ship?
Do you see the plane?

Point to the succeeding pictures and signal the class to continue at the same conversational speed.

> CLASS: *Do you see the bus?*
> *Do you see the bird?*
> *Do you see the fish?*
> *Do you see the elephant?*

When the class is doing well, the teacher calls on individual students and points to pictures in any order. The student is forced to give his attention to the pictures cueing the substitutions while practicing *do you*. This may seem overly simple to an English speaker, but it is quite a task for one who is learning the language. Try a Spanish pattern practice on the same model:

EXAMPLES:

¿Ve usted el tren?

¿Ve usted el barco?

¿Ve usted el avión?

Continue with the remaining pictures: *autobús, pájaro, pez, elefante, camello, luna, estrella, sol, nube.*

Simple substitution: realia The same type of practice can be conducted by pointing to real objects in view of the class.

Substitution in variable slot To direct the attention load away from the problem, the substitutions may fit a different slot each time.

> [Cue and response by the teacher]
> Do you see the train?
> Hear.
> Do you hear the train?
>
> Ship.
> Do you hear the ship?
>
> He.
> Does he hear the ship?

> [Cue by the teacher, response by the class]
> s: Did.
> R: *Did he hear the ship?*
> s: Plane.
> R: *Did he hear the plane?*
> s: They.
> R: *Did they hear the plane?*
> s: Like.
> R: *Did they like the plane?*

s: Bus.
R: *Did they like the bus?*
s: You.
R: *Did you like the bus?*
s: Do.
R: *Do you like the bus?*

This exercise includes changes at the problem point (the use of *do* before the subject to signal a question), but these changes may be cued at any time and the student cannot concentrate on the problem. Notice also that the cue *he* forced a change from *do* to *does*.

Multiple substitution The teacher supplies two or three cues instead of only one. The cues may be oral, pictured, prompted by realia, or any combination of these.

EXAMPLE OF DOUBLE SUBSTITUTION WITH ORAL AND PICTURE CUES:

[Cues and responses by the teacher]
    You.   [pointing to the train]
    Do you like the train?

    He.   [pointing to the ship]
    Does he like the ship?

    She.   [pointing to the plane]
    Does she like the plane?

[Cues by the teacher, responses by the class]
s: You.   [pointing to the bus]
R: *Do you like the bus?*
s: They.   [pointing to the bird]
R: *Do they like the bird?*
s: She.   [pointing to the fish]
R: *Does she like the fish?*
s: You.   [pointing to the elephant]
R: *Do you like the elephant?*
s: They.   [pointing to the camel]
R: *Do they like the camel?*
s: She.   [pointing to the moon]
R: *Does she like the moon?*
s: You.   [pointing to the star]
R: *Do you like the star?*

Transformation In simple transformation, a cue sentence is changed into another. For example, *John saw the elephant. Did John see the elephant?* This tends to become conscious-choice drill, since the student

knows he must turn each sentence into a question using some form of
the verb *do*.

To make this into a pattern practice, one includes a substitution of
any of the preceding types. Transformation and double substitution are
included in the following:

[Cues and responses by the teacher]

     John saw the train. Mary. Ship.
     Did Mary see the ship?

     John liked the plane. Peter. Bus.
     Did Peter like the bus?

     John caught the bird. Robert. Fish.
     Did Robert catch the fish?

[Statements and cues by the teacher, questions by the class]

s: John rode on the elephant. Joseph. Camel.
r: *Did Joseph ride on the camel?*
s: John saw the moon. Albert. Star.
r: *Did Albert see the star?*
s: John liked the sun. Charles. Clouds.
r: *Did Charles like the clouds?*

Conversation Controlled short dialogues that force the use of a
problem pattern and draw attention to a set of pictures is a good pattern
practice. The fact that English requires *do* for negative statements but
not for affirmative ones is something of a learning problem. Compare
non-English *I no understand*, with *I don't understand*, and *I understand*.

[The teacher points at or covers the pictures, asks the questions, and
responds]

     [Points to the train]
     Do you see the train?
     Yes, I do. I see the train.

     [Covers up the ship]
     Do you see the ship?
     No, I don't. I don't see the ship.

     [Points to the plane]
     Do you see the plane?
     Yes, I do. I see the plane.

[Now after each question the teacher gives a hand signal to the class
to respond or says, "Respond."]

s: [Covers up the bus]
     Do you see the bus?
r: *No, I don't. I don't see the bus.*

s: [Points to the bird]
   Do you see the bird?
r: *Yes, I do. I see the bird.*

s: [Covers up the elephant]
   Do you see the elephant?
r: *No, I don't. I don't see the elephant.*

s: [Points to the camel]
   Do you see the camel?
r: *Yes, I do. I see the camel.*

s: [Covers up the moon]
   Do you see the moon?
r: *No, I don't. I don't see the moon.*

Addition   Increasing the length of the sentence increases the attention load away from the problem.   Each cue is added to the previous sentence instead of being substituted for some part of it.

The problem is the verbal phrase *must go* which some students render as non-English *must to go*.

EXAMPLE WITH THE CUE ADDED ALWAYS AT THE END:

[Examples and responses by the teacher]
   I must go to the bank.
   I must go to the bank.

   Before lunch.
   I must go to the bank before lunch.

   To cash a check.
   I must go to the bank before lunch to cash a check.

[Cues by the teacher, responses by the class]
s: I must go to the bank.
r: *I must go to the bank.*
s: Before lunch.
r: *I must go to the bank before lunch.*
s: To cash a check.
r: *I must go to the bank before lunch to cash a check.*
s: Because I need money.
r: *I must go to the bank before lunch to cash a check, because I need money.*
s: To buy a shirt.
r: *I must go to the bank before lunch to cash a check, because I need money to buy a shirt.*

More difficult but more flexible and probably more effective are additions and substitutions that fit in varying slots.

[Examples and responses by the teacher]
I must go home.

Have.
I have to go home.

Very soon.
I have to go home very soon.

You.
You have to go home very soon.

[Cues by the teacher, responses by the class]
s: I must go home.
r: *I must go home.*
s: Have.
r: *I have to go home.*
s: Should.
r: *I should go home.*
s: Very soon.
r: *I should go home very soon.*
s: We.
r: *We should go home very soon.*
s: To study.
r: *We should go home very soon to study.*
s: Geography.
r: *We should go home very soon to study geography.*
s: To school.
r: *We should go to school very soon to study geography.*

The Place of Pattern Practice Some teachers become so enthusiastic over pattern practice that they attempt to do all their teaching through it. This is not justified, since not all language learning is of the pattern type. Pattern practice fits between practice with conscious choice and free selection. The major stages of teaching a second language can be listed in order as follows: (1) mimicry-memorization, (2) conscious choice, (3) pattern practice, and (4) free selection.

This listing does not imply that all mimicry-memorization must be completed before going on to conscious choice, etc. It does mean that each stage has a role to play in language teaching which it performs most effectively. When forced into roles it is not fitted to play, it may do more harm than good.

Reading and writing, an introduction to the culture, literature, and technical vocabularies may be started in limited fashion fairly early in connection with any of these four stages of language teaching. Full development of reading, writing, etc., must await mastery of a good deal of what is involved in these four stages.

Free Selection   At the end of pattern practice the student is not ready to speak freely. He has the patterns ready as habits, but he must practice using them with full attention on purposeful communication. This is free selection.

Even at this stage, we must somehow force the student to use the problem patterns. Showing a sound film once, then showing it again silently and asking the students to supply the commentary or a dialogue for memorization permits some control.

Discussion topics, a story, a composite picture, and a film strip are means of controlling the free use of the language at this stage.

Pattern Practice and FLES [1]   Elementary school children have greater power to learn a second language through imitation in meaningful situations and less power for conscious-choice learning than adults. Consequently, some pattern practices can be introduced without the intermediate stage of conscious choice. Also, the play motive is strong and the work motive is weak among children. FLES therefore concentrates on mimicry-memorization as a dramatization game. If the situations are clear, the pupils will do the rest.

[1] Foreign Language in the Elementary School.

Live Words
and
Their
Meanings

Chapter 12

Various definitions of the word and of lexical units have been given else-where and need not be elaborated here.[1] The lexical units of a language —chiefly its words—have a form or expression which is associated with a content or meaning. The form, which may appear in more than one shape, e.g., *will, 'll,* is expressed in phonemes. The meaning or content is found in the culture. The units of expression and content can occur in certain positions and situations and not in others. These privileges and restrictions of occurrence constitute the distribution. Expression, content, and distribution of words and lexical units are different for each language.

In English, for instance, the word *friend* (expression) can be used rather freely to refer to any acquaintance with whom one has frequent and pleasant relations (meaning). One speaks not only of close personal friends, but of friends in business, at the club, and in the bowling league (distribution). By contrast, Germans use the word *Freund* in a far more limited sense, restricting it to a close personal friend whom one has admitted to his intimate circle after prolonged association and proven

---

[1] For example, Leonard Bloomfield, *Language;* C. C. Fries and A. Aileen Traver, *English Word Lists;* C. F. Hockett, *A Course in Modern Linguistics;* R. Lado, *Linguistics Across Cultures;* Edward Sapir, *Language* (see Bibliography for complete references).

experience. All others included under the English term *friend* are known as *Bekannte,* "acquaintances."

Lexical units may be words (e.g., *telephone*), parts of words (*un-* in *undo*), or composite expressions (*Statue of Liberty, devil-may-care, Jack-in-the-pulpit, merry-go-round*) with some unit of lexical content not deducible from its parts.[2]

Some lexical units such as *do, the, not,* or *with* in English are used chiefly to express grammatical functions and are called function words. Others express cultural content, e.g., *house, sleep, quietly, peaceful,* and are called content words. The vocabularies of languages are collected in dictionaries, of which there are many kinds.[3]

Vocabulary of the first and a second language The core vocabulary of the first language is learned at home in the great struggle of the child to communicate his needs. Neither he nor his family have much to say about the words he must learn; they are given by his immediate environment and the culture. He learns words for the persons with whom he lives, for the things he needs, for the actions he wants performed or stopped, and he learns function words that enable him to construct the sentences he says. In school he learns to write the words he knows, and he expands his vocabulary more arbitrarily, following the school curriculum.

In learning a second language in school, the student is not usually forced to acquire the same sort of vocabulary that he needed for the first language. Although the function words necessary to express sentences are usually the same as for the native speaker, the content words—for actions, things, qualities—are different, since the second language serves a different purpose from the first. For example, the student does not need to address his family in the second language; he does not have to use it to fill his basic needs, and he does not have to communicate socially with his fellow students through it.

The vocabulary of a second language can be decided by the teacher, the textbook, or the school; it is in fact so selected. Criteria for vocabulary selection are discussed later in this chapter. The function words necessary for the grammatical patterns should be selected in connection with the teaching of the patterns. The contextual areas in which the student is to gain fluency can be selected on the basis of importance to the students. Words of the immediate environment may be chosen for the early stages because of ease in showing their meaning, or they

[2] Hockett calls these units "idioms." See his lucid discussion in *A Course in Modern Linguistics.* New York: The Macmillan Company, 1958, chapters 19, 36, and 37.
[3] Monolingual, bilingual; unabridged, research, scientific, students', children's; etymological, dialectal, conversational; rhyming, synonym-antonym; word, phrase, idiom; etc.

may be rejected in favor of situations that reflect the environments characteristic of the new language.

The words of a second language are not translations of the words of the first language. Even when they are borrowed from it, they develop differences in meaning, distribution, and form which are characteristic of their language. Both *library* in English and *librería* in Spanish are ultimately derived from the Latin word *liber*, "book." Yet the Spanish word most frequently means "bookstore"; it takes a feminine article (*la*) and is replaced by a feminine pronoun (*ella*). Whereas the English word *library* is a place to read and borrow books, and it is referred to by the pronoun *it*. The pronunciation of the two words differs as to vowels, the [r] sound, and the position of the stresses.

Knowing the Vocabulary of a Language When do we know the vocabulary of a language? This question has several important aspects: size of vocabulary, the degree of knowledge required, and whether the vocabulary is for speaking, listening, reading, writing, and/or for specialized or technical uses.

A limited vocabulary No one knows all the words of any of the major languages of the world. We all know limited vocabularies. The physician, the sailor, the philosopher, the engineer have limited vocabularies, and each knows words that the others do not.

All of the speakers of a given language know, however, its function words, whose role is chiefly grammatical. All of them likewise know a core of content words which have wide currency in the speech community. There have been various estimates of the size of these limited vocabularies, but we need to clarify the problem further before the size of a vocabulary can be made meaningful.

Speaking, listening, reading, and writing The idea of a minimum vocabulary necessary for speaking, listening, reading, and writing is not new, but the problem is complex. In speaking and writing, one can choose his words and use a paraphrase where a specific word is not known. But in listening or reading, one cannot choose the words. Thus a minimum vocabulary for listening and reading will be larger than one for speaking and writing.

The 850-word vocabulary of Basic English [4] is a minimum vocabulary which might be adequate for speaking, if considerable violence to normal use of words is accepted, but it is not adequate for reading or listening. The 2,000 entry vocabulary of *A General Service List of*

---

[4] C. K. Ogden, *Basic English*. London: Kegan Paul, Trench, Trubner & Co., Ltd., 1930. I. A. Richards, *Basic English and its Uses*. New York: W. W. Norton & Company, Inc., 1943.

English Words [5] is a more adequate one for speaking and limited writing, but it is far from adequate for listening and reading.

Reading studies of the size of the vocabularies of native speakers of English in the United States show that much larger numbers of words are known than was previously believed. According to these studies, first-grade children have a vocabulary of some 16,900 basic words, and twelfth graders know some 46,500 basic words and 80,000 basic and derived words. [6]

We know very little about the reading, writing, speaking, and listening vocabulary of foreign students who know English as a second language and are successfully studying in English-speaking schools and universities. In the absence of such information we can only give an opinion as to what their vocabulary might be. At present it is possible to guess that a speaking vocabulary of 2,000 words like that of *A General Service List of English Words* is an adequate minimum for the purposes of basic communication. For reading, however, a vocabulary of 7,000 words is closer to minimum needs. Vocabularies for writing and listening should better be set at 3,000 to 4,000 words than at 2,000.

Three levels of vocabulary To clarify further the idea of the vocabulary of a second language, three levels are distinguished for the reader: (1) vocabulary to operate the patterns and illustrate the pronunciation of the language, (2) vocabulary for communication in areas of wide currency, and (3) esthetic and technical vocabularies.

The first stage, vocabulary to operate the patterns and illustrate the sounds of the second language, should be kept as simple as possible in order to allow the teacher to concentrate on the grammatical patterns and the sound system. For this reason, some authorities advocate using at this stage content vocabulary from the immediate environment—the classroom, the home, the family, etc.

When the roles of the two languages can be defined so that the first language, for example, is the language of the home while the second language is used for cultural development as a school subject, it may be better to use vocabulary from the second culture that does not refer to the immediate environment of the home to avoid duplication and possible conflict for the learners.

At this early stage, one teaches most of the function words, that is, the interrogatives, prepositions, auxiliaries, etc. One also teaches a small number of content words of particular grammatical classes; for

[5] Michael West, *A General Service List of English Words.* London: Longmans, Green & Co., Ltd., 1953.
[6] R. Seashore, "How Many Words Do Children Know?" *The Packet:* Heath's Service Bulletin for Elementary Teachers, vol. 2, no. 2, pp. 3–17, Boston: D. C. Heath and Company, 1947.

example, adjectives when teaching the modification pattern with adjectives, nouns when teaching number, etc. In this stage the teacher can come close to teaching the full core-structure of the language.

In the second stage, vocabulary for communication, the student acquires the vocabulary items he needs to converse on contextual areas of wide currency. The particular areas will vary depending on the age and education of the students and on whether the teaching takes place in the country where the language is spoken or in that of the students. If the language is taught in the country of the students and the goal is a liberal education, the contextual areas can be heavily weighted in that direction. If the language is taught in the country where it is spoken, there may be good reason to deal with contextual areas of everyday chores since the students will have to use the language for this purpose as well as for further intellectual growth.

The third stage, esthetic and technical uses of vocabulary, must not be confused with the first two. It presupposes, however, that the other two stages have been mastered. Artistic expression deals in part with selective uses of words, and the esthetic effect is lost if the basic communicative use is not known. In technical and scientific vocabulary, words are defined for particular purposes and the attempt is made to achieve precision by limiting use to these definitions. This is not learned by the native speaker of the language through enculturation; he must study the technical matters and the technical vocabulary that goes with them.

The meaning of knowing Since the word "knowing" can have many meanings, its technical use here has to be stated. In speaking it means that the forms of the words can be expressed at will almost instantaneously when their meaning is available. This must be in appropriate sentence structure, sound, stress, and intonation. Speed must be normal, with attention on the meaning.

In listening it means that when the expression is heard in context, it will recall its meaning almost instantaneously. In both speaking and listening the form includes various shapes of the word in different environments as, for example, the full and abbreviated forms of *will* and *he* in *will he* and *he'll*.

Knowing live words The meaning of words is much more fluid than is usually realized by most people. In a sense, words mean the memory of the situations in which they have been observed and understood, brought out by the context in which they are used. The meaning of a word has a variety of features. When the word is used in context, some of these features are brought out, and others remain dormant. To know a live word is to be able to use it or to understand it in situations in which the person has not experienced it before.

The word *reading* shifts meaning in the familiar contexts that follow:

John is *reading* a novel.
He is *reading* the dialogue of the play.
The doctor is *reading* the X ray.
The pilot of the plane said, "Do you *read* me?"
John was *reading* aloud without knowing what he *read*.
Don't *read* any hidden meanings into this.
She *read* his fortune on the palm of his hand.
Read between the lines.

It can be used and have meaning in a context that probably rarely occurs to anyone:

He *reads* stones, bones, and broken pots and makes sense of them all.

Knowing words in isolation is less than knowing the vocabulary of a second language. The words must be taught and learned in context.

Vocabulary difficulty It has been demonstrated that the chief source of both ease and difficulty in learning the phonology and grammar of a second language is their similarity to and difference from the first language. The same is true in learning the vocabulary of a second language although the evidence for this statement is based on less formal observations.

Ser and *estar* in Spanish are difficult for English speakers because the area of these two verbs corresponds to that of the single verb *be* in English. German has the two words *essen* and *fressen* for what in English is expressed by the verb *to eat;* the first is used only for human beings and the second only for animals. These German words will, therefore, be difficult for an English speaker to learn to use. On the other hand, *presidente* in Spanish is easy for an English speaker because he has the word *president* which resembles it in form, meaning, and distribution.[7]

Vocabulary Selection The teacher needs to rely on certain criteria of vocabulary selection in order to meet the needs of various goals and conditions. If materials are to be prepared, the criteria can be used in selecting the vocabulary for them. If materials are available already, they can be supplemented on the basis of the criteria given.

In the first stage of vocabulary for speaking, the chief criteria should

[7] The systematic comparison of the vocabulary of the first and a second language to determine the patterns of difficulty of words has been described elsewhere. See, for example, R. Lado, *Linguistics Across Cultures.* Ann Arbor: The University of Michigan Press, 1957, chap. 4.

be range of usefulness and regularity of fit in the patterns taught. In the second stage, range of usefulness should be the chief criterion. Thus a word that can be used in more than one area will be preferred to one that is restricted to a single contextual area. For listening and reading, on the other hand, the chief criterion should be frequency of occurrence, since the student will usually have no control over the words that he will encounter.

For the third stage, esthetic use of the words, selection has to take into account the style that is involved.

Once the vocabulary has been selected, it needs to be graded as to difficulty on the basis of similarity to and difference from the first language. Words which are similar in form and meaning can be used freely with little effort given to their presentation or learning. Words that differ in form or meaning, however, have to be taught more formally.

Once the selection has been made, the vocabulary must be assigned to appropriate lessons. Function words will be introduced in connection with the grammar patterns with which they are associated. The content words selected to operate the patterns will also be introduced in conjunction with the grammatical patterns for which they have been selected. Other content words are assigned to the contextual areas selected.

HOW TO TEACH VOCABULARY

In the past, vocabulary was taught mostly by translation: either a list of words with their translation at the beginning of the lesson or the translation of the material containing new words or glossaries at the end. The error in this was to confuse translation with language use, and to assume that putting across the meaning was the whole of teaching vocabulary.

Actually, putting across the meaning is only a small part of vocabulary teaching. To use a word, the form of the word must be taught; and making the new word easily available may require a great deal of practice for fluency in speaking and quick understanding in listening. The emphasis, therefore, should be on learning to use the words rather than merely on grasping the meaning.

Recognizing Degrees of Difficulty Teaching vocabulary varies for (1) easy words which resemble those of the first language in form, meaning, and distribution; (2) words of normal difficulty which have a form that does not resemble that of the first language; and (3) special problems, which are particularly difficult to master. Some examples from German for an English speaker are the following: (1) easy words: *die Hand, die Lampe, die Demokratie, sehen* (to see), *hart* (hard); (2) words of normal difficulty: *der Regenschirm* (umbrella), *die Kraft* (power), *bewachen* (to guard), *plötzlich* (suddenly); (3) special problems: *der Betrag, der Beitrag, der Vertrag, der Vortrag* (amount, contribution, treaty, lecture), *verhältnismässig* (relatively), and the use of the prepositions *an, auf, bis, zu, nach,* etc.

In every case, however, the following steps will be involved.

Hearing the Word Let the students hear the word in isolation and in a sentence. If the sounds of the word have been mastered, the students will hear it correctly with two or three repetitions. If new sounds or new sequences of sounds are involved, more exposures will be necessary. Slow pronunciation without distortion will help. Breaking the word into parts and building up to the whole word will also help. If major trouble persists, it is a matter for the pronunciation lesson rather than for vocabulary.

Pronouncing the Word Let the students pronounce the word even if their aim is only reading or listening. Pronouncing the word helps them remember it longer and identify it more readily when they hear or see it. Seek pronunciation accuracy in individual items even in anticipation of pronunciation drills. Some compromises will have to be allowed temporarily, however, in sounds that will be taught later. Contrary to common belief, a few more repetitions of a mispronunciation caused by native language habits will not increase the difficulty of the pronunciation problem to any measurable or relevant degree.

Grasping the Meaning Get the meaning to the class without using translation, except possibly as a last resort. This is not advocated on the ground that translation may or may not render the meaning of the word accurately. It is proposed because if we use the first language every time any real communication is necessary, the target language will remain a useless curiosity rather than the vital communication system that it is. It will usually be preferable to let the class go without grasping the meaning of a word they have learned to pronounce rather than resort to translation.

It is surprising how many ways there are to put across the meaning of a new word to a class, and teachers soon realize how often a class will grasp the meaning of new words when they are taught to pronounce them and put them in sentences. Here are a number of ways:

Self-defining context The context makes the situation clear, and this in turn illuminates the meaning of the new word.

ENGLISH EXAMPLE:

Late. The class is at 10:00. Peter comes at 10:15. He is *late.*

Early. The class is at 10:00. John comes at 9:45. He is *early.*

On time. The class is at 10:00. Mary comes at 10:00. She is *on time.*

SPANISH EXAMPLE:

Tarde. La clase es a las 10:00. Pedro llega a las 10:15. Llega *tarde.*

Temprano. La clase es a las 10:00. Juan llega a las 9:45. Llega *temprano.*

A tiempo. La clase es a las 10:00. María llega a las 10:00. Llega *a tiempo.*

FRENCH EXAMPLE:

En retard. La classe est à 10 heures. Pierre arrive à 10 heures 15. Il est *en retard.*

En avance. La classe est à 10 heures. Jean arrive à 10 heures moins le quart. Il est *en avance.*

A l'heure. La classe est à 10 heures. Marie arrive à 10 heures. Elle est *à l'heure.*

Definitions Definitions in the target language may be used effectively if they are expressed in terms that are better known or more easily guessed than the word that is defined.

ENGLISH EXAMPLE:

Ladle. A large spoon with a long handle, used to serve soup, etc.

FRENCH EXAMPLES:

Une louche. Grande cuillère pour servir la soupe, le potage, etc.

Courrier. Il se compose de lettres, de télégrammes, de journaux, et de revues.

SPANISH EXAMPLE:

Cucharón. Cuchara grande para servir sopa, etc.

GERMAN EXAMPLE:

Fussball. Ein Sport, wo man den Ball mit dem Fuss oder mit dem Kopf schlägt.

Opposites When one member of a pair of opposites is known, the meaning of the other can be made clear through it.

ENGLISH EXAMPLE:

Empty. The bottle is *empty* (opposite of *full*).

GERMAN EXAMPLES:

Jung. Hans ist *jung.* (Er ist nicht *alt.*)

Dumm. Der Junge ist *dumm.* (Er ist nicht *klug.*)

Sale (*salir*). María *sale* de (lo contrario de *entra* en) la escuela.

Synonyms A synonym may be used to approximate the meaning if the synonym is better known than the word being taught.

FRENCH EXAMPLE:

Étaler. Le vendeur nous a étalé (montré) les gants.

ENGLISH EXAMPLE:

Enough. One minute is enough (sufficient) for this problem.

SPANISH EXAMPLE:

Basta. Basta (es suficiente) un minuto para resolver este problema.

Pictures Pictures of many kinds have been successfully used to show the meaning of words and utterances. They are particularly effective to cue the meaning-stimulus in practice exercises. The pictures need not be elaborate or very artistic. A circle and some lines, for example, can be used for prepositions as in the figure below.

into. Peter goes *into* the circle.

in. He is *in* the circle.

through. He goes *through* the circle.

out of. He goes *out of* the circle.

around. He goes *around* the circle.

Drawings can be used to illustrate the meaning of things, actions, qualities, and relations. A line drawing of a head, for example, provides many useful nouns and verbs.

A picture (as on page 124) can be used to illustrate the meanings of the words listed and later to practice their recall by covering the words and remembering them with the picture as the only stimulus.

Pictures can be ambiguous, of course, and they can mean many things. Frequently they must be edited and adapted for use. Pictures with some simple context help to overcome the problem of ambiguity,

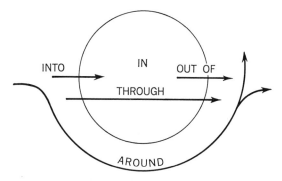

Picture illustrating meaning of particles.

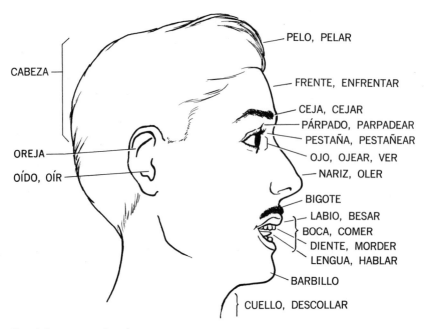

Spanish nouns and verbs.

and once identified, they can elicit meanings quickly and precisely. After the vocabulary has been learned with the aid of a picture, the same picture may be used to test vocabulary and as a visual image around which to use the vocabulary in short sentences.

Dramatization Many actions can be acted out or demonstrated.

ENGLISH EXAMPLES:

Sleep. [Lean head on hand to one side and close eyes]
Walk. [Walk]
Stand up. [Stand up and have class stand up]
Sit down. [Sit down and have class sit down]
Shake hands. [Shake hands]
Open. [Open a book]
Close. [Close the book]
Kill. [Action of stabbing or shooting, then fake fall and close eyes]

Actions and dramatizations, however, can be ambiguous, as is seen in the parlor game of charades. In it, a member of one of two teams is told a secret word or well-known title of a book by the opponents. He then proceeds to act out this word until his team guesses it. In spite of the effort of the player to make the meaning clear so that his team will win the point, many unexpected misinterpretations occur that enliven the game. The words chosen are of course as difficult to act out as the opposing team can make them, but ambiguity occurs in everyday words as well.

Children enjoy dramatizations and can learn through them. They play games in which they sing and merely suggest the actions mentioned in the song. A good example is the one that says, "This is the way we wash our clothes" [hands move as if rubbing clothes against wash board], "wash our clothes, wash our clothes, . . . so early in the morning. This is the way we wash our face" [hands move as if pouring water on face and rubbing], etc.

Realia Real objects or models of real objects are effective in showing meanings. For example, names for food appearing in stores and on restaurant menus can be learned with plastic toy models of the hundreds of foods now available. Using real money, both paper and coins, is another good device.

Series, scales, systems The meaning of such words as the months of the year, the days of the week, the parts of the day, seasons of the year, ordinal numbers, cardinal numbers, etc., that form part of well-known series can be made clear by presenting them in their usual order in the series.

FRENCH EXAMPLES:

janvier, février, mars, avril, mai, juin, juillet, août, septembre, octobre, novembre, décembre

dimanche, lundi, mardi, mercredi, jeudi, vendredi, samedi

printemps, été, automne, hiver

le matin, le midi, l'après-midi, le soir, la nuit

un, deux, trois, quatre, cinq, six, sept . . .

premier, second, troisième, quatrième, cinquième . . .

SPANISH EXAMPLES:

enero, febrero, marzo, abril, mayo, junio, julio, agosto, septiembre, octubre, noviembre, diciembre

domingo, lunes, martes, miércoles, jueves, viernes, sábado

primavera, verano, otoño, invierno

la mañana, el mediodía, la tarde, la noche, la medianoche

uno, dos, tres, cuatro, cinco, seis, siete . . .

primero, segundo, tercero, cuarto, quinto . . .

Parts of words The parts of complex and compound words may be more common than the words themselves. Separating such words into their component parts often clarifies the meaning.

SPANISH EXAMPLE: *incondicionalmente* [in-condición-al-mente]

condición

condicional

condicionalmente

incondicionalmente

La ciudad se rindió *incondicionalmente*.

Illustrative Sentences   Most words have a variety of restrictions on their use and at the same time have certain special uses that represent survivals from an earlier period in the history of the language.   Systematic descriptions of these restrictions and idiomatic uses would be laborious and ineffective in teaching the words for use.   It is better to give several examples that illustrate the range and variation of usage. This is particularly useful in learning words for speaking and writing. Let the students repeat these sentences.

> ENGLISH EXAMPLE: *think*
> Peter *thinks* clearly.
> *Think* before you speak.
> I *think* so.
> Did you *think* he was here?
> I can't *think* of his name.

> GERMAN EXAMPLE: *los*
> Der Hund ist *los!*
> Was ist hier *los?*
> Es muss was *los* sein.
> Eins, zwei, drei, *los!*

Practice from Meaning to Expression   Having put across the meaning of the new word, one is ready to lead the class in practicing its use to reinforce the trace and turn it into a habit.   There are many types of practices for this purpose.   They vary as to the stimulus by which the meaning is suggested to elicit the expression.   Pictures, realia, context, and dramatization can be used.   Series and systems can be used also. This is controlled practice in which the class does not create new uses or new contexts but merely remembers the ones presented.

Reading the Word   Now that the class have heard and pronounced the word and know what it means, they should see it and read it aloud. Interference from the writing system will eventually have to be faced. If it is faced while the memory of the sound is fresh, it can be overcome.

   Writing the word   It will help to have the class write the new word while the auditory memory is fresh, even if the goal is only to read. Copying the word from the blackboard will do, but the class should have always pronounced the word before copying it.

Using the word more freely This step can lead to trouble with some classes that become too bold and start exploring the vague outer limits of the words. The result may be that they misuse the words too often and derive more harm than good from the practice. The degree of freedom permitted must be carefully geared to the proficiency level of the class, but practice with increasing freedom of choice is essential for full mastery.

Shift of attention Eventually the student will have to use the word for some communicative purpose in which his attention will not be on the word itself. At this stage the teacher provides a context by description or through reading which elicits the use of the word. The student should be encouraged to take an attitude or a point of view which he defends or attacks. This lends further realism to his use of the word.

Strategy for Special Types of Words The steps described above for the teaching of vocabulary are stated in general terms applicable to all vocabulary. Special techniques or special combinations of the above techniques may be applicable for particular groups of words. Some of these special cases are discussed below. Others can be developed by the resourceful teacher.

Words that are easy to learn As we have noted repeatedly, words that are similar in form and meaning to the first language are easy to learn. They usually fall into patterns of correspondence of sounds and stress and can be taught quickly in such patterns. They should be taught for listening and reading rather than for speaking and writing because of traps involved in such use.

For each pattern of correspondence, two or three examples are given to the class. Complete regularity of correspondence is unnecessary since the words are presented for recognition only.

ENGLISH:	SPANISH:
nation /néyšən/	nación /nasyón/ or /naθyón/
constitution	constitución
mission	misión
multiplication	multiplicación
combination	combinación
division	división
variation	variación
complication	complicación
emotion	emoción
condition	condición
substitution	substitución
etc.	etc.

A pattern of correspondence such as this can be used to teach English to Spanish speakers or Spanish to English speakers. After the examples, the list is given in the target language only. The class may repeat them to reinforce their hearing, and they may read them for the same purpose. If anyone does not grasp the meaning from the similarity to English, he raises his hand. The item is repeated and may be given in the native language if need be.

Another pattern is then taught.

ENGLISH:	SPANISH:
animal /ǽnɨməl/	aniɹal /animál/
criminal	criminal
constitutional	constitucional
conventional	convencional
missal	misal
commercial	comercial
brutal	brutal
personal	personal
etc.	etc.

Other patterns are taught, and, finally, a connected passage is given in which the students identify items from any pattern by repeating them aloud or underlining them while reading.

Words of normal difficulty Words of normal difficulty are best taught in contextual areas, such as food, clothing, sports, work, school, shopping; music, language, literature, art; the human body, a person, a city, a country; a discovery, an exploration, geography; a newspaper, education, and government.

There are advantages to using a connected context illustrating the words that are to be taught. This connected context should be presented orally to the class. Then the words are taught following the steps described above. Additional words can be taught as alternatives to those chosen in the connected context. For example, if the area is food, various dishes can be learned as alternatives to the single selection in the passage. If the conversation gives *coffee* as the choice of the speaker, *tea, milk, chocolate, water, wine, beer,* etc., can be learned as alternatives.

A composite picture of people sitting at table with a variety of food set before them can be used as stimulus in connected meaning-to-expression practice.

Practice can be controlled in varying situations by changing a key word or phrase. This change forces the use of the words that have to be practiced. For example, in practicing the words *lunch, breakfast,* and *dinner,* the key situation words might be *morning, noon,* and *evening.* The teacher might thus say, *It's morning; he's eating break-*

fast. It's noon; he's eating lunch. It's evening; he's eating dinner. He might then cue the class by saying *It's morning, it's evening,* or *it's noon,* and have them respond by saying, *He's eating breakfast, lunch,* or *dinner.*

Series, scales, systems Probably the easiest way to learn such series as counting, the days of the week, the months of the year, etc., is to memorize them. Additional practice in using the items is necessary. Such sentences as *Today is _____, Yesterday was _____,* and *Tomorrow is _____,* can be used as general frames.

Pictures can be used to practice contrasts such as *tall:short, heavy:light, sick:well,* etc., or double contrasts such as *old:new—old:young.*

Difficult words Because of differences with the first language, some words and sets of words are especially difficult to teach and to learn. They have to be taught as special problems with the strategy determined by the particular problem in each case.

The use of *in, on, at* for location is a problem for Spanish speakers learning English. Spanish prepositions do not coincide with these three prepositions in English. Students can remain confused for years on this little problem. It is therefore necessary to bring it to consciousness showing the distribution in English and practicing it until students can use the prepositions accurately without having to think about them.

In teaching this problem, begin by giving the words for recognition and repetition as usual. Select the examples, however, to show the difference in distribution.

in Washington	I live *in* Washington.
on Main Street	I live *on* Main Street.
at 1212 Main Street	I live *at* 1212 Main Street.

MORE EXAMPLES:

in the United States	*on* Miller Street	*at* 212 Miller Street
in Mexico	*on* Fifth Avenue	*at* 2341 Fifth Avenue
in Chile	*on* Loyola Avenue	*at* 16 Loyola Avenue

Comment: Use *in* with large areas, *on* with lines, and *at* with points.

Expanding Vocabularies At the advanced level of language teaching, one devotes considerable time and effort to expand the vocabulary of the students. The class supplies additional words on a theme or context. The total list compiled by the class is larger than the vocabulary of any single student and represents an expansion for each. For example, the class can be asked to name the parts of the human head and face and to list the various actions associated with these parts.

Vocabulary expansion for and through reading Reading is the best source of vocabulary for expansion. Reading selections are taught and the vocabulary contained in them is learned in the process. A different type of vocabulary exercise is proposed here, however. The difficult words are presented in sentences for practice before the class reads the selection in which they appear. Then the selection is read through, and the new words are reinforced in their proper context.

Expansion through patterns of form Vocabulary is increased by giving examples of a derivation pattern and asking the students to build derived words by analogy.

EXAMPLE:

Noun	Adjective
faith	faithful
fear	fearful
doubt	doubtful
cheer	_____
hope	_____

Expansion through families of words The student can be asked to build several derived words from a basic one by analogy.

EXAMPLE:

reason	reasonable	unreasonable	reasonably	reasonableness
profit	profitable	unprofitable	profitably	profitableness
work	_____	_____	_____	_____

cheer	cheerful	cheerfully	cheerfulness	cheerless	cheerlessly
hope	hopeful	hopefully	hopefulness	hopeless	hopelessly
care	_____	_____	_____	_____	_____

Expansion through programming In view of the very large vocabularies needed for full use of the second language in university study in the country where it is the medium of communication, it may be profitable to give intensive doses of vocabulary for college-level students who have mastered the structure for use within a limited vocabulary. This can be done with programmed frames in which one frame defines, and the other reinforces by eliciting a recall. For example:

A sea animal valued for its fur is the *seal.*
On a rock we saw a _____ with a fish in its mouth.
The circus had two trained _____ that swam gracefully.

Chapter 13

Reading

We should never confuse a language with its writing system. Learning a writing system differs basically from learning to speak or understand a language. Learning to speak and understand means learning the language, whereas reading and writing imply that the language is known and that we are learning a graphic representation of it.

Because of the redundancy in language, it is possible to grasp whole sentences from partial identification of their parts. Thus it is possible to read a second language for limited purposes superimposing the native-language sound system upon it. This is sometimes taken to mean that the spoken language is not involved in reading. Actually, readers will put sound into the sentences subvocally anyway. By imposing the native-language sound system on the reading, many distinctions of the target language will be maintained and many morphemes will be identifiable. For full reading, however, this is inadequate since some distinctions will be made which are not relevant, and other distinctions that are relevant will be leveled.

It is something of a contradiction to teach writing before the student knows the patterns he is to write. When the written symbols of the native language are the same (as in French or Spanish for English speakers), to teach reading and writing before the student knows the language may seem reasonable, but it gives the students the false idea that the sound systems of the two languages are the same and that the letters represent the same sounds in both.

Most languages have never been written down, and writing systems never have developed before language in a culture. Man has the capacity to learn language as it is spoken. Writing attaches to the spoken forms in the process of learning to read and write the native language.

Definition   To read is to grasp language patterns from their written representation.   In a second language, reading is usually taught to students who are already literate in the source language.

Spoken Form Most Complete   Only spoken expression shows the full intonation, stress, juncture, and consonant and vowel systems of a language.   Spoken utterances express the language code fully and completely, although they are not limited to the code only but contain elements of expression such as voice qualifiers that are outside the code.

  • Written expressions are partial representations of the spoken forms. The written phrase *the dog* could be read in a variety of ways because it is incomplete.   In answer to a question, it might have a matter-of-fact statement intonation.   If it referred to a person who might have acted in an unfriendly manner toward the speaker, it would have a low intonation throughout.   If an animal is found after having been missing for some time, the phrase might have a high to extra-high intonation sequence ending in a drop.   In expressing incredulity, the intonation would rise from mid to high in the middle of the second word.

Writing Systems   Writing does not represent meanings or ideas directly; it represents language units.   The cave drawings of Altamira convey vivid images of primitive hunting, but they are not writing.   It is essential for writing to represent language units.

  When the graphic symbols represent consonants and vowels, we have an alphabetic system.   When they represent syllables, we have a syllabic system.   When the symbols represent words or morphemes, we have a logographic system.   The classic example of logographic writing is that of Chinese.   Some systems use a combination of these, as does Japanese, which uses Chinese characters and two syllabaries.   The graphemes of an alphabetic system are letters, and the list of the letters of a system is an alphabet.   The most widely used alphabet is the Latin one.   The oldest to represent consonants and vowels is that of Greek.   Russian uses the Cyrillic alphabet, named after its developer, St. Cyril.   Very different in appearance from any of these are the Thai, Korean, and Burmese alphabets, but all are basically representations of the phonemes of the respective languages.

  Syllabaries, lists of symbols or characters of a syllabic writing system, are less common. The Indian chief Sequoia developed a syllabary for his language. Japanese uses one syllabary for grammatical function words and another for borrowed items—*katakana* and *hiragana*.

The writing of any language is a self-contained system. The symbols have value internally within the system. Even when two languages use the same symbols, such as the letters of the Latin alphabet, their value in one language is independent of their value in another. The fact that the letter *h* often represents a velar fricative phoneme in English as in *house, hope, have* is irrelevant as to what it represents in Spanish,[1] where it is silent as in *hombre, honda, hacer.*

The value is still independent when symbols represent similar sounds across languages because of common origin or borrowing.

Imperfect Fit   We noted that writing does not represent all of language. In addition, the same letter may represent now one phoneme, now another, such as *i* in English *fine, machine, chin.* Similarly, the same phoneme sequence /iy/ may be represented by different letters: *ee: feet, ea:seat, ei:receive, ie:achieve, i:machine, e:even.*

The fit of the writing system of English is quite irregular chiefly because the language has evolved, and the writing system has failed to keep pace. Better fit is found in Finnish, Turkish, Spanish, and others; a perfect fit is not to be found in any language because of borrowings, changes, and imperfections in the original design.

Habit   Try writing any sentence backwards and notice how slowly you write and how insecure and childish your handwriting looks. Try reading a page from right to left by means of a mirror and see how slowly you read, and notice that you understand and remember little (to say nothing of the eyestrain you will feel). Using a writing system involves habit.

Literate Arabs read from right to left with the same ease that we read from left to right. The difference is bridged by habits formed through long practice. Chinese readers find it easier to read from top to bottom for the same reason. Each may argue that his direction of reading is easiest, but it would be difficult to prove the point. For language teaching purposes, "habit" is a necessary and sufficient explanation.

Transfer   The habits involved in reading and writing the source language tend to be transferred to the target language with resulting

---

[1] Except insofar as the words may be cognates and an unbroken spelling tradition may have been maintained for both languages.

interference where the two systems differ and with facilitation where they are parallel. The force of this transfer is much stronger than we realize, and it persists into advanced stages of mastery.

This fact has obvious implications for teaching how to read and write a foreign language. These implications will be developed more specifically in the treatment of reading and writing that follows.

· · · **TEACHING READING**

The task of teaching reading can be divided into parts as follows: (1) Prereading: identifying the graphemes. (2) Fit: associating the graphemes and the language. (3) Habit: reading what is spoken. (4) Reading aloud: speaking what is written. (5) Reading for information: technical, cultural, recreational. (6) Diversification: reading different styles of graphemes and of language. (7) Reading power: vocabulary building and speed. (8) Literature: esthetic experience.

Prereading: *The graphemes*   In French, Italian, Portuguese, or Spanish, since the alphabet is the same as that of English, teaching the graphemes is of minor importance and may in fact be overlooked without major consequences. A brief presentation of the few symbols that differ from those of the native language writing will be helpful to the reader. For Spanish this means ñ (*n* with a tilde), 1 (1 with a slanting stroke), 7 (crossed 7), ¿, ¡ (upside down question mark and exclamation point), ' (acute accent mark). In Portuguese it means ã, õ (vowel with a tilde), etc. In French: ç (*c* with cedilla), ' ` ^ (acute, grave, and circumflex accent marks), etc.

Russian with its Cyrillic alphabet requires the teaching of unfamiliar Cyrillic letters such as ж, ф, ю. And although they often represent different sounds, some of the letters are similar enough to Latin letters to be identifiable by association: a, B, e, K, M, H, o, p, c, T, y, x.

In Arabic, whose alphabet shows no obvious resemblance to the Latin one, all the letters have to be identified not only in isolation but in connected writing where the absence of short vowel marks, the location of long vowel marks above or below the consonants, and the direction of writing from right to left will be noted.

In Chinese, with its completely different system, the need for delaying the teaching of reading is readily granted. When Chinese reading is taught, the characters have to be presented a few at a time. To identify even the 2,000 characters needed for minimum reading is a formidable undertaking.

To teach English or Spanish reading to readers of Arabic, Chinese,

Japanese, Russian, or other languages with very different writing systems requires prereading instruction to identify the letters of the Latin alphabet.

Teaching graphemes by contrast When the problems are few, present the new symbols and check their identification by the students without further ado. With a few spaced repetitions, the symbols will be learned.

When the writing system is quite unfamiliar, do not teach each symbol as if it were completely different and unrelated. This increases the learning burden. Even Chinese characters show recurring partial elements and minimal contrasts. Take advantage of the recurring partials and highlight the contrasts.

For example, in teaching the Latin alphabet to Japanese readers not familiar with it, do not present *o, l, b, d, p, q* as if they were completely different. Show that they are a circle, a line, and combinations of the two in different relative position to each other—circle at the right or left of the vertical line, and the line reaching above or below the horizontal level of the letters. Practice identifying them, perhaps by name. Similarly, the broken circle of *c* may be contrasted with the full circle of *o* and with the broken circle and small upper loop of *e*.

Thus highlighting the minimal contrasts serves to guide the student and helps him overlook the irrelevant stylistic frills of the letters, for example, the corners in *b* and *d* that are nondistinctive.

In Chinese writing, there are 214 recurring partials used to classify the thousands of Chinese graphemes. These recurring partials have to be learned, but they in turn show minimal contrasts and similar elements.

Fit: *Associating the graphemes and the language* Fit is the relation between a writing system and the spoken language it represents. When the student can speak a pattern and can identify the graphemes separately, it is time to associate the language with graphemes.

Teaching the regularities of fit When a letter regularly represents the same sound, tell the student so. The fit of English writing is very poor; yet there are phonemes regularly represented by the same letter, e.g., /m/:*m*, /v/:*v*.

There are many other regularities of English spelling, although they are not simple one-phoneme-to-one-letter associations. Some letters always represent the same phoneme, but the phoneme can be represented by other letters, e.g., /f/:*f*, also *gh, ph*; /ǰ/:*j*, also *dg, g*. Some letters represent a phoneme under given conditions, e.g., /l/:*l, ll*, but not in *walk, calm*. Some combinations of letters represent a particular phoneme, though not completely, e.g., /iy/:*ee*.

In Spanish, the proportion of regular spelling representations is much greater, and more can be accomplished by pointing out and practicing these associations. In Finnish and Turkish, the proportion is even greater.

It will usually be profitable to teach the alphabet or syllabary by heart. The names of the letters often illustrate the regular sound-symbol associations. Care must be taken to show that the phonemes are central and regular and that any discrepancies are imperfect representations, rather than the other way around.

Teaching the problems in patterns Once the major regularities of fit are taught, the problems have to be taught more gradually. The problems arise from irregularities of fit or from interference from the source writing system. For example, the fact that English /k/ can be represented by *k* and *ch* as in *king, chemistry,* and the *ch,* in turn, can represent /č/ in *church* and /š/ in *machine* is a problem of irregularity.

On the other hand, for a Spanish reader, the fact that Spanish /č/ is always represented by *ch,* which can stand for /k/ in English, results in interference. The Spanish reader will repeatedly read chemistry as /čémistriy/.

Taking up each word as a separate problem is inefficient. Teach patterns of representation. For example, English /i/ is most often represented by *i* between consonants: *bit, fill, win, principle.* Teach this pattern as such.

Say, for example, "/i/ is often represented by the letter *i* plus one or more consonants: *bit, sip, fill, win.*" Then write these words on the board. Ask the students to read them aloud. Write other words they know, e.g., *him, his, Miss, six, ship,* and ask them to read them aloud.

Then to test the generalization, write some words they may not know, e.g., *rift, Tim, wit,* and ask them to pronounce them if they can.

English /ay/ is most often represented by *i* + consonant + *e: five, nine, mile.* Teach it as a spelling pattern that fits a part of the sound system.

Teaching the exceptions as needed Nothing can be more deadening than having to recite all the exceptions to a rule or pattern. Such memorization is painful and useless for the most part, since the students do not need to know the exceptions as a list, but individually as items.

When particular words are needed, if they have exceptional spelling representation, teach them as items: /ə/ represented by *e* in *the* before a consonant; /i/ represented by *o* in *women.*

Programming You cannot teach all the patterns, problems, and exceptions at once; something must come first, something second, and something last.

There is no need to postpone reading until complete mastery of the language has been achieved. The principle of teaching the language first is maintained in teaching reading of each pattern immediately after it is mastered orally.

The program moves on a double track. On one track is laid out systematically the association of sounds and symbols. On the other is handled the reading of sentences already mastered orally. The second track cannot wait for all the elements to be taught in the first; when something is needed out of normal sequence, teach it without analysis.

The order of presentation on the graded track cannot be prescribed in any single sequence; various cumulative arrangements are equally defensible. In general, regular patterns can be taught first, followed by problems due to interference from the source writing; next, problems caused by multiple patterns of fit can be presented and the exceptions taught as needed.

Habit: *Reading what is spoken* Reading is grasping the language patterns from their written representation quickly without analysis of what symbols represent what sounds. This is a skill that comes through habit. As soon as possible, preferably the first time reading is introduced, present the written representation of patterns after they are spoken by the students. For practice, have the students speak the patterns using the written representation as stimulus. The symbols and problems they do not yet understand will be carried by identifying the pattern from the symbols that are regular and the problems that have been studied.

Reading Aloud: *Speaking what is written* Reading aloud clearly and interestingly is an artistic skill. Not all the native speakers of a language are able to read aloud effectively. Reading aloud is therefore not easy to justify as an end in itself in teaching a foreign language. It is, however, an effective practice and test of a student's ability to read in general.

In reading aloud, the student is confronted with written sentences that he has not spoken immediately before and with sentences which he has never spoken but whose elements he can speak. This practice becomes genuine reading since he must grasp the patterns he is to speak at some normal speed from the incomplete clues of their written representation.

Material which has been mastered orally can be rearranged into somewhat different sentences and read aloud for practice in reading.

The common practice of having each student in succession read aloud a sentence or two to the class seems inefficient. Choral reading allows everyone to practice every sentence. We do not have experimental evidence to show that listening to another student recite with the expectation that one will recite in turn is as effective as reciting in chorus. The statement that the practice is inefficient will therefore remain impressionistic until some simple experiments are conducted and reported.

When the each-one-read-one practice permits a student to know ahead of time what sentence he will recite, some students concentrate on preparing their own sentence and do not listen to any other sentence. This is obviously unsatisfactory.

We are of course talking of reading aloud as an exercise in reading, not as a pronunciation or rhythm exercise. Eventually there is a point where reading must proceed with constructions and vocabulary that are not common in speaking. The value of reading aloud obviously ends at this point.

Reading for Information Up to this stage the student has been chiefly learning to read. Now the task shifts to reading to learn. Or more accurately he now reads for information, since he is still learning to read but at a more advanced level at which his attention is on the information he can gather rather than on the graphemes or the fit.

Grading and selection Subject matter becomes important at this stage. Tremendous nonsense has been perpetrated in this area: children's stories are used for adults because the language is supposedly simple; quaint stories that are an insult to the intelligence of children and adults keep appearing again and again; stories completely out of touch with the world of thought or experience of the target culture are read and become the caricature of a people.

Reject such nonsense. Here are some obvious principles of selection. The subject can be worthwhile *and* interesting—there is no necessary conflict between the two. The subject must be adapted to the maturity of the students. The language must be graded for their level of proficiency. Serious literature is usable at this stage only insofar as the language lies within the power of the students and the content is worthwhile as thought or information. Serious literature should not be simplified in order to make it usable. It should be postponed until the students are ready for it as an esthetic experience in itself.

Among the topics of worthwhile content at this point are cultural patterns, customs, cities, heroes, and products of the countries where the language is spoken; these countries' institutions, educational systems, monuments, great achievements, artists, musicians, painters, leaders, leading newspapers, and magazines; their religion, history, beliefs, and characteristics; topics of universal human value, such as discoveries and inventions.

These and many others can contribute to the education of the students as well as to his improvement in reading. Such reading selections can be prepared for the students of the foreign language, or they can be selected and adapted from the wealth of material that is printed yearly in many languages.

Full reading in class In the early part of reading for information, one must move slowly. A page an hour is not too slow. At this point, a single reading program handled completely in class is indicated.

Combining class reading with outside reading Eventually, more reading will be necessary than can be done in class. This can be done through a single reading program for everybody as follows:

Read a page aloud in class. Make sure it is fully understood by asking questions and /or by other means. Assign the next two pages for outside reading. Check each assignment at the next class to find out if the students did the reading and understood it. Read the next page aloud in class with student participation in chorus, checking comprehension; then assign the next two pages. Check the homework as before; read the succeeding page in class; assign the next two, and so on. As the students' skill increases, the outside assignment is increased. Through some such program, a substantial amount of reading can be done.

Extensive outside reading Diversified extensive outside reading is achieved by letting each student read books, magazines, and newspapers outside of class and having him give oral reports on them in class. This can be combined with writing practice by assigning a book review or composition based on the reading.

The teacher should have an extensive list of titles with an indication of level of difficulty. Cultural readings to provide information and understanding of the target culture are recommended at this stage. Professional and technical material is permissible for mature students studying the language as a tool in their professional training.

This outside reading can be very flexible. Each student can read an entirely different list of titles on different technical subjects. In a mixed group, the reports to the class must be in nontechnical terms to permit comprehension and discussion by the other students.

With large classes, the reports can be limited to a page or two, and the oral presentation restricted to a couple of minutes if need be.

This combination of uniform and diversified reading with oral and written reports and discussion lends itself to courses in reading, composition, and conversation for students who have learned to speak the language and wish to penetrate the culture and maintain and expand their language skills.

Diversification Just as speaking style changes according to the situation, purpose, and persons involved, so reading varies according to subject, readers, and purposes. A light detective story is read quickly for the plot and suspense. A book on mathematics has to be read gradually, step by step. A newspaper may be scanned selectively for news of interest, for ads if the purpose is to buy something, etc. A dictionary is consulted for specific items. A poem can be read over and over thoughtfully, taking in the sound, the thought, the feeling. This diversification of reading is necessary for the native speaker as well as the foreign one. Learning to skim, to read quickly for specific facts, and to read critically are discussed in various works and will not be elaborated further here.

Reading Power   As we have already noted, recognition vocabularies are much larger than previously suspected. Seashore found the vocabulary of twelfth-grade students in the United States to be about 80,000 basic and derived words. He found that first graders know some 16,900 basic words. To think, then, of 2,000 words in a foreign language as an adequate reading vocabulary is untenable. We must expand the vocabulary of our students if we expect them to read effectively.

Vocabulary building   Intensive and extensive reading is admittedly one of the best ways to increase vocabulary power. We find we do not achieve this, however, when teaching stops with a simplified textbook and reader in the foreign language.

Concentrated readings with a deliberate vocabulary overload might help. (Some individuals read a dictionary to increase their vocabulary.) We would propose a programmed approach with each frame introducing, testing, or reinforcing a vocabulary item or an extension of one. For example,

> Columbus *discovered* America in 1492.
> Columbus ———— America in 1492.
> His *ship* was the Santa Maria.
> The Santa Maria was his ————.
> He *sailed* from Spain.
> America was ———— by Columbus in 1492.
> His ship ———— from Spain.
> He sailed on the ———— Santa Maria.

The items can be completed by writing the missing words or by rehearsing them silently.

Speed   Modern education and society require that we read quantities of material to keep informed. Rapid reading with comprehension has become a necessity. How can we achieve it?

A considerable literature is available on reading, and machines and courses are offered to improve reading speed. The basic ingredient is accelerated practice free from improper habits. Specific attention is given to eye span and eye movements, pacing, and testing for comprehension. Not sufficiently emphasized is the role of language in reading. Even less stressed is the role of language and writing systems in reading a foreign language.

Efficient reading for information occurs when the written symbols trigger the language patterns in the reader, who then grasps the stream of total meaning. If he is aware of the written symbols, of his eye movements, or even of the sounds of what he reads, he is doing less than fully efficient reading. This awareness of the process or the means constitutes noise, or interference in communication. To this we add the interference from the native language and writing systems. The interference from the native language is overcome by better mastery of the target language. Interference from the background writing system and from awareness of sounds and symbols is overcome by extensive selective practice with pressure to increase speed.

Reading pacers, reading films, tachistoscopes, and other devices are in use to speed the reading of native readers. They can be used also in a foreign language. The materials should ideally be adapted to the students' needs, at least in the intermediate stage between slow, word-for-word reading for information and the more or less efficient reading of a literate native speaker who concentrates fully on content whether or not he reads very fast.

Literature Literature is widely used and widely abused in foreign language teaching. The first abuse comes from offering courses in literature to students who do not know enough of the language to understand its literature. This results in either talking about the literature in the student's native language without reading it or in a painful translation or in deciphering of small bits of literary items. This is hardly reading literature.

Another abuse is to simplify some well-known literary work and read it as if it were the real thing. If a work has achieved immortality, it should not be simplified or in any way distorted, or it ceases to be that work and becomes an impostor.

A more "justifiable" abuse of literature in a foreign language is to simplify a literary work and use it not as literature but as reading for information about the target culture.

Perhaps the worst abuse of literature in a foreign language is to take a masterpiece from some earlier period and use it as the model for students in learning the language. Such would be the case if Shakespeare were used today as the model to be imitated in a class in English as a foreign language.

Proper use of literature We should teach literature when the student is advanced enough in his control of the language and his understanding of the culture to experience it somewhat like the native reader.

This does not imply a fixed and specific level of control. Some literary works are easier to understand than others. Selection and arrangement of titles on the basis of difficulty for the students permits the appreciation of literature at a level of mastery of the language within the reach of the nonnative student. Furthermore, instead of doctoring a work of art to bring it down to the level of the students, it is better to prepare the student to understand and experience a particular piece of literature. Vocabulary and cultural items can be treated beforehand so that when the literary work is read, it can be read through, understood, and appreciated.

Under these conditions it is possible to introduce students to a foreign literature in a way that preserves the values of such an experience, so generally accepted as part of a liberal education in one's own language and so highly humanizing and powerful in a foreign one.

Chapter 14

Writing

To write is to put down the graphic symbols that represent a language one understands, so that others can read these graphic symbols if they know the language and the graphic representation. Pictures may convey meanings, but they do not represent language units. Writing is a partial representation of units of language expression. This is the essential difference between drawing and writing.

Drawing pictures is not writing. Drawing letters is, strictly speaking, not writing. A sign painter might paint Chinese characters, but he is not writing unless he knows how to write Chinese, i.e., unless he understands Chinese and the characters. By the same criterion, copying letters or setting a text in type for printing is not writing unless the person knows the language and its representation.

Learning to Write Learning to write a foreign language is learning to put down at a speed greater than that of drawing the conventional symbols of the writing system that represent the utterances one has in mind. This is divided into several stages: prewriting, copying read texts, transcribing, composition, and literature. Literature is discussed in Chapter 15. The other stages are treated here.

Prewriting The task of preparing students to learn to write in a foreign language varies according to what the student knows from his native language writing. Being sufficiently prepared involves knowing the symbols that will represent the utterances he has in mind and how to put them down.

A person literate in English, learning to write French or Spanish, knows how to write the letters because they are the same as his own except for a few details. Teaching him to write one of these languages means merely teaching him to choose the letters that represent the French or Spanish sentences he has in mind. The same is true in teaching a literate French or Spanish speaker to write English.

Teaching a literate Arab, Chinese, or Korean to write English requires teaching him how to write the letters of the Latin alphabet before he can write anything.

Copying the symbols   Preschool children and illiterates are usually first taught a form of printed letters because the component parts and contrasts are more easily learned. Students who are literate in their own language can begin with cursive writing just as easily.

The basic strokes   In teaching cursive writing, the student has to be shown where to begin each letter, which way to move, and how to connect the strokes and the letters. The arrows show this in the following:

Teaching the fit   Since writing follows or accompanies reading but does not precede it, the regularities of fit and the exceptions learned for reading will transfer to writing so that a step-by-step presentation is unnecessary. The problems will vary somewhat since there may be more than one spelling representing a sound but only one sound for a particular spelling, and vice versa. For example, the English phoneme /f/ can be represented by *gh* (*enough*), *ph* (*photo*), *f* (*food*), but the letter *f* represents the single phoneme /f/. And the letter *h* can represent the phoneme /h/ as in *house* or represent no sound as in *honor*, but the phoneme /h/ is always represented by *h*.

Letter styles and contrast   Show the student what parts of the letters are distinctive and what are matters of style. For example, show him that the loop of the *e* is distinctive because without it the single symbol becomes an undotted *i*, and two loopless *e*'s become a *u*. The

double wave ⸾ of cursive *k* is in contrast with the single one ⸯ of *h*.
Clearness of contrast is the dominant virtue at this level.

Writing Chinese The task of teaching the characters in Chinese
writing is incomparably more difficult than teaching the letters of any
alphabet. A decisive difference is the number involved: while there
are fewer than 50 letters in most alphabets, in Chinese it is estimated
that between 70,000 and 125,000 characters exist. Nevertheless, teaching
a useful number of characters can be greatly simplified by showing the
recurring parts of the characters and highlighting the minimal contrasting elements, rather than by teaching each character as an entirely
different and unrelated symbol.

For example, 土 and 王 have 土 in common; the contrast is in
the additional horizontal bar of 王 . 古 and 杏 have 十 and 口 as
recurring parts in common; they contrast in 八 which appears only in 杏 .
杲 and 杏 have identical recurring parts, 木 and 口 ; they contrast in
the position of one above the other.

Copying Read Texts There is a long road between writing the symbols
slowly and carefully, with full attention on the strokes, and writing at
a useful speed for communication. We must help the student establish
the habits involved in writing, from the initial traces up to a point
when the particular strokes are handled automatically without awareness.

To dramatize and bring home the importance of habit in writing,
attempt to write this sentence from right to left. You will go very slowly,
start and stop many unnecessary times, make mistakes, get tired soon,
and produce a handwriting like that of a beginner.

Copying as an exercise We are convinced, though experimental
evidence is lacking, that a very good way to provide extensive early
writing practice is to have the students copy large amounts of text that
they have read. Instruct the student to take a phrase at a time, write
it down, then check it against the text. This provides a model, exercise,
and reinforcement.

The chief drawback of this practice is monotony. Students soon tire
of this and find excuses not to continue. Additional motivation can be
provided, however, by giving short dictations from the text as quizzes
and showing the students their own progress.

Transcribing A more advanced practice in learning to write is to put
down utterances in script without a written text as a model. This
requires that the association between language units and script be recalled,
not merely recognized.

Dictation The simplest practice is to give the students an utterance they know how to say and read, and ask them to write it down. Their written response is then corrected by the students themselves against a model.

Transcription of own utterances An interesting variation widely used to teach reading to native speakers of English is as follows: A story or some other topic is suggested. The students then propose sentences for the composition of a story. The teacher accepts those that fit the reading vocabulary of the students and seem interesting. The students write them down in their notebooks. One student writes on the blackboard to permit group or teacher correction of his effort as a model. Variations of this exercise are numerous and desirable in teaching writing.

Composition Thus far, the student has been learning to write; he now writes to inform. He is still learning but at a more advanced stage. He already knows the language, and he knows how to represent it in script. Now he must be taught to present his information in a format acceptable for the occasion, be that an informal friendly letter or a matter-of-fact business communication, a report to the teacher, or an article for publication.

Teach him that to write a communication he must (1) have something to say on some topic, (2) have a point of view and focus, (3) follow accepted conventions of format, and (4) be effective.

Topics Here are some topics for practice compositions for students who cannot think of one of their own: describe a city, a house, a monument, a building, a cathedral or church, a ship, a person, the furniture of a house, a mountain, a river, a bay, a street, etc. These will make heavy use of nouns.

Narrate the activities of a specific, a typical, or a composite day, week, month, season, year; life stage, such as childhood, youth, adulthood, middle years, old age; or the entire life cycle for a man or a woman. Narrate the life of a hero or other notable person. Narrate the story of a historical event, a battle, a discovery, an exploration, etc. This will make heavy use of verbs.

Tell of a specific, a typical, or a composite meal, or a celebration, such as a wedding, a saint's day, a birthday, etc. Tell of a specific, a typical, or a composite dress worn by somebody or on particular occasions. Tell of a ceremony such as a mass or church service. Tell of a vacation with emphasis on means of transportation, activities, or the people. These topics will encourage the use of adjectives and adverbs, especially if the student is told to express his point of view.

Describe or tell about the schools, occupations, government, beliefs, customs, religion, language, leisure activities, values, etc., of a culture or a country.

Interpret something of your native culture for readers of the target language.

Write about some of the great human truths beyond a particular culture, e.g., the meaning of life, truth, liberty, death, beauty, love, or God.

Point of view The same subject may be written about from a variety of points of view and focus. Teach the students to adopt a clear and consistent point of view and purpose. Here are some: sympathetic and friendly, antagonistic and unfriendly; encyclopedic and detailed, or scientific, humorous, apologetic, protesting, educational, or esthetic.

The student should decide if he is the protagonist or an observer and if the subject is completed and past, in process at present, or expected, hoped for, or feared. He should choose whether to treat the subject from close range in great detail or at a distance and in swift outline.

Style conventions A friendly letter may begin with "Dear John, I am writing from the steps of the Lincoln Memorial," and end with "As ever," but not so a formal business letter. It is not that one is correct and the other incorrect; each is correct in its own situation according to the style conventions of the language at the time. These conventions include language forms such as contractions, and vocabulary selection such as *it rained cats and dogs* versus *it rained heavily*. They include fixed formulas of address, etc. There is little choice in the salutation and complimentary close of each type of letter. The student cannot invent these or attempt to be very creative about them.

Teach the special formulas and format of various letters, notes, and invitations. Teach something of the characteristics of newspaper writing, reports, plays, digests, abstracts, and outlines, and perhaps teach prose styles versus poetic styles as well.

Clarity and effectiveness Since the object of writing is to communicate information with a point of view in mind, clarity and effectiveness are desirable. The composition must be well organized so that it can be followed readily by the intended reader, and within this organization, the content must be so selected that it will have the desired effect upon him.

There are limits to the ways in which a composition may be arranged. The principal arrangements are logical, chronological, spatial, causal, esthetic, and various combinations of these. History is narrated chiefly on a chronological basis, though, within this arrangement, logical, causal, and spatial subarrangements are fitted.

The description of a machine, a game, or a species in biology might be organized on a logical basis, taking the various components at one level, identifying them by their essential features, then moving to their subcategories, etc.

A geographical description might be arranged spatially, say, for example, clockwise down the Atlantic coast of South America and up the Pacific coast, ending in the interior.

The effectiveness of the composition will depend on such matters as order of presentation, emphasis, point of view, and style, but there is no single way to be effective.

Chapter 15

Cultural Content and Literature

We cannot teach a language well without coming to grips with its cultural content. There can be no real learning of a language without understanding something of the patterns and values of the culture of which it is a part. Fries states this strongly: "To deal with the culture and life of a people is *not just an adjunct* of a practical language course, something alien and apart from its main purpose, to be added or not as time and convenience may allow, but an *essential feature of every stage of language learning....*"[1]

Every time that the textbook or the teacher mentions a word or describes or refers to something that the American student does not understand culturally or misunderstands because its cultural content differs from his native patterns, there is immediate need to deal with the cultural difference involved. This need is present even if we teach the language exclusively as a tool and not as a complete educational experience. When the language is taught for its educational value, understanding cultural content is much more important.

If we teach Spanish language forms but refer to American cultural

[1] C. C. Fries, "American Linguistics and the Teaching of English." *Language Learning,* vol. 6, no. 1–2, p. 14, 1955.

meanings, values, and patterns of behavior, we are not fully teaching Spanish. The mere mention of wine at table, the United States, a bull-fight, an examination—frequent items that might occur as part of an elementary dialogue—involves cultural differences which, if ignored, are understood by the student in the cultural meaning of his native patterns, and therefore misunderstood. Wine at table, for example, might be understood by the American student to imply a special occasion, when it does not have that implication in Spanish. The United States means "my country" to the American student but means a foreign country to the native of Spain or Latin America. A bullfight, something exotic, rather cruel, to the American observer, is a gala show of bravery and art in the face of death in Spanish culture. An examination usually means a written exercise to the American, but to the Spanish student, it is an oral confrontation with a tribunal of professors. Thus, even if we succeed in teaching the Spanish sound system and grammatical structure, the student may make Spanish noises but he will not speak Spanish; he may hear Spanish noises but he will not really understand them.

When, on the other hand, we succeed in teaching cultural content with the language, the student not only acquires that knowledge but increases his understanding of his own culture as well.

The question is not whether we must tackle cultural content or when we should tackle it, since we must come to grips with it from the beginning. The question is one of determining what the learning prob-lems involved are and how we may teach an understanding of one culture to another.

Different Objectives   Differences in the purpose for which the language is taught influence the cultural content of the course. Let us consider briefly a foreign language as part of the general education of students, as a stepping stone to a foreign literature, as an instrument for inter-national communication, and as a reading tool for scientists.

As part of education   To become truly educated, it is necessary for a student to absorb the full cultural meaning of the target language where it differs significantly from the native one. A student cannot achieve this objective without breaking free of the EMUs of his native language, or without realizing that much of what he has learned through his native language represents custom and habit and that there are other custom and habit patterns that are also valid.

In addition, an educated person must go beyond the habitual cul-tural molds that are learned by everyone in the process of enculturation. The man in the street may know that a certain painting is the picture of a room with some people in old costumes, while another, looking at the same object, knows that it is Velazquez' famous painting, "Las

Meninas," and that the painter who appears in it is Velazquez himself. The man in the street may believe that all Mexicans wear wide-brimmed sombreros and spend their lives dancing and playing the guitar, while another knows who wear these sombreros and when, who the great guitar players are, and who cannot pluck a chord on a guitar.

There is no limit to how much an educated person may know; nor can anyone know everything, but a foreign language for education must involve cultural patterning plus something beyond.

To read literature Since literature is expressed through language, one cannot understand it unless he understands the meanings of the culture expressed by the words of the language and unless the values and cultural experience against which the literature is written are also understood. One cannot jump from the structure of a language into its literature without passing through the basic cultural content of the language.

For international communication Limited international communication can occur without detailed reference to the specific culture of which the language is a part, but the contrasts among words and the shades of difference among synonyms cannot be resolved without reference to some body of usage. The touchstone should be the present-day usage of educated native speakers of the language.

As an adopted national language In such countries as India, Ghana, and the Philippines, English is taught as a means of communication among nationals. In this case, the language must express the cultural meanings current in the host culture. If, in addition, it is to be used as a foreign language for educational purposes, the foreign cultural content should also eventually be taught.

To read scientific reports Greatest resistance to learning cultural content might be expected when the objective is the limited one of reading scientific papers in a foreign language. This is in part proper, since scientific terms are defined for the sake of precision. Some understanding, however, of the content of the language is still necessary, because not all the words used in scientific papers are fully defined. Merely to translate the word *bones* into Spanish as *huesos* may lead the Spanish reader to think that the English original did not apply to fish bones, since the Spanish form does not.

The Problem What specifically should we teach as cultural content?

Elementary meaning units and patterns The cultural content and the connotations of the words and idioms selected for teaching will have to be made clear to the students. These units of cultural content (EMU) vary from culture to culture. Whenever the native and target words differ significantly in content, we should teach the target cultural content;

when they do not so differ, we may present the linguistic item without further ado. The difference may be in coverage (*hueso* does not cover "fish bone"), in cultural content (a Spanish *desayuno* bears little resemblance to a typical American breakfast), or in cultural function or significance (*vino* in Spain and *wine* in the United States have a different function and a different connotation).

When the differences fall into a pattern, teach them as a pattern. Note, for example, that Spanish has separate sets of terms for the anatomical parts of humans and animals.

False clichés Where the native image of the target culture contains false clichés, we should substitute accurate information. In teaching English as a foreign language, it may be necessary to show that battles between Indians and cowboys are to be found today only in the movies.

Great achievements Just as we teach our students the great achievements of our culture as inspiration and education, we shall want to teach something of the achievements of the target culture. We cannot understand another people's language fully until we know through their eyes those whom they call their heroes, what these people have fought for and what they stand ready to defend again, what accomplishments they prize, and what they consider virtuous, courageous, honorable, and of good report.

The Declaration of Independence is more than a historical document; it is part of the living tradition that makes the United States what it is. Gibraltar is more to the living Spanish culture than merely a fortified rock occupied by England. Babe Ruth is more than a professional baseball player with a high batting average. You cannot teach in a few class hours everything that a person experiences in a lifetime as a member of a culture, but some selected experiences will do much to achieve understanding.

How to Teach Cultural Content and When How do we teach one culture to understand another? Where do we begin?

Setting the stage Begin with a film, pictures, music, or something else that will forcefully make the students sense that they are entering another culture, not merely taking up strange noises for familiar things. A good film in the target language seems best, even though the students will not understand what they hear and see. Good music from the target culture will increase the desire to get into the language of these people. Attitude toward the culture has been found to correlate significantly with learning.

Supply an introductory sketch of the culture and its people. Who are they? What are their outstanding characteristics? What have they done? Where are they located? What are their religious beliefs, their form of government, and their educational system? The point of view might be that of the target culture itself or an objective one. These things may have to be presented as a reading assignment in the native language, but there can be objections to having it presented in the native language by the teacher, since this will weaken the identification of the teacher with the target language. There is much to be said for having the students think of communication with the teacher as being always in the target language both in and out of class.

Ad hoc cultural notes In the early stages of teaching language, the ordering of material is decided on the basis of language structure, because this is the primary learning burden. One cannot grade assignments on the basis of language and systematically cover the culture as well. Introduce cultural content as needed to make the language material meaningful and to avoid misinformation.

When a word or expression must be taught that differs in cultural content from the roughly equivalent term in the native language, explain its meaning as a cultural note or an aside without going into the entire structure of the culture. If possible, do this in the target language itself. If not, let the students read to themselves the explanation or note in the native language. This will preserve the foreign language atmosphere of the class and the unbroken identification of the teacher with the foreign language.

Contextual areas Careful selection of contextual areas for the dialogue and reading material permits full use of the language in limited areas early in the course. Pictures, slides, or a film may help significantly to provide cultural content for observation by the students. Observation alone, of course, may mislead. Explain or clarify the cultural content of the material presented.

Cultural topics as content Thus far we have been discussing ways of using cultural items to teach the language. When the students have reached an intermediate level of mastery, the teacher can switch emphasis and use the language to teach cultural matters. The object is still to teach the language, but to teach it at a higher level where the language is used to acquire information, and the information deals with the target culture.

Selected topics are used at this stage, rather than any full treatment of the entire culture. Food, holidays, specific heroes, institutions, or customs may be taken up as the context in the target language. A reading selection is often the means of presenting the information. A conversation on the topic in the target language provides practice with attention on the content.

Particularly valuable at this stage are sample selections from the leading newspapers and magazines, professional and religious publications, and entertainment and political press releases to provide not only some cultural content from the target culture point of view but also to show the chief forces and publishing enterprises of the society. Samples of editorial writing, feature stories, columns, etc., will, if judiciously chosen, make good reading and become a source of authentic views revealing values and issues of the day. Preparation for each selection should be provided before the student tackles the selection.

Civilization courses Language teaching, strictly speaking, ends before the civilization course begins. As a matter of fact, civilization courses may be taught—though not with best results—in the native language. The guidelines and criteria determining excellence in a civilization course are outside the scope of this book and will therefore not be treated here.

Experiencing the Culture   Much can be done to understand the target culture through the study of the language. Moreover, by mastering the language, we gain the freedom to penetrate further into the culture through what the people themselves write and say. Full experience, however, is difficult if not impossible without living in that society for at least a year. Students cannot be expected to do this in any great number. It is highly recommended, however, that the language teacher make every effort to spend a full year there and to pay shorter visits from time to time to revive fading memories and to learn of new developments.

TEACHING THE LITERATURE OF A FOREIGN LANGUAGE

A literary piece is a unique, esthetically notable expression of some content through language. A piece may achieve the esthetic level of literature through the qualities of its expression, the significance of its content, or both. Shakespeare's *Hamlet* and Cervantes' *Don Quixote* are notable for both expression and content. "The Raven" by Edgar Allan Poe is literary in its expression rather than in its content. St. Teresa of Avila's *Autobiography* is more notable for its content than its expression.

Purpose   The objective in teaching a foreign literature is not as a rule to train writers for the production of literary masterpieces in that language. Few have achieved the ability to write literature in a foreign language. Joseph Conrad represents an exception rather than the rule. And it is doubtful that the ability to write literature can be imparted through an ordinary foreign language course.

The chief objective should be to teach appreciation of a foreign literature, i.e., capacity to experience it fully. This should also increase the students' appreciation of their own literature.

Another objective is to experience artistically something of the target culture. Mere knowledge of facts is less valuable than imaginative realization of the culture as a way of life. This will give perspective on, and fuller appreciation of, one's own culture.

For this objective, however, the material is chosen rather on the basis of what it reveals of the culture than of its literary merit, and so it is not, strictly speaking, being used to teach literature.

Prerequisites   To experience a literary work, it is necessary to understand the language in which it is expressed, the cultural meanings which it contains, and the circumstances surrounding it.   If it is a contemporary piece, ordinary proficiency and cultural information are usually sufficient.   If it belongs to an earlier period, special preparation and annotation will be necessary.

Point of View   Fullest appreciation cames through adopting the point of view of the target culture itself, rather than that of an outsider looking in.   "Chicago" by Carl Sandburg or "Oh Captain, My Captain" by Walt Whitman remain pretty superficial exercises without involvement from the inside.   You cannot enter into the experience of the poet by coolly observing the forms used and the facts enumerated.

Technical criticism of the literary piece is useful insofar as it will permit a fuller appreciation of it on the part of the student.   Beyond this, such information and analysis become a professional matter for the literary critic and lose relevance for the student seeking to become an educated person and not a literary critic.

Selection versus Simplification   The widely used practice of simplifying literature by restricting its vocabulary and grammar complexity is questionable.   If "Chicago" has earned a place in the literature of the United States, can we simplify its vocabulary and teach it as Sandburg's creation?   Can we simplify "The Raven" and teach it as the poem that Edgar Allan Poe wrote?

We can, on the other hand, select literature that is within the linguistic range of the students, and we can prepare the students to experience specific literary works.   It seems more justifiable to prepare the student for the literary piece than to doctor the work to bring it down to the level of the students.

The student can be prepared by dealing with the annotations and language problems before tackling the piece itself.   The words that may be difficult are taught ahead of time.   They are seen in the sentence in which they will appear later in the text. This way, when the literary selection is presented, there need be no interruption to explain or look up words or to solve grammatical problems.

Simplification is useful in other than artistically immortalized writing. A feature article, an editorial, or a factual discussion of some topic can be simplified down to the level of the students without literary loss and with obvious gain for the students.

Sample Presentation   Suppose, for whatever reasons, we have chosen "Chicago," Sandburg's vigorous poem, as the subject to be taught to advanced students of English as a foreign language. We assume they know enough English to justify the selection. We have decided to prepare the students to appreciate the poem rather than to doctor it to fit the students.

Vocabulary and structure   Any words or idioms that the students are not familiar with should be taught first. If *wanton* is not known, for example, it might be presented thus.

Wanton:
unjust, inhuman
wanton cruelty
wanton hunger
I have seen the marks of _____ hunger.

Background for appreciation   The students should find out before they read the poem that Carl Sandburg was born in Illinois, so that Chicago is not only his city as an American but as a son of its state. He worked as a laborer, porter, dishwasher, newspaperman, and editor there. He loves it as it is.

The students should know something about Chicago as a transportation center and as the city where the stockyards handle huge quantities of cattle for butchering, processing, packing, and distributing to all parts of the United States and abroad. They will probably know stories of gangsters and gangster wars in Chicago; the movies and the sensationalism in the news will have seen to that.

Sandburg's style is vigorous, using strong everyday words. The students should know that the poem is in free verse so that they will not expect rhyme and measured rhythm.

How much to explain will depend on the students and the time available. Too much explanation will kill the students' interest in the poem. Explain enough to help with appreciation without falling into technical information of interest chiefly to the critic. With this, read the poem aloud to the class, or play it from a professional quality recording.

CHICAGO by Carl Sandburg[2]

Hog Butcher for the World,
Tool Maker, Stacker of Wheat,
Player with Railroads and the Nation's Freight Handler;
Stormy, husky, brawling,
City of the Big Shoulders:

They tell me you are wicked and I believe them, for I have seen your painted women under the gas lamps luring the farm boys.

And they tell me you are crooked and I answer: Yes, it is true I have seen the gunman kill and go free to kill again.

And they tell me you are brutal and my reply is: On the faces of women and children I have seen the marks of wanton hunger.

And having answered so I turn once more to those who sneer at this my city, and I give them back the sneer and say to them:

Come and show me another city with lifted head singing so proud to be alive and coarse and strong and cunning.

Flinging magnetic curses amid the toil of piling job on job, here is a tall bold slugger set vivid against the little soft cities;

Fierce as a dog with tongue lapping for action, cunning as a savage pitted against the wilderness,

Bareheaded,
Shoveling,
Wrecking,
Planning,
Building, breaking, rebuilding,

Under the smoke, dust all over his mouth, laughing with white teeth,
Under the terrible burden of destiny laughing as a young man laughs,
Laughing even as an ignorant fighter laughs who has never lost a battle,
Bragging and laughing that under his wrist is the pulse, and under his ribs the heart of the people,

Laughing!

Laughing the stormy, husky, brawling laughter of Youth, half-naked, sweating, proud to be Hog Butcher, Tool Maker, Stacker of Wheat, Player with Railroads and Freight Handler of the Nation.

Allow questions after the reading. Read it or play it again. Have the class participate in the reading as they can. Have a discussion on the poem afterwards.

[2] From *Chicago Poems* by Carl Sandburg. New York: Holt, Rinehart and Winston, 1916. By permission of the publishers.

Chapter 16

Language Testing

ON SOME CURRENT VIEWS AND PRACTICES

Discussions of testing tend to deal with techniques as the chief concern, without sufficient thought for the linguistic problems involved. The following questions are often asked: Should we use a composition as a test? Should we use translation? Are objective tests easier? Are they valid? Can we give oral examinations objectively?

More meaningful would be, Does translation measure auditory comprehension? Does grammatical analysis measure speaking ability? These are questions of validity and administration.

With this type of question in mind let us look at some common testing practices.

Translation As a test of ability in speaking, listening, reading, and writing, we notice the following limitations in the use of translation:

1. The most proficient students do not translate when they use the language.

2. There are various ways to translate and to judge a translation: for artistic purposes, for accuracy of information, for grammatical exactness, or for vocabulary equivalence. A translation can be judged from these and other points of view. If the student is forced to translate for vocabulary or grammar, his literary appreciation may suffer.

3. The grading of translations tends to be unreliable because of the

various ways to translate and the variations that the scorer may or may not allow.

4. Translation is a special skill different from speaking, listening, reading, and writing.

5. Translation is slow as a test. Unless he has had special training, a good student takes longer to translate a letter than to write one. In the time that it takes him to translate a passage, he can cover more material using other techniques.

6. Translation is slow to grade, since the examiner has to weigh each response to see if it is allowable.

7. The use of translation in tests encourages the abuse of translation in the classroom.

Perhaps the only favorable things to be said for translation as a test of language proficiency are that translation questions are easy to set and are compact. The price paid for these is high.

Grammatical analysis Tests that ask for grammatical analysis were at one time widely used. Labeling the parts of speech, defining grammatical terms, giving the rule, and supplying examples for grammatical terms were used as tests, probably because these were the tasks regularly performed in class. They are of doubtful validity as a measure of proficiency.

1. The ability to analyze a language and the ability to use it are very different things.

2. Most of those who use the language well cannot analyze it accurately or completely, and those who can analyze it, often cannot use it.

3. Differences in terminology among grammarians and linguists are to be expected, but they complicate the instructions to the students and the scoring of their answers.

Grammatical analysis, partly because of these considerations, is no longer widely used or defended in tests.

Words in isolation Words in isolation are used extensively in foreign and native language tests. To predict school success and measure general ability, such tests show good results. Yet, as measures of proficiency in a foreign language, one can find objections to them. The words of a language are much more flexible than one suspects. Meanings change subtly and radically from sentence to sentence according to the context. Thus to identify a word in isolation by a synonym, an antonym, a translation, or even a dictionary definition, tests only a fraction of the control of that word in its full range of use. To identify, for example, the word *right* out of context as the opposite of *left* is no indication that the student will understand the expression, *yield the right of way,* in connection with driving an automobile.

Flexibility in bringing out different features of a word in new usages through metaphor and metonymy applies to the everyday use of the language as well as to literature. When words are used in special ways by the literary artist, the problem of understanding them becomes almost insurmountable for those who know only the standard meaning attributed to the words in isolation.

The technique is also faulty because it does not force a choice between two possible meanings of the word. *Right* means "opposite of left," but it also means "legal privilege" and a hundred other things. Listing these meanings as choices still leaves the student helpless to decide which one applies since there is no context.

Objective tests Objective and short-answer tests are widely used. They are attacked or defended as a technique without reference to linguistic content. The fact is, however, that objective items having the appearance of a good language test may be fully effective or quite ineffective.

An example will illustrate this point with regard to auditory comprehension. The examiner reads aloud the sentence, "The man is looking at a new car," and the student is asked to indicate which of four pictures the sentence describes: in one a man is looking at a car; in another, at a ship; in a third, at a house; and in a fourth, at a train. On the surface this is a good item to test auditory comprehension: the student listens to an utterance and shows that he does or does not understand it by the picture he chooses. On more critical inspection, however, one realizes that to choose the picture of the car, the student need only identify the word *car,* which is so different phonologically from *house, ship,* and *train* that he might do it even if his contact with English has been only through reading.

In contrast, such items can be made to test important phonological problems. If, for example, the sentence is "The man is washing the dog," the student can be asked to choose between pictures representing, respectively, a man washing a dog and a man watching a dog. The student then has to hear the difference between the /č/ of *watching* and the /š/ of *washing,* which is an important problem in auditory comprehension if the native language does not make such a distinction.

Another example illustrates how an objective technique for testing reading comprehension becomes useless as a result of inadequate choices. In this test the student was given a reading passage dealing with the story of fire in Greek mythology. After reading the passage he had to answer a series of three-choice items that supposedly tested his understanding of the passage. Here is one item that can be answered even without reading the passage, since only the third choice is possible:

"(1) A man can lift a mountain. (2) A bird can lift a mountain. (3) A bird can lift itself into the air." It is difficult to know what this item was supposed to test.

The validity of objective tests cannot be judged on the appearance of the items but must be determined on the basis of linguistic content or by statistical analysis.

Dictation   Liked by many because it is an auditory technique and involves writing, dictation is so well established that one hesitates to question its effectiveness. Yet, when one looks at dictation critically, one is surprised to discover its limitations.

1. It does not test word order because the examiner reads the words in their proper order.

2. It does not test vocabulary recall because the examiner gives the words.

3. It does not test sound discrimination sharply because (a) the context often gives away the difficult sounds, (b) the examiner reads more slowly than he speaks, and (c) he frequently repeats the reading.

Dictation does test spelling, recognition of the forms of words, and some problems of inflection, but it is slow for these purposes, since they can be tested rapidly by other techniques. Dictation is not a bad technique and should not be abandoned, but there are better ways.

Usage and correctness tests   Correct usage items that give the student one choice that is correct and others that are not are acceptable as a technique. The question is, what are the correct and incorrect choices? If they merely perpetuate the bugaboo of artificial correctness that has no currency outside the classroom, they are worse than useless.

"Commonsense" techniques   Still preoccupied with the appearance and outward reasonableness of the test rather than with its linguistic content are those who think of commonsense tests of speaking, listening, reading, and writing as the total and final answer to the problems of language testing. The validity of a test cannot be judged on the superficial appearance of the task but on the linguistic content and on performance. Let us look at these commonsense techniques separately.

Speaking   In tests of speaking, where the present state of the art is generally one of failure, the attempts move blindly in the direction of having the student speak. This reflects again the tendency to think of the technique itself and its appearance of validity rather than of the linguistic problems involved. The unreliability of general impressions of speech restricts the value of these tests.

1. The personality of the student colors the impression of his ability to speak.

2. The tense situation under which the student is tested produces nontypical performances that unduly influence the over-all impression.

3. Scoring oral responses is a highly subjective affair even under well-controlled conditions. The differences are great among different examiners and for the same examiner at different times.

4. Individually administered oral tests are time-consuming for the examiner and as a result tend to be made so short that they become useless. A 15-minute test administered to 100 students takes 3 full days and 1 hour of a fourth day for an examiner working 8 hours a day without time off for coffee. By contrast, a 1-hour group test given to 100 students and scored objectively can be handled in 1½ or 2 hours.

Listening The examples on page 160 show that listening to an utterance and understanding it, though having the outward appearance of a valid test, may not be a good indicator of auditory comprehension. The fact of listening is not enough. The utterance heard and the choices of the response must be such that the right answer reveals control of the crucial elements of listening comprehension.

Reading The appraisal made of listening tests obtains also in tests of reading. It is not simply a matter of having the student read and checking his comprehension. It is a question of what he is asked to read and what items of comprehension we ask.

Written composition The writing of an essay on an assigned topic enjoys great prestige not only as a test of ability to write but as a sign of intelligence, education, and academic achievement as well. Historically, the ability to write has been the chief sign of learning. In defending the use of compositions as tests, it is usually adduced that they force the student to think, to organize what he knows, and to deal with mature topics rather than trivial detail.

Under linguistic scrutiny some limitations appear, however.

1. A single composition is usually a poor sample of the sentence patterns of the language, its vocabulary, and the problems of spelling and punctuation. The usual composition test may not elicit a single question or request. The particular vocabulary needed for one essay may be limited and specialized. The spelling and punctuation problems are similarly restricted, and the student avoids those that trouble him.

2. A single composition is a poor sample of the student's ability to organize his thoughts or to deal with mature topics. It so happens that the topics set for composition tests have to deal with matters that are familiar to the student, and differences in the amount of information the student may have on the topic will be reflected in his organization and treatment of it in his essay.

3. From a practical point of view, the scoring of compositions is a

very complex problem, and as a result, it is slow and inaccurate. The problem is decisively put in the following statements:

> If the essay examinations are somewhat unreliably written, they are even less reliably read. The basic problem is that teachers do not agree with themselves when they read papers, much less with other readers. In one study, for example, an eighth-grade composition was graded twice by 28 teachers. Fifteen who gave it passing marks the first time failed it on the second round, while 11 who failed it the first time passed it on the second. As for different readers' opinions of the same paper, they have on occasion provided grades ranging from 50 to 98 on the same paper, as read by 142 teachers. . . .
>
> To keep 150 readers grading according to a common standard is essential but well-nigh impossible. In spite of the fact that they are a highly selected group of teachers—expert readers brought together under one roof and given a day's training and practice in grading sample papers before they start on the examinations, and then supervised closely by veteran "table leaders" whose sole function is to iron out problems of consistency in grading—they still do not agree enough to permit one to view the resulting grades with confidence.[1]

THE NEW VIEW

The new view in language testing differs from present general practice in the more specific description of what is to be tested.

Situation versus language In addition to the fact that we must decide whether or not a test involving listening or speaking tests listening and speaking, we have to decide what relative importance to assign to language and to the situations in which language is used.

If we begin with what appear to be valid situations, we have a *situation approach*. To know, for example, if a student will understand university lectures in English, we choose a number of sample lectures and test the student's comprehension of them. On the other hand, in a *language approach*, we choose items that test control of the language units and patterns. The situations are chosen to fit the language problems, rather than the other way.

Although initially one may favor the situation approach, a closer

---

[1] Henry Chauncey, "The Plight of the English Teacher." *The Atlantic Monthly*, vol. 204, no. 5, p. 123, November, 1959. By permission of the author.

look should change that opinion. In the situation approach, the situations in which a language may be used and tested are potentially infinite. On the other hand, the language units and patterns through which all the meanings must be conveyed are limited by the system of the language. In the situation approach, the problem is to find a representative sample of situations which will be valid in and of themselves, and there can never be complete agreement on this. A physician cannot be satisfied that a situation involving highway engineering reveals his command of a foreign language. And it is easy to mention situations in which native speakers will not understand everything.

In a language approach, on the other hand, it is possible to test the entire sound system, all the major grammatical patterns, and a valid sample of the general vocabulary that the student may be expected to know. The choice is between testing an infinite variety of situations and testing a limited number of linguistic units and patterns. The situations, even if sampled adequately, do not insure coverage of the language system, while the language system will be adequate in all situations with which the student is familiar.

The new dimension The most important single thing that produces dramatic advances in language tests is the structural understanding of language. Some of the techniques used in these tests are also new, but what makes them valuable is not so much the newness of the technique as the linguistic problems which they test.

Structural understanding of language problems Of the thousands of different sounds in any language, only a small number of contrasting differences constitutes the system through which all the meanings of the language are transmitted. In English, for example, although the phoneme /p/ shows different pronunciations by different speakers as well as by the same speaker, as in *picture, capture, camp, supper, pray,* it remains a single contrasting unit. In other languages a /p'/ released with a puff of breath similar to that in *picture* may constitute one phoneme, while a /p/ without the puff, like that in *supper,* may constitute an entirely different phoneme, a difference equal in importance to the difference between /p/ in *pill* and /b/ in *bill* in English. Many of the regional differences in the sounds of a language are of secondary importance because they represent only subphonemic variations.

The structural view of language has shown that this distinction between elements that constitute phonemes, on one hand, and variations that do not represent different phonemes, on the other, applies not only to the consonants and vowels but to the intonation, stress, rhythm, and pauses as well. And the grammatical constructions, word formation, and lexical units also show these two levels: the structural ones, constituted by those differences that can change one unit into another, and the substructural ones, made up of the differences that are stylistic options or usage requirements within structural units.

Native speakers reduce much of the operation of the language system to automatic habits through which they react almost instantaneously to the structural contrasts and overlook substructural variations.

The native language factor Learning a foreign language can be defined for testing purposes not only as learning to understand and be understood, but more specifically as learning to use the structural units and patterns of the foreign language in valid situations. Those units which are sufficiently similar to the native language are known by the student from the beginning. The critical area of learning is limited to those units which cannot be transferred from the native language because they are nonexistent in it or are different enough to cause interference. When the student masters these difficult units in actual use, he will have "learned" the foreign language.

Testing the problems as testing the language The new tests, then, attempt to test mastery of the units and patterns that are different from those of the native language and constitute the learning problems. In the preparation of the new tests, therefore, the first consideration is not how to test, but what to test. We begin by considering the native and the foreign language systems to obtain a list of the learning problems which will be tested.

The comparison produces lists of problems of pronunciation, grammatical structure, vocabulary, and cultural meanings related to language. We then prepare tests that measure degree of mastery of these problems. Following are some samples of the newer techniques used to test problems.

Sample Techniques to Test Problems If we know the specific consonant and vowel phonemes that will be difficult to learn, and if we know the learning problems in intonation, stress, rhythm, and juncture, we can test these problems in a variety of ways. We can test the students on hearing the difference through understanding of spoken sentences or by stating "same" or "different" without having to go through their meaning.

Pronunciation through auditory comprehension This example, given earlier, illustrates the technique that goes through meaning: the student hears the sentence, "The man is watching the dog," and has to choose between a picture of a man watching a dog and one of a man washing a dog. The student has to understand the words and hear the phonemic difference between /č/ and /š/. Many variations of this technique are possible, but we must proceed to another type.

Auditory perception An example of the same-versus-different technique to test auditory perception is as follows: The examiner reads aloud the three sentences,

(1) The man is watching the dog.
(2) The man is washing the dog.
(3) The man is watching the dog.

The student has to give the number of the sentences that are the same. The first and third sentences are the same, so he says, or marks, (1) and (3).

To a native speaker of English this type of item seems overly simple. To speakers of a language that does not have a phonemic contrast between /č/ and /š/, it is a difficult test. An easier variation gives the key word only: *watching, washing, watching.* Even easier is a minimal pair, *watching, washing* instead of the three items. In this case, the student merely says "same" or "different."

Production technique When we know what the problem is, we can test it accurately. We elicit an utterance that contains the problem sound and listen only for that one sound. Since the ear of a native speaker is sharply aware of phonemic contrasts such as that between /š/ and /č/, the examiner has little trouble scoring the responses. Non-native teachers who have mastered the language can do the same. Pictures are desirable as stimuli because they give no clue to the sounds tested. When a picture does not elicit the desired utterance, use reading or even translation, the object being not to pass on the adequacy of the translation or the style of the reading but on the pronunciation of an affricate /č/ or a fricative /š/.

Paper-and-pencil techniques Because it is not always possible to have a qualified examiner read the test and listen to the student's responses, there are paper-and-pencil techniques which are reasonably valid and simple to administer. The techniques consist in comparing sounds in words in which the letters that represent them have been omitted. For example, the student is given three sentences:

(1) Everything was underst - - d.
(2) The cook would prepare the f - - d.
(3) We start a fire with dry w - - d.

The student is asked which of the sounds represented by the missing letters are the same. He indicates his response by giving the number of the sentences. In the example, the response would be (1) and (3) since the last vowel of *understood* and that of *wood* are the same. The vowel of *food* is a different phoneme even though it is represented by the same letters.

A rhyming technique asks the student if two words rhyme, or which of three choices rhymes with a model. Still another variation asks which of several choices is most like a sound omitted in the lead word. The choices are words with underlined letters. Some of these techniques and many others like them can be used informally in a class; others are more reliable and have wider application.

The position of word and sentence stress can be tested by a paper-and-pencil technique also. Numbers are placed above the syllables which are to be compared. The numbers serve to refer conveniently to the syllables on a separate answer sheet. The student decides on the basis of his pronunciation which syllable receives the most prominent stress and checks or circles the number representing the syllable on the answer sheet.

EXAMPLE:

$$\overset{1}{\text{I}}\ \text{saw}\ \overset{2}{\text{his}}\ \overset{3}{\text{sister}},\ but\ \overset{4}{I}\ didn't\ \overset{5}{see}\ him.$$

In this context the peak of prominence among the numbered syllables is on *him*. The student circles the 5 on the answer sheet.

EXAMPLE:

$$\overset{1}{\text{He}}\ \text{understood}\ \overset{2}{\text{the}}\ \overset{3}{\text{ideas}},\ but\ \overset{4}{he}\ \overset{5}{forgot}\ them.$$

In this case, the peak of prominence is on the second syllable of the word *forgot*. The student must decide which word and within that word which syllable receives the peak of stress. He circles the 4 on the answer sheet to indicate that syllable 4 receives the primary stress.

Correlations between scores obtained through these paper-and-pencil techniques and the scores given by the examiner when the student reads the test aloud are high enough to make the techniques useful under proper conditions. Other variations have been developed and still others will surely be invented by teachers who know what they are trying to test.

Grammatical structure The new recognition techniques for grammatical structure test understanding of the grammatical signals in utterances. This is quite different from asking the student which sentence is correct or what rule has been broken. The single-word modifier precedes the head in English: *sky blue* is a color, and *blue sky* is a sky. If in the native language the direction of modification is opposite that of English, as it is in Spanish and other languages, the test would consist in checking to see if the student understands *blue sky* to mean sky or if he is confused by the word order signal and takes it to mean a color. Such checking can be made through multiple-choice items.

The choices can be given in writing, e.g., "(1) a color, (2) the heavens." They can be given in pictures or in the native language.

A *watch pocket* is a pocket; a *pocket watch* is a watch. In a test item the examiner might say, "Which is the watch pocket?" The student is made to choose between the phrases, "(1) a pocket," and "(2) a watch," or between pictures of a watch and a pocket.

Vocabulary and cultural meaning In testing vocabulary we force a choice between minimally different items in context. For production, items involving partial recall of a limited vocabulary are useful. Items checking comprehension of a wider range of units are needed to test vocabulary in reading or listening. Here is an example of a partial production item.

To cook meat by dry heat is to _____ it.
(1) f - -.   (2) b - - l.   (3) r - - - t.   (4) b - - e.

The best choice is *roast,* represented by "(3) r - - - t." The other choices, *fry, boil,* and *bake,* are not quite satisfactory. The student merely checks (3) on the answer sheet to indicate his response.

A recognition item searching an extended meaning of a common word is the following:

He *read* the expression on their faces carefully.
(1) spoke words
(2) understood spoken words
(3) studied
(4) understood printed words

The four skills Testing the four skills consists of controlled samples of those skills containing the specific learning problems that the students are likely to have. Under auditory comprehension we include pronunciation, grammar, lexical items, and cultural meanings if relevant. All of these are tested in utterances under essentially normal conditions. In speaking, the same elements are involved, and the test elicits utterances from the students. Techniques which correlate highly with these skills but are less elaborate can be used effectively under special conditions.

In writing, the primary elements are grammatical structure and lexical content, with spelling and punctuation as additional criteria. In testing spelling, a better technique than dictation is one in which a sentence identifies an incomplete word which the student is asked to complete from memory or from several given choices. The letters omitted are those that constitute the spelling problems, thus giving more density of test elements. In dictation, the student and the teacher waste time with words that do not constitute problems and with letters that do not constitute problems in the words that are problems.

EXAMPLE:
Write the missing letters.

He teaches at the university; he is a pro ___ e ___ or.

He is riding his new b ___ c ___ cle.

Please accept my sincere a ___ ology.

EXAMPLE:

Write the number of the best choice.

The room has good a___ oustics for music.

(1) q   (2) k   (3) c   (4) cc

Putting a Test to the Test Ultimately, the proof of a test is in its performance.   There are many commonsense questions one can ask of a test before accepting it.   Can it be given under the circumstances in which it must be given?   Is it too long?   Is it too easy?   These can usually be answered by the user through inspection of the test or its description.   Two aspects require more technical study: reliability and validity.

Reliability No matter how convincing a test may appear, if the scores obtained vary greatly without apparent reason, the test is unreliable and cannot be used.   A test is reliable if the scores obtained with it are steady.   The degree of reliability of a test is usually given as a correlation.   Perfect reliability would be indicated with a 1.00.   This degree of reliability is not expected on normal tests.   Complete lack of reliability would appear as .00.

There is no single point between .00 and 1.00 where we can say that a test is reliable.   Satisfactory reliability depends on the use to be made of the scores, the skill or element being tested, the length of the test, etc.   A reliability coefficient of .70 might be satisfactory for an interview test of speaking ability, while a full-length paper-and-pencil test of vocabulary might be expected to show a reliability coefficient of .98 or .99.

Validity No matter how steady the scores on a test of arithmetic may be, the test is not valid as a measure of proficiency in Spanish or French.   Validity is the degree to which a test measures what it claims to measure.   A test of translation may be valid as a test of translation but not valid as a test of auditory comprehension, and vice versa.   Validity can be measured by content or by correlation with a criterion that we know is valid.   Validity is often expressed as a coefficient of correlation between the test and the valid criterion.

Norms Raw scores on a test have limited meaning until we can compare them with other raw scores.   The collected scores of groups of students whose performance is known are called norms.   There are various types of norms, each of which offers advantages and disadvantages according to the uses to be made of them. Percentile norms classify a raw score into one of a hundred numerically equal groups of students from high to low.

Grade norms are the average scores of students at each grade level. Progress norms give average increase in scores by semesters, years, or credits. Prognostic norms give expected performance of subjects who place at various levels on the scale of the test.

Part **3**

Technological
Aids

Chapter 17

The Language Laboratory

Technological aids in language teaching are a major force today, and among these aids, the language laboratory occupies the most prominent place. Two conflicting attitudes toward the role of the language laboratory are prevalent: one regards the lab as the center of language teaching, with the teacher assisting the lab operation and adjusting to it; the other regards the lab as a teaching aid, with the class as the center.

Few would admit even to themselves that they look upon the lab operation as the central part of language teaching. Everyone is quick to state that the lab is not intended to replace the teacher but to take away the drudgery of drill so that the teacher may devote his time to more intellectual or literary activities. Yet the materials and plans produced may in fact be directed toward the lab as the center of teaching. Two criteria seem to characterize the lab-as-the-center attitude: (1) The recorded materials are complete lessons, which attempt to do all the teaching. (2) The accompanying explanations and the advertisements state that the lessons do not require a trained teacher.

This point of view that the lab is the center of teaching is rejected here for the following reasons: (1) It is more difficult and expensive to produce good materials that attempt to do everything than to produce materials that supplement the work of the teacher. (2) Complete materials age rapidly and soon become dated. (3) Such complete materials are inflexible and awkward without a teacher to control them and adapt them to the students.

The statement that such a lab will take the drudgery out of language teaching is problematical at best. Drudgery can never be completely taken out of teaching, because teaching will always involve working with those who know less than the teacher. A teacher who feels so strongly that drill is a boring chore should seriously consider whether he should remain in the profession. One of the chief satisfactions of teaching is observing how the students learn what to them is new material, however old and familiar it may be to the teacher. By relegating all learning and drill to the language laboratory, the teacher can become merely a baby-sitter and examiner.

In the lab-as-an-aid point of view (1) the teacher is clearly thought of as the central figure teaching the student. (2) The lab is one more aid, not the central component of teaching. (3) The lab materials are designed to supplement class work selectively. (4) The materials are not complete lessons.

With the explosion in demand for more education for more people, there is a critical shortage of good teachers everywhere. It is sometimes thought that by providing language labs anybody will be able to teach a language and the teacher shortage will be solved. The fact is that language labs require better-prepared teachers who can put the new equipment and techniques to good use as well as conduct a class. Labs do not solve the teacher shortage. When used properly, they can increase greatly the effectiveness of good teachers, whether or not they are native speakers of the target language.

Definition of a Language Lab There are laboratories designed for research on the analysis and description of languages and labs designed for the teaching of languages. The language-research or speech-research laboratory may contain such equipment as the sound spectrograph and the oscillograph. The language-teaching laboratory usually contains playback and recording equipment for students to practice the languages they are studying. This chapter is concerned with language-teaching laboratories.

There is great variety in equipment and facilities in language laboratories. Some may have a single playing machine with earphones for the students, while others have semiprivate booths with a tape recorder for each student. Some have a soundproof recording studio, and others are merely listening rooms.

The language lab is a special room for practice with sound equipment. The tape recorder used by the teacher in connection with the lesson in class does not constitute a lab, although every teacher should have ready access to a tape recorder for teaching. What constitutes a language lab is a special room with necessary equipment set aside for practice by the students. A separate room with a single tape or disc playback apparatus where the students may practice is the most rudimentary lab, but it is a lab. A classroom can become a lab after class hours, or the lab can be used as a classroom by the teacher, but the distinctive characteristic is the separate room where students may practice the language.

The Scope of the Lab The language lab can provide good models of the speech of the target language for imitation and manipulation by the student. This increases the power of the teacher who is not a native speaker of the second language and who has not achieved complete native pronunciation. It also increases the power of the teacher who is a native speaker by permitting the students to hear a variety of speakers of the language.

The lab permits audio-lingual practice outside of class. When the lab allows individual selection of exercises, it provides for individual differences so that each student can repeat an exercise as many times as necessary. Labs with recording equipment for the students permit recording the students for more objective and accurate criticism and correction by the teacher. Labs that have the proper equipment can be used for listening tests given individually or in groups and for group speaking tests, which the teacher can correct individually later.

How to Use the Lab We have stated that lab materials which attempt to teach complete lessons are expensive to produce, become dated quickly, and will not succeed ultimately without direction by a teacher, who cannot be relegated to the role of baby-sitter. For these reasons, the materials for the language lab should be partial materials rather than complete lessons. They should be, for example, exercises for the difficult problems that will require extra work or a variety of voices on longer passages that would take too much time in class, etc.

The myth of a lab method The idea that electronic recorders in the lab constitute a revolutionary method of teaching a second language is a myth. In the lab, no matter how expensive the equipment, there can be good materials, bad materials, and impossible materials. A forty-five-minute commentary on the subjunctive in Spanish without a single example and therefore without practice by the students is bad teaching whether in a classroom or in a modern lab.

Lab materials have to be prepared with as much if not more care than any other materials for teaching: they must be clear, graded, purposeful, and based on linguistic facts and psychological laws of learning. Merely recording something for use in the lab does not make it a good exercise. It must be a good exercise to begin with.

Adapting classroom drills to lab use The question, What does one do in the lab? can be easily answered. Almost any practice one does in the classroom can be adapted to lab use for extra practice. Lab exercises can be those described above in the chapters on pronunciation, grammatical patterns, pattern practice, vocabulary, and writing and reading, and they can be directed toward listening, speaking, reading, and writing. The adaptation is not difficult, and it will be illustrated below. Lab exercises can involve the following as well as other activities: listening, listening-repeating, mimicry-memorization, listening and identifying by number, listening and comprehending, pattern substitution, addition, synthesis, oral composition, transformation, dictation, reading paced by a recording, etc.

Any recorded materials that the student can listen to in the lab and use for some learning experience are lab materials. More strictly speaking, however, lab materials are practice exercises in which the student may (1) listen and speak to show improvement in the classroom later, (2) listen and speak with self-correction from the reinforcing response that follows his own attempt on the tape, or (3) listen and write either in dictation or in a response of some kind, such as identification of a number or a word.

How to Prepare Lab Materials There are commercially available tapes and records to accompany language textbooks or to supplement the language course. They usually have adequate instructions for the teacher and need no further elaboration here. Publishers often give the user the choice between purchasing a set of the tapes or records or borrowing the master tapes for the purpose of making one's own copies. It is preferable to purchase the commercially made copies unless one has superior copying equipment and technical assistants. Making one's own copies will take considerable time, and they may not be of the best technical quality. Many schools do not have the money to buy expensive sets of materials, however, and the teacher will then have to make the copies for his students.

In addition to the regular tapes, the teacher will need to prepare supplementary tapes to be used as a regular part of the course, an extra assignment for slow students, a bonus for the better students, etc. The language teacher should, therefore, be able to prepare such tapes. The following discussion gives step-by-step suggestions and examples. They are intended to be suggestive rather than restrictive. As his experience develops, the teacher will be able to introduce variations and original ideas to suit a particular class or problem and to explore more effective materials.

The discussion is divided into the following steps: (1) Identify the problem that needs lab practice. (2) Choose the type of drill best suited for the purpose. (3) Prepare the tapescript. (4) Make the recording. (5) Check it. (6) Evaluate the exercise in actual use with the class.

Identifying the problem that needs lab practice Before beginning preparation of a drill, one must know what the drill is to accomplish, that is, the learning that is to result from it. This could be, among other things, the memorization of a dialogue, the perception or production of a sound or contrast, mastery of a grammatical pattern, vocabulary use, cultural content, reading, or writing. And within any of these, it will be a specific dialogue, a specific sound or contrast, a specific grammatical pattern, etc.

Choosing the type of drill The type of drill to be chosen depends in part on the problem to be mastered. Drills are of three general types with regard to the basic recording format: The most complete—one developed for language laboratories with a theory of learning in mind— is the *anticipation mode*. In this mode, the student is given a model and cues and is asked to respond before the correct answer is heard on the tape. This elicits active responses and enhances learning.

A less elaborate mode consists of a model with pauses to allow the student to respond but without any confirming or reinforcing clue on the tape itself. The third mode is simply a straight recording on tape for the student to hear, without pauses or reinforcing comments.

The following discussion will illustrate the anticipation mode most completely because it is the most effective and the most complex to prepare. The other two modes will be illustrated briefly later.

Preparing the tapescript You cannot improvise a good lab drill that will be used over and over again by the students. It is standard practice to prepare a tapescript. The amount of detail to be included depends on the intended use of the tape and the experience of the teacher in preparing tapes. The tapescript will have five components: information for classification and reference by the lab staff, instructions to the student preferably in the target language, notes to the one making the recording, examples, and the body of the drill. In addition there should be a standard phrase to signal the beginning and closing of each drill or tape, e.g., "Beginning of tape," and "End of tape." These should appear on the script the first time and can be omitted from it in successive drills with the understanding that they will be recorded on the tape.

Following is a sample tapescript for a mimicry-memorization drill to learn the French dialogue of Chapter 6. The use of a second voice (that of Jean Levet in this case) to give the responses in the examples makes it easier for the class to understand what their responses will be in the body of the exercise. When a good second voice is not available, the teacher records both the cues and the responses in the examples.

INFORMATION FOR CLASSIFICATION AND REFERENCE

COURSE ___Introductory French_____ DATE _____

SUBJECT ___Dialogue No. 4_____

TEXT REFERENCE ___Experimental French Materials, Unit 4_____

PREPARED BY ___John Doe_____

VOICES ___Teacher: John Doe. Student: Jean Levet_____

RECORDING SCRIPT

	TEACHER: Beginning of tape. [breaking silence]
	[very brief pause]
Identification	French Dialogue No. 4
	[very brief pause]
Instructions	Apprenez le dialogue.
	Écoutez.

Examples

TEACHER: C'est vous Jean Levet?
JEAN: Oui, c'est moi.
TEACHER: Oui, c'est moi.   [reinforcement]
JEAN: Oui, c'est moi.

TEACHER: Vous êtes étudiant?
JEAN: Oui, je le suis.
TEACHER: Oui, je le suis.   [reinforcement]
JEAN: Oui, je le suis.

TEACHER: Vous avez des frères?
JEAN: Oui, j'en ai.
TEACHER: Oui, j'en ai.   [reinforcement]
JEAN: Oui, j'en ai.

Body of drill   TEACHER: Répondez.

TEACHER: C'est vous Jean Levet?
[Pause—STUDENT: *Oui, c'est moi.*]
TEACHER: Oui, c'est moi.   [reinforcement]
[Pause—STUDENT: *Oui, c'est moi.*]

TEACHER:	Vous êtes étudiant?	
[Pause—STUDENT:	*Oui, je le suis.*]	
TEACHER:	Oui, je le suis.	[reinforcement]
[Pause—STUDENT:	*Oui, je le suis.*]	
TEACHER:	Vous avez des frères?	
[Pause—STUDENT:	*Oui, j'en ai.*]	
TEACHER:	Oui, j'en ai.	[reinforcement]
[Pause—STUDENT:	*Oui, j'en ai.*]	

At this stage we either reverse the parts and have the student ask the questions, or we instruct him to anticipate the questions as well as the answers, thus coming closer to our intended goal of complete memorization of the dialogue.

The tapescript for the pattern drills on the agreement and position of adjectives and nouns in Spanish (Chapter 10) might be as follows. Notice that the student does not learn the linguistic facts in the laboratory; he practices what he has learned in class.

RECORDING SCRIPT

Instructions   TEACHER: Práctica de adjetivos con substantivos. Observe los ejemplos femeninos.

Examples

Me gusta la casa blanca.
Torre.   [substitution]
SECOND VOICE: Me gusta la torre blanca.
TEACHER: Me gusta la torre blanca.   [reinforcement]

SECOND VOICE: Me gusta la torre blanca.
TEACHER: Verde.   [substitution]
SECOND VOICE: Me gusta la torre verde.
TEACHER: Me gusta la torre verde.   [reinforcement]

SECOND VOICE: Me gusta la torre verde.
TEACHER: Silla.   [substitution]
SECOND VOICE: Me gusta la silla verde.
TEACHER: Me gusta la silla verde.
SECOND VOICE: Me gusta la silla verde.   [reinforcement]

Body of drill   TEACHER: Responda: Nueva.
[Pause for student to respond]
Me gusta la silla nueva.   [reinforcement]

[Pause]

Casa.
[Pause]
Me gusta la casa nueva.
[Pause]

Blanca.
[Pause]
Me gusta la casa blanca.
[Pause]

Mesa.
[Pause]
Me gusta la mesa blanca.
[Pause]

Nueva.
[Pause]
Me gusta la mesa nueva.
[Pause]

Ejemplos masculinos:
El libro.
[Pause]
Me gusta el libro nuevo.   [reinforce-
[Pause]   ment]

Vestido.
[Pause]
Me gusta el vestido nuevo.
[Pause]

Blanco.
[Pause]
Me gusta el vestido blanco.
[Pause]

El papel.
[Pause]
Me gusta el papel blanco.
[Pause]

Verde.
[Pause]
Me gusta el papel verde.
[Pause]

Ejemplos masculinos y femeninos:
La casa.
[Pause]

Me gusta la casa verde.   [reinforce-
[Pause]   ment]

Nueva.
[Pause]
Me gusta la casa nueva.
[Pause]

El vestido.
[Pause]
Me gusta el vestido nuevo.
[Pause]

Blanco.
[Pause]
Me gusta el vestido blanco.
[Pause]

La torre.
[Pause]
Me gusta la torre blanca.
[Pause]

Something that comes closer to a conversational exercise is the following in which the model makes a statement and prompts the student to ask a question with regard to the same matter but about a different person.

RECORDING SCRIPT

Instructions   TEACHER: Controlled conversation. Examples.
Listen.

Examples   John went to class today. Peter.
SECOND VOICE: Did Peter go to class today?
TEACHER: Yes, he did.

TEACHER: John knew the lesson well. The students.
SECOND VOICE: Did the students know the lesson well?
TEACHER: Yes, they did.

TEACHER: John was tired after class. Albert.
SECOND VOICE: Was Albert tired after class?
TEACHER: Yes, he was.

Body of drill   TEACHER: Continue the exercise.

John went home. Peter.
[Pause for student to respond]
Did Peter go home?   [reinforcement]
Yes, he did.

John ate lunch at home.   Mary.
[Pause]
Did Mary eat lunch at home?   [rein-
                                forcement]
Yes, she did.

John went to the library after lunch.
Peter.
[Pause]
Did Peter go to the library after lunch?
                                [reinforcement]
Yes, he did.

There is no single ideal number of items for all drills. The number should be determined in part at least by the difficulty of the problem.

The discrimination of difficult sound differences can be practiced in the laboratory very effectively. Compare the following variation of the anticipation drill.

RECORDING SCRIPT

Instructions   TEACHER: Say, "Same," if the two sentences are the same.
Say, "Different," if they are different.
Listen. Participate when ready.

Examples   I can't leave alone.
I can't leave alon .

SECOND VOICE: Same.
TEACHER: Same.   [reinforcement]
I can't leave alone.
I can't leave alone.

Don't fill the plate.
Don't feel the plate.
SECOND VOICE: Different.
TEACHER: Different.   [reinforcement]
Don't fill the plate.
Don't feel the plate.

Body of drill   TEACHER: The sheep moved.
The ship moved.

[Pause for student to respond]
Different.   [reinforcement]
The sheep moved.
The ship moved.

Hit the water.
Hit the water.
[Pause]
Same.   [reinforcement]
Hit the water.
Hit the water.

Any narrative or conversation in the present tense can be segmented into phrases of five to nine syllables and recorded with pauses to permit the student to transform each of the phrases into the past. Following each student response, the correct response is given on the tape so that the student may confirm or correct his response immediately.

Less complicated than the anticipation mode is the model-with-pauses mode, which allows time for the student to produce some active response but does not provide an immediate check on the correctness of it. This results in a faster moving drill and provides extensive practice which can be checked occasionally by the teacher when he monitors the students in the lab. Substitution, transformation, conversation, and other exercises can be presented in this mode with considerable benefit to the student who practices and makes the effort to learn.

It is possible to take an uninterrupted recording of a play, a story, or a conference and insert into it pauses at frequent intervals to permit the students to imitate each phrase immediately after it is uttered through the recording. For this purpose, two tape recorders are connected together so that the output of the first becomes the input of the second. Pauses are marked in the transcription of the material at permissible breaks every five to nine syllables. The two tape recorders are then set in motion so that the program in the first recorder is transmitted to the tape of the second. At each pause mark, the first recorder is stopped instantaneously for a length of time that permits the repetition of the preceding phrase.

Even less complicated than the model with pauses is the continuous recording mode. Such recordings are valuable for a variety of uses in the lab. In the first place, it is highly desirable to hear extensive amounts of authentic speech of the target language both for nonselective listening and for selective listening. The over-all rhythm and intonation, the transitions, and many of the sound segments will become familiar through successive approximations that result from hearing great amounts of recorded material in the target language. But in addition, such recordings can be used to practice choral reading with the recording, and they can be used as pacers in silent reading for slow readers.

Do's and don'ts in recording Many more teacher-made tapes fail because of unnecessary flaws than because of poor equipment. When the time comes to record the drills, you may wish you had access to high fidelity equipment. If you do, fine. If you do not, make sure that your equipment is in good repair and clean, and see to it that the human factor does not introduce unnecessary flaws.

Here are things that will enhance the recordings. Become thoroughly familiar with the tapescript so that you do not have to read every word but can speak the material with ease. Relax, be natural, not tense. Tenseness will show in your voice, and it will become tiresome to the students. Be alive; be interested in what you are saying.

Make the length of the recording no more than half that of the lab period to permit the students to play it through at least twice. Bring in other voices besides your own. Although a variety of voices is not linguistically essential, it helps to maintain interest, and interest increases learning. Make all explanations as brief as possible and even shorter. Anything beyond a single explanatory sentence without intervening examples tends to be lost.

And here are some things to be avoided. The timing of the pauses for student responses must not be so long that the student becomes impatient waiting for the next item nor must the pauses be so short that he cannot finish his response before the next item begins. A rule of thumb is to repeat silently the response twice before going on to the next item. This is based on the fact that we know the response better than the student and that saying it silently goes faster than speaking aloud.

Do not change the volume of your utterances, and do not change the distance to the microphone. Do not speak so low that the recorder has to be turned to its highest volume. It will then pick up other disturbing sounds as well. Do not rattle papers in front of the microphone, or you will hear them amplified in the recording. If the script can be spread on the table, do so, and you will not have to turn pages or even touch them. Cellophane wrappers will dampen the noise from paper handling. When you are through with a page, set it gently aside; do not put it under the pile of other sheets.

Do not place the microphone directly in front of your mouth, or you will blow up the sound of your breathing and the hissing of the sibilants. Set the microphone to the side of your mouth, and keep it at an even distance. Do not worry if you have to clear your throat; just do not do it directly into the microphone. With all these cautions crowding for attention, it is doubtful that your first attempts to record will be very relaxed and natural. With a little practice, you will avoid these possible pitfalls and will be able to concentrate on the positive qualities of a good recording.

Checking the recording It is always necessary to play back the recording. If you forgot to turn on the recording switch and have produced a blank tape, you might as well be the first one to know. In addition, you will be able to check the length of your pauses and any extraneous noises that may have crept in.

Evaluating the drill Observe the students as they use the tape on their own. This will show if the drill is too slow or too fast, too easy or too difficult, or if the signal quality is within the range of tolerance of the class. You will also notice if the length of the drill is satisfactory for the time that the student has in the lab.

In addition to being acceptable to the students, the tape should be evaluated for effectiveness in teaching what it is supposed to teach. This evaluation must remain on an informal basis of observation of the performance of the students in class. Rigidly controlled experiments cannot be conducted for every tape we must prepare and use in the language laboratory.

Student Activity in the Lab Depending on the equipment and the drills in the lab, the student may merely listen or listen and do something other than speak; he may listen and speak, and he may listen and/or record. There is a good deal of listening in any lab drill, even when speaking and recording are also involved. The amount of recording that the student normally does is only a fraction of his total lab work.

For the listening activity in the lab, so-called audio-passive equipment will suffice. With such equipment, the student can listen, or he can listen and respond in written form as in taking an auditory comprehension test or taking dictation. The audio-passive lab is not fully satisfactory when the student is expected to respond orally to the drill. The earphones clamped down on his ears do not allow him to hear his responses at all well. Since he is already handicapped in hearing the sounds of the foreign language because of the interference of his native language habits, this further interference from the clamped earphones is all but fatal. When the students are expected to respond orally to the drills in order to achieve some sort of proficiency in speaking, a so-called audio-active lab is highly desirable. In such a lab, each student position is equipped with a microphone and a preamplifier (an electronic device to enlarge the power of the signals coming from the microphone). The student's responses are picked up by the microphone and transmitted to his own ears through the earphones. This gives him a better check on his responses than if he were speaking freely in a room.

The audio-active lab also makes it easier to wire the system to enable the teacher to monitor the student's responses from a console and to speak to the student through the earphones, offering corrections of his mistakes. The audio-active lab may also be set up so that the teacher can record samples of the student's responses as they come from his booth.

With an audio-active lab, the student can perform almost any practice activity he needs, except that he normally cannot control the lesson that is being played to him from a central source. To practice the drills at his own speed, going back over those parts that are difficult and skipping lightly over those that are easy, the student needs a tape recorder in his own booth or position. This will also permit him to record his responses as needed. In this type of lab, the dual-channel tape recorder gives him maximum flexibility. These machines play back on two channels simultaneously and record at least in one. Thus the master is, let us say, on channel A; the student hears it, and he responds, recording his response on channel B. He can then play back both the master and his response and more objectively compare his performance with the master. He can erase his response on channel B without erasing the master on A, and he can then record a second attempt.

It has been argued that the student should not listen to his own mistakes but should listen only to the master recording. This is hardly relevant, since the student listens to his mistakes in the audio-active laboratory anyway. It is true, however, that there is no point in recording the student's responses when he feels he is still struggling to improve them and knows what he is doing wrong. When the student has progressed as far as he is able in discernment and thinks he is right, the full value of the dual-channel recording equipment is reached. At that point, he should record his responses and compare them objectively with the master. He will detect problems he is not able to detect otherwise. And when the teacher points out his mistakes to him, he can concentrate on observing them on the tape without having to devote his attention to the complex operation of speaking the foreign language.

Operation and Administration A language lab requires three types of work: (1) language teaching and direction; (2) electronic design, supply, repair, and maintenance; and (3) routine handling of tapes and traffic.

A language teacher must select or prepare the materials for use in the lab. He should monitor the work of the students and should decide what operations the lab must be designed to perform, even if he cannot express in electronic terms what this means by way of equipment.

A technician with knowledge of electronics and some experience in language lab equipment will be needed for planning, supply, and maintenance. The language teacher should become informed on these matters in order to know what he needs, but more knowledge is necessary to decide on installation and equipment and to maintain the tape recorders in good repair, help in making tapes, etc.

There is also considerable routine work connected with running a language lab. Tapes must be obtained, distributed, collected. Lesson material must be put on the console spools for listening from the booths. For these activities, part-time work by interested students might do.

Planning a Lab The components of a language lab usually include earphones, microphones, preamplifiers, tape recorders, booths, central console, monitoring system, control switches, tape duplication facilities, recording studio, tape library and supply, and sound conditioning. Besides such general considerations as the need for simplicity and ruggedness and adequate lighting, temperature, and ventilation, special considerations, such as frequency response and range of the equipment, have to be looked into carefully.

A commonly held error maintains that audio equipment for speech requires much less fidelity than for music. This myth has some basis in fact as do all myths. Dictating machines and the telephone require less frequency range than equipment intended to play fine music. But dictating machines and the telephone are designed for use with the first language, where the listener needs only part of the signal to understand the whole pattern. In the early stages of learning a second language, on the other hand, the student needs the whole signal, since he cannot fill in the missing parts as he normally does in the native language. As the student advances in his control of the second language, the need for high fidelity of reproduction decreases.

The *minimum* acceptable frequency response range for language laboratories is 250 to 8,500 cps (cycles per second) ± 2db (decibels).[1] The vowels are reproduced accurately within a frequency range of 250 to 3,500 cps, but the voiceless sibilants /s š č f θ/ are reproduced at much higher ranges.

Balance in the equipment is important. If the tape recorder reproduces 250 to 12,000 cps but the headphones handle only 250 to 3,000, the students will hear only 250 to 3,000, and the fine quality of the

---

[1] More specifically the range is 250 to 6,000 cps ±2 db with no peaks or valleys greater than 1 db, and with permissible variation up to ±5 db in the range 6,000 to 8,500. These data were supplied by Alfred S. Hayes. For additional information see his *Technical Guide for the Selection, Use, and Maintenance of Language Laboratory Facilities.* Prepared under a contract between the U.S. Office of Education and the Electronics Industries Association. Washington: U.S. Office of Education, 1963.

recording is lost. Similarly, if the microphone picks up everything up to 15,000 cps, but the recording equipment handles only 250 to 3,500 cps, the fine microphone is superfluous.

The components of the lab will vary according to what it is expected to do. A major difference in labs involves having or not having tape recorders in each booth. When the lesson is piped in from a central console, we have a broadcast type of lab. When the student has his own lesson in the booth, we have a library type of installation.

In the broadcast type of lab the standard installation has headphones, a microphone, and a preamplifier in each booth. If more than one program can be sent out from the console, there is also a selector knob in the booth for the student to switch to the desired program. A volume control is sometimes standard equipment. The student can regulate the volume of the program and the volume of his responses back to his headphones.

To eliminate the microphone and preamplifier from a lab reduces the value of the lab unduly. When the student has the headphones on, he cuts out his own voice and has very little chance to notice his own mistakes. If he wears a one-ear headphone, the responses of his classmates interfere with listening to his own responses.

In the library type of lab there is usually a tape recorder in each booth, and the student has his own program source in the form of a prerecorded tape. This offers the great advantage of permitting him to repeat any part of the exercise that troubles him as many times as needed. The library type of lab usually has facilities for broadcasting from a central console also.

The equipment in each booth is then a set of headphones, a microphone, and a tape recorder, preferably a dual-channel one, with one recording head for the student band and two playback heads, one for the program band and the other for the student band. The student can control volume through the tape recorder.

Often the lab will have a majority of booths with broadcast-type equipment and a small number of booths with library-type equipment, namely tape recorders. Economy of installation would be the only justification for this arrangement since a library-type of lab can be used for broadcast purposes if needed and still be available for full operation in a library mode.

Through proper wiring and design the lab can allow the teacher to listen in on any booth and speak to any booth or to any combination of booths. The monitoring system can be provided with an outlet for a tape recorder, and the teacher can record any booth. This design and wiring should be considered when the lab is built, because the same wiring installed later will be more expensive.

As the center of the monitoring system, the standard lab has a central console, with one or more program sources, as well as recording facilities in some cases. The central console is sometimes provided with a switch to start all the tape recorders in all the booths or to turn them off simultaneously. A master on-off switch for all power to the lab is usually available either at the console or near the exit from the room. The console usually overlooks the lab to facilitate visual control of it.

The usual semiprivate lab booth is table high for reading and writing while listening. Sound isolation is achieved by sound-treated head-high side partitions and by a similar partition facing the student and separating him from those in front. The back of the booth is usually left open. Transparent material is sometimes used in front of the student to permit visual communication with the teacher in front. Similar visual contact can be achieved by a nose-high front partition and a platform-high console.

For the preparation of master tapes, there is need of a completely closed sound-treated recording studio connected visually by a double-glassed window with the control room where the technician sets the recorder and controls the equipment.

The control room can be at the same time the repair shop for the technician. No matter how good the equipment may be, a steady amount of maintenance and repair work will be necessary to keep the laboratory in good working order.

The master tapes and sometimes the student tapes must be kept in a convenient location. A separate small room should be set up for this. The master tapes should be classified according to some practical system and a list or card file kept for easy reference.

How Many Booths? The first approximation to the number of booths needed for a lab is obtained by dividing the number of students to be served by the number of lab periods per day or week. If the number of students is 480 and the number of periods the lab will be open is 8, the number of booths would be 480 ÷ 8 = 60. To make the formula meaningful we have to know how long the lab periods are and whether they will be each day or each week. Eight 50-minute periods a day would keep the lab open 8 hours allowing 10 minutes between periods for students to leave and others to enter. Each student would have 50 minutes of lab work a day, 5 days a week.

If a 60-booth lab is too large for the space available or too expensive, the number of booths can be reduced by increasing the number of lab periods. This can be done by reducing the length of each period or by increasing the cycle from one day to two days, three days, or a week. Reducing the length of the lab period to 25 minutes instead of 50 would double the lab periods per day. With 16 lab periods, the number of booths needed to give each student a 25-minute lab period a day would be $480 \div 16 = 30$.

If we wish to keep the length of each period at 50 minutes but reduce the number of periods per student to one period a week, the number of periods per week would be $8 \times 5 = 40$. The number of booths needed for one period per student per week is $480 \div 40 = 12$.

These figures do not indicate any standard. The length of the lab period may have to be determined by the length of the class periods. It is sometimes stated that a 30-minute lab period a day is ideal for a nonintensive language course.

Merely counting students and lab periods does not solve the problem of scheduling whole classes in the lab. For this purpose the lab should be large enough to accommodate the largest standard class, allowing it to meet together with the teacher in the lab as needed. If the largest standard class is 30, then the lab should have at least 30 booths, even if the students could be accommodated individually with fewer.

The number of different classes (sections) in the school is also to be considered. If, for example, there are 48 different sections and each section is to meet in the lab once a week for 50 minutes, then 30 booths would not be enough. We would have to reduce the length of the period, increase the time when the lab will be open per week or double the number of booths to 60 in order to accommodate two classes simultaneously.

If the cost of 60 booths with full equipment (listen-speak-record) in each is too expensive, then planning 30 booths with full equipment and 30 with only listen-speak facilities might be considered. Each class could be in the listen-speak-record boths 25 minutes and in the others the remaining 25 minutes. Other combinations can be considered to suit the particular needs of each school.

A Standard Plan Many lab plans are possible to fit the available space and the preferences of the users and planners. A standard plan that might fit a variety of needs is the following:

The booths are arranged in rows facing the console, four rows of six booths each, for a 24-booth lab. Each booth is allotted 3×6 feet of space including the aisle between rows. The 24 booths occupy 24×21 feet of floor space.

The booths should be low enough to permit visual contact with the teacher at the console and high enough for privacy. Transparent plastic or glass as the booth front permits only partial visual contact and that only from the center front of the room.

Booths are available commercially and should not be built locally

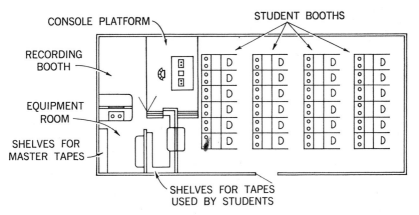

CONSOLE PLATFORM

STUDENT BOOTHS

RECORDING BOOTH

EQUIPMENT ROOM

SHELVES FOR MASTER TAPES

SHELVES FOR TAPES USED BY STUDENTS

Floor plan for 24-booth laboratory.

unless a very favorable construction situation exists. A standard booth is shown in the figure on page 192.

The console should be on a platform 18 to 24 inches high to permit visual contact above the partitions of the booths. The console position permits the teacher to face the class in the lab.

A sound-conditioned small room 6 × 8 feet is provided for the teacher to make tapes. The entrance to this room is not directly from the lab but through another small room where the recording equipment and a work bench are located.

The collection of master tapes needs to have a special space accessible only to the teachers and the lab technician and not to the students. Blank tapes and copies of the master tapes used by the students should be stored in a contiguous space with a window to the general lab space so that students may receive tapes there.

The Lab of the Future Labs have been standardized along the lines described above, but they will change in the rapid evolution of technology. Changes could follow the pressures now felt in lab space, manipulation of equipment by students, and the problem of scheduling everything in a central all-purpose lab. Three labs are now possible experimentally in these three directions of pressure: a dial-selector type of lab, a radio broadcast station, and individual tape recorders with individual tapes.

Dial lab Labs with tape recorders for each student require substantial care and maintenance. Manipulation of the recorder and the tapes by the students takes skill that some would like to make unnecessary. To overcome these matters there is an experimental lab with nothing but a telephone dial in addition to the headphones and microphone in each booth.

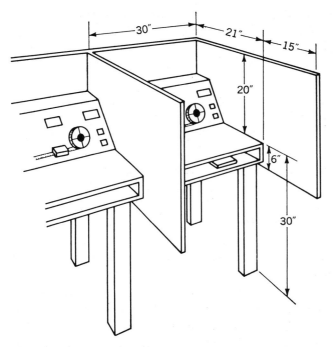

Booth unit.

The drill material is in a central tape recorder with capacity for many channels. The student dials the number of the exercise he wants to study, and the material is played through the earphones. Dialing a different number, the student records his answers through his microphone but on the central tape recorder. Dialing still another number, the student can hear his recorded response.

Cost of the central recording machine and dial system, technical difficulties in making such equipment operate smoothly, the need for a well-trained technician for such a lab, and resistance to extreme mechanization may keep the use of this type of lab restricted for some time.

Radio broadcasting station　To overcome the problem of space and cost of equipment, it is possible to broadcast language drills from a radio station and have the student practice through a simple radio receiver tuned to that station. The space problem is indeed overcome by this arrangement, but only one lesson may be broadcast at a time, and of course the student can only listen and repeat, not record or play back.

Individual tape recorders　Duplicating individual tapes for the students makes it possible to have each student do his lab work anywhere, even in his room, if we supply him with the tapes he is to study. Cost and maintenance of dual-channel tape recorders runs relatively high. A combination of a small, well-equipped central lab plus rental of tape recorders for those students who can afford them may be a good practical plan. In this arrangement, good duplicating equipment becomes more important than in others, and the cost of such equipment is a factor.

Live Issues Whether or not to have a lab is no longer an issue in the United States. If a school does not have a lab, it is most likely because of lack of funds.

Passive versus active labs The issue of a broadcast lab with listen-repeat equipment versus a library type of lab with listen-repeat-record equipment is still a live one. The movement seems to be in favor of the latter on the grounds that the more complete lab can also be used for the simpler type of operation but not vice versa.

Some simple experiments comparing effectiveness of the two types of lab would be an important contribution to second language teaching.

Preparing for the lab versus preparing for the class A vital issue is the relative importance given to the lab and to the class. Is the class to be used as a preparation for the lab, or is the lab a preparation for the class? In many instances, it makes little difference as long as the student is given the opportunity to practice in both. In other instances, a basic difference is involved. In this book we have assumed that the lab is a supplement to and a preparation for the class. Experiments to determine this issue would be difficult, and the conclusions would probably remain indecisive.

Chapter 18

Pictures Visual aids in teaching are well established. Their usefulness in second language teaching needs no defense. Yet any visual method is bound to be misleading, for visual stimuli bear no necessary relation to language. They can be attached to almost any language and to many structures of the same language. A scientific approach to language teaching is almost forced to depend primarily on the structure of the language. Visual aids must remain aids.

Pictures provide a great deal of information at a glance, but when used to illustrate the meaning of a particular expression, they can mislead. A word printed across a full color picture of a corn stalk might be expected to mean corn or corn stalk, yet it was intended to mean fertilizer in a primer for immigrants. To the illustrator it seemed obvious that a fine specimen of corn should mean fertilizer. To the reader it did not.

Even imperfect pictures, once assigned a meaning, however, have great power to elicit that same meaning again and again. If, for example, the series of drawings that follows is assigned the meanings given, the drawings will elicit these same meanings later, even though the drawings bear only a remote likeness to the objects named.

_____ train	__▫__ ship	◯ orange	◌ watch
⌒ house	⧄ paper	⊓ chair	⌣ plate
⊞ window	⊍ glass	⋏ man	⌒ cat

Test yourself by covering the above and attempting to recall the words from the pictures below.

This power extends to false meanings, that is, meanings whose relation to the pictures is deliberately distorted.

EXAMPLES: It's raining.    A beautiful automobile.

 Resting nicely.

Some experiments should be set up to explore this power of pictures to elicit meanings defined by context.

We sometimes erroneously assume that pictures have the same meaning everywhere in the world. This is false. Pictures are culture-bound in at least two ways. (1) The objects and people shown in the pictures have different functions and connotations in different cultures, and (2) experience in understanding pictures varies from culture to culture. The convention by which a balloon above the picture of a person can mean speech, a dream, or a thought, is a cultural convention. Even the habit of understanding a line drawing to show three-dimensional space is restricted culturally.

Cultural Content, Structure, and Pictures   Pictures can be used effectively to teach language and cultural content. They have often been used to elicit conversation on topics such as shopping, a vacation, or a party. This use of pictures without control of the grammatical structures being taught tends to be more vocabulary rehearsing than language teaching. Nevertheless, some good materials along these lines have been developed by teachers who graded the language to be practiced on the basis of their experience.

More productive is the use of pictures to practice the language structures systematically. In this approach, the sentence patterns are selected beforehand. A model is given or elicited, and then series of pictures provide substitution elements that the student incorporates in the sentence pattern he is practicing. There are many types of such picture exercises. They are described in the appropriate sections of this book, i.e., pattern practice, vocabulary, pronunciation, etc.

In the structural approach to the use of pictures for language teaching, the pictures are selected to fit the structure taught and the lexical substitutions that will fit those structures. Cultural content must be dealt with *ad hoc* from the beginning to prevent gross cultural misunderstanding. Later, pictures can be used to provide more systematic cultural experience necessary for a full understanding and use of the language. Again the use of pictures will differ according to whether it is topic centered or structure centered.

A structural selection of pictures is more effective for teaching at this stage than merely dealing with miscellaneous pictures on a given topic or topics. A vacation in the area of the second culture may be an interesting topic and one that affords flexibility of use, but it will not be as effective as a field trip in which the subject specifically seeks out the cultural units that are difficult to understand because of structural differences between the target and native cultures.

Selection of pictures and the order of presentation can best be made on the basis of the second culture and the ways in which it is different from the first culture. Presentation as well as selection must take into account these differences. Merely to show pictures of a children's birthday party in the United States to children in India will not constitute a meaningful experience for them.

The Blackboard The blackboard has been rightly termed the most versatile visual aid. It is standard equipment in every classroom. There is no blackboard method of teaching language, of course, but most language lessons make use of the blackboard. This use should be deliberately planned, leaving informal recourse to the blackboard only for unexpected problems encountered during the teaching of the lesson.

Begin with a clean slate. The blackboard should be completely erased before beginning any new lesson or new point in the lesson. By the law of contiguity, there will be associations made between whatever is on the board and the material practiced. If the material on the board has no relation to the lesson, the associations thus established will interfere with the desired learning.

Write an attention pointer when new material is taught. An attention pointer is not a full explanation; it is a hint as to where to look for the crucial point in the lesson or exercise. For example, if the problem being taught is the difference in the sounds between the vowel of *eat* and that of *it*, the attention pointer might be, "Notice the difference in the vowels." A brief outline of the lesson can profitably be written on a corner of the board to guide the students in listening.

Teachers in the primary grades make very effective use of colored chalk. Secondary school teachers and even college and university lecturers could benefit from similar use of color.

Writing more than a word or short sentence on the board during the presentation of a lesson is slow and ineffective. The class tends to lose interest while the teacher writes. It is more effective to write the material on the board before class and to cover it until it is needed in the lesson. It is then uncovered at one sweep, and the class becomes absorbed with its content.

Excellent use of the blackboard can be made for memorization of a text. The material is written on the board and covered before class time. For memorization it is uncovered and read through by the teacher with the class following silently or in a low voice. The material is read again by the teacher with the class attempting full simultaneous reading. This choral reading may be repeated until the students read smoothly together. The teacher then erases some of the nouns and leads the class in reading everything, including the erased words. Verbs are erased, and another reading is conducted, with the teacher abstaining while the class reads and supplies the missing words. Additional readings follow, with more and more material erased until even the function words are erased, and the class repeats the text, looking at the blank board where the text appeared previously.

To have the class correct their own dictation exercises, one of the students can write his dictation on a board that is not visible to the rest of the class. When the dictation has been finished, the blackboard can be turned around or otherwise put in full view of the class. Corrections are made on the dictation, and the class can correct their own from the sample on the board.

Minimal contrasting pairs written on the blackboard can clarify the contrast. For this purpose the significant elements of the pattern are written one under the other. Vertical lines separating the contrasting elements will further highlight the point.

Flash Cards Flash cards for teaching or self-study have been used for years and can still be bought easily in bookstores. Essentially, they are sets of cards with a word or phrase on one side and its meaning— usually in translation—on the other.

For self-study, the student looks at the word and attempts to recall the meaning. If he succeeds, he discards the item. If he fails, he puts it at the end of the pile for another attempt when it comes up again. This is essentially the same process used in teaching machines. With proper instructions, the student could proceed to write the answers before turning the card over.

For active recall of vocabulary, the flash cards may have a picture or the native language word on one side and the second language word on the other. The student sees the picture or word and attempts to recall the second language word. He checks his response against the back of the card.

To practice pronunciation and the symbols of a phonetic alphabet, the cards may have individual phonetic or phonemic symbols and words in phonetic or phonemic transcription. The cards are shown to the students, who attempt to pronounce what they see. The back of the cards may give the words in ordinary spelling as a check. When the problem is a single sound, it can be identified by underlining the appropriate letters in the word. Properly designed and used, flash cards can be very helpful in teaching and studying a language.

Charts Wall charts of many types have been used successfully for years. They have great advantages for oral practice. They keep the attention of a whole class together on the same stimulus, whereas individual pictures in the students' books tend to scatter the attention of the class. Charts can be used repeatedly in full daylight, while other aids require electric connections, darkening of rooms, special equipment, etc.

Materials that make various uses of wall charts are advertised and described by publishers. Two types are particularly effective: mimicry-memorization conversation charts and pattern-practice charts.

In the first step of learning a second language, a dialogue containing key examples is memorized. Such a dialogue can be illustrated by a single picture on a wall chart or by a series of pictures. The student memorizes the conversation, attaching each sentence or utterance to a point on the chart. The dialogue is recalled by looking at the chart and successively concentrating on the point of each next sentence. Placing numbers on the chart to indicate the sequence of the points eliciting sentences is a further mnemonic device.

The pattern-practice chart is basically different from the mimicry-memorization chart. The pattern-practice chart provides substitutions within a given structure pattern in order to practice the same pattern with a variety of elements. The series of line drawings given on page 199 to show the permanence of word-to-picture associations can be a pattern-practice chart.

The chart can be used to practice almost any sentence pattern. For example, it can be used for the English sentence pattern illustrated by *It's a train.* The teacher points to the first picture and says, *It's a train.* The class repeats, *It's a train.* The teacher points to the next picture and says, *It's a ship.* The class repeats. The third picture will elicit, *It's an orange,* when the teacher points to it. And so on to the end of the series.

The same chart can be used to practice the question pattern illustrated by *Is it a train?* Questions and affirmative short answers can follow: *Is it a train? Yes, it is.* Affirmative and negative short answers can be practiced by pointing to the wrong picture now and then, e.g., pointing to the train and saying, *Is it a ship?* to elicit, *No, it isn't. It's a train.*

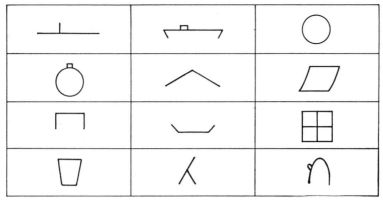

Improvised pattern practice chart.

More complex patterns and sequences of patterns can be practiced speedily with the same chart, e.g., *He didn't want the train; he wanted the ship. He didn't want the orange; he wanted the watch.*

Slides and Slide Projectors Slides or transparencies are mounted single picture films for projection on a screen or wall by means of a slide projector. Although there are slides of various sizes, the most common size is the 35 mm film mounted on 2- by 2-inch frames. These can be made on any 35 mm camera and mounted on cardboard frames by the producer or laboratory that develops them.

Slides are relatively easy to make with one's own camera or are readily obtainable commercially on subjects and places of general interest. Their effectiveness is no longer a matter of the slide as a device for teaching, but of the content of the particular slides to be used. They can show cultural subjects in full color and provide the stimulus for controlled speaking practice or free conversation. Available slides for language and culture teaching are listed in bibliographies and advertised by manufacturers. Slides for the enrichment of the language class can be used to project the types of wall charts we have discussed.

Since the slide projector has become standard equipment in all schools in the United States, many manufacturers produce them. Selection will depend on budget considerations and intended use. Newer models have remote control devices which make it possible for the teacher to move about in the room and change slides as needed. These newer models have clock mechanisms that can be set to change the slides automatically every few seconds.

The light power of the bulb is an important consideration, especially if the room cannot be darkened completely or if semidarkness is preferred to permit the students to take notes. Standard acceptable power is 500 to 750 watts.

The screen, too, is important. Beaded screens have considerably more brilliance from the center, but this brilliance is lost from the sides of the viewing room. Nonbeaded screens show a more even image on a large picture. A blinder covering the light side of a screen in a semi-darkened room has been found to increase the definition of the picture significantly.

Film Strips Film strips can be very useful. They can be used alone for informal conversation with the aid of the teacher. They can be coupled with a tape recording or a record. A beep on the recording lets the teacher or the operator know when to change to the new frame. The beep may activate the slide projector or film-strip projector and change the picture automatically. The film strip is essentially a series of picture frames on one roll of film.

Opaque Projector The opaque projector takes any page in a book or any sheet and reflects it on a screen in a darkened room. The chief advantage of the opaque projector over slides and film strips is that any material can be shown as it is. If the teacher wishes to show a photograph, a chart, or a paragraph, all that is needed is to place it in a tray under the projector, and it will be reflected on the screen. Slides and film strips have to be prepared beforehand at considerable cost and effort.

Shortcomings of the opaque projector are the need for considerable darkening of the room, which is sometimes difficult to achieve in the classroom and which interferes with writing and other class activities. In addition, the change of one exhibit to the next on the opaque projector tends to be slow and awkward. The cooling system has to develop considerable power to keep the heat of the bulb from damaging the paper. As a result, the cooling system tends to be noisy in some models.

For these and other reasons, for example, their bulkiness, the use of opaque projectors tends to be restricted to the display of illustrative materials in lectures.

Overhead Projector To overcome the problem of having to turn one's back to the class to write on the blackboard, the overhead projector projects what the teacher writes on a transparent plastic film in front of him onto a screen behind him as he faces the class. A special pencil is required. This kind of projector also permits a larger image than can be written on the board.

Since the drawings and writing on the plastic roll or sheets can be prepared in advance to be projected at the desired time, considerable flexibility and power can be achieved. For example, if the teacher gives a dictation and wishes to have the class correct their own papers, the material can be projected on the screen at the appropriate moment.

By using several transparent sheets superimposed on each other, parts of a dialogue to be memorized can be gradually withdrawn from view while the class attempts to reproduce the entire material.

For whatever reasons, integrated graded language materials for use through overhead projectors have not been developed, and the use of the overhead projector remains limited to illustrative drawings and notes in connection with public lectures and papers read at professional conventions.

Motion Pictures The motion picture is in theory at least the most powerful of the visual aids. It combines pictures with movement, color, and sound. Theoretically, one can have on film the best materials presented by the best teacher. With this in mind a number of motion pictures for the teaching of foreign languages and English as a foreign language have been produced and will continue to appear.

With all these potential advantages one would expect motion pictures to have taken the field by storm. Yet this has not happened. Why? It may be that the cost of producing these films renders them prohibitive. A few reels to supplement a course are used, but whole series covering an entire course are rare, and even when available are not widely purchased or used.

In addition, it is easy to disagree at least in detail with the way the picture teaches something, and the picture is then seen and abandoned. Motion pictures date rapidly, and methods and props soon look out of fashion and in fact are. The very teacher who appears in the picture modifies his methods each year, yet the lessons of the picture are frozen.

Also, because traditionally the motion picture has been used for entertainment, those who produce them for teaching insist on the entertainment aspect and blunt the teaching impact.

With secondary school and university students, the classes are expected to be approximately an hour in duration. Watching a motion picture in semidarkness for that long a period tires the students. Motion pictures of less duration, which are the majority, require a good teacher to teach the class the remainder of the period. If a good teacher is available, the importance of the picture recedes, and it tends to be shown as supplementary material occasionally.

Motion pictures depicting the culture and people as well as the language are used as supplementary material for enrichment. They should be used more, for they bring to the classroom a realism that cannot be attained otherwise. The selection of appropriate films and their availability are serious matters that take time on the part of the teacher.

Television   Television has become increasingly important in second-language teaching. It is used widely in FLES. The case for television in FLES considers that there are not enough qualified teachers to introduce foreign languages in a whole school system. Native speakers of foreign languages in the community are not qualified professionally to teach, and qualified teachers do not speak the language well enough to be imitated.

Through television, it is argued, a good teacher and a good model can be used for all the pupils, and this plus their superior power of imitation will enable the children to learn well. The cost of introducing foreign languages through television on a large scale is relatively small compared with providing qualified teachers. It is true that the teacher already in the classroom is qualified to direct the pupils in various activities, and to supply a specialist in language is an expensive duplication of personnel.

The case against television argues that television without a qualified language teacher is ineffective or harmful, and with a qualified teacher, television is not necessary. The program is scheduled for all pupils at the same hour at the same pace. Even though a school misses a class—as is sometimes inevitable because of weather, special holidays, equipment failure, etc.—the lesson continues, and the class must skip in order to keep up. Faster classes must go slowly, and slow classes must speed up to the fixed norm of the television lesson. Since television lessons are complete, self-contained units, the classroom teacher can easily feel superfluous and settle down to correcting papers or some other unrelated activity, leaving the class to fend for itself.

Experiments are being conducted by school systems to compare the effectiveness of the use of television (1) without a teacher, (2) with the regular classroom teacher, (3) with a specialist, and (4) with untrained native speakers, and to compare these results with foreign language teaching without television. It is difficult to predict which way the pendulum will go. The results of these experiments will often be indecisive, because of the many factors involved, and the decision made by school systems will not be guided by effectiveness alone.

The use of two teachers, a specialist and the classroom teacher, is preferable, but cost and availability of personnel may prove decisive. The gradual training of the classroom teacher to follow the set of materials used on television may be the path of least trouble and least resistance. If television continues to be used for other subjects, it will be used for foreign language as well, instead of some autonomous equipment and materials, such as film strips and recorded tapes, which might be more flexible and effective in the hands of the classroom teacher.

A survey sponsored by the U.S. Office of Education and the Modern Language Association of America led to the following conclusions:

> A single, skillful, inspired teacher, on a city-wide or nation-wide network, can not and will not be able to do the work of several hundred, or a hundred, classroom teachers—or of one classroom teacher. Such a television teacher can, however, do *a significant part* of the work of several hundred teachers.
>
> Television is not *the answer* to the shortage of teachers, but insofar as TV teaching of foreign languages is done by skillful, inspired teachers, backed by sound advice from linguists and producers, and by a sound program in the schools, television can be *a major part* of the solution to this problem.[1]

[1] J. Richard Reid, "An Exploratory Survey of Foreign Language Teaching by Television in the United States." *Reports of Surveys and Studies in the Teaching of Modern Foreign Languages,* New York: Modern Language Association of America, 1959–1961, p. 207.

Chapter 19

Teaching Machines and Programmed Learning

Teaching machines have received a great deal of publicity in recent years. Sensational statements are made about them without substantiation. Here is one that appeared in the daily press. "Never before has an innovation [teaching machines] so swiftly captured the fancy of public and educators. First described three years ago . . ." How new is this new development, and of what does it consist?

Pressey's Teaching Machines Nearly a third of a century ago, in 1924, Sidney L. Pressey exhibited and described "a simple apparatus which automatically gives *and* scores a test, and which will also automatically, teach. . . ."[1]

The characteristics of modern objective tests gave Pressey the idea of using a mechanical device to administer and score such tests, as well as to teach.

[1] S. L. Pressey, "A Simple Apparatus Which Gives Tests and Scores—and Teaches." In A. A. Lumsdaine and Robert Glaser, *Teaching Machines and Programmed Learning*. Washington, D.C.: National Education Association, 1960, p. 35. (Pressey's article first appeared in *School and Society*, vol. 23, no. 586, Mar. 20, 1926.)

The apparatus is about the size of an ordinary portable type-writer. . . . The person who is using the machine finds presented to him in a little window a typewritten or mimeographed question of the ordinary selective-answer type, for instance:

"To help the poor debtors of England, James Oglethorpe founded the Colony of (1) Connecticut, (2) Delaware, (3) Mary-land, (4) Georgia."

To one side of the apparatus are four keys.[2]

The person presses the key representing his reply. This turns the drum of the machine so that the next question comes up, and the reply is automatically recorded.

The above paragraph describes the operation of the apparatus if it is being used simply to test. If it is to be used also to teach then a little lever . . . shifts the mechanism so that a new question is not rolled up until the correct answer to the question to which the sub-ject is responding is found . . . the counter counts all tries.[3]

Pressey improved the machine the following year so that:

. . . as each item is learned to the point where two successive right answers are made, the apparatus revolves past it.

The apparatus thus keeps the subject at each question until he masters it and, when the mastery is achieved, takes the subject's time with that item no more. And as the learning progresses, the subject's attention is concentrated more and more on those items which are most difficult for him.[4]

These Pressey teaching machines were already of a fairly sophisti-cated design. In a sense, all other teaching machines derive from them. Some simplified the mechanism; others developed more elaborate devices.

It should be noted that there is nothing mysterious about a teaching machine. The same teaching effect is achieved without a teaching machine, though less automatically, by a two-ply answer sheet with easy cutout peepholes for the choices. The student removes the cover of the choice he considers best. If it is the best answer, a proper mark shows through the peephole on the second sheet. If it is not, a blank is seen, and the student tries other choices until he finds the right one. As with the teaching machine, the total number of tries is the raw score.

[2] *Ibid.*, p. 36.
[3] *Ibid.*, p. 37.
[4] *Ibid.*, p. 43. This is from another reprinted article by S. L. Pressey, "A Machine for Automatic Teaching of Drill Material." Originally published in *School and Society*, vol. 25, no. 645, May 7, 1927.

Skinner's Teaching Machines   There are other similar and simply operated teaching machines, two of which are described here for the reader.

Written-answer machine   One of the simplest teaching machines is a box in which the program, one item at a time, shows through a window covered with transparent plastic or glass.   The student reads the lead and writes his answer on an answer tape through an open slot. A lever or knob moves the correct answer into view and slides his answer under the transparent glass or plastic.   He compares the answer with the correct one but cannot erase it.

The student marks himself right or wrong by pressing the pencil through a special hole that activates a counter in the machine, or he marks the paper for easy counting of correct or incorrect responses later.

Constructed-response machine   Although different in appearance from Pressey's devices, the machine developed by B. F. Skinner is essentially a modification of it.

> The device consists of a small box about the size of a small record player.   On the top surface is a window through which a question or problem printed on a paper tape may be seen.   The child answers the question by moving one or more sliders upon which the digits 0 through 9 are printed.   The answer appears in square holes punched in the paper upon which the question is printed.   When the answer has been set, the child turns a knob.   The operation is as simple as adjusting a television set.   If the answer is right, the knob turns freely and can be made to ring a bell or provide some other conditioned reinforcement.[5]

Audio Models   Combinations of the teaching machine with a tape or disc recording device give an additional dimension to teaching machines. The audio material is presented on tape, for example.   The student responds in writing through a slot on the box and moves it forward to check his answer.

Anticipation drills on tape are essentially teaching-machine exercises since the student's oral response is immediately followed by the answer on the tape for correction.   The scoring and tabulation of correct and incorrect oral answers, however, has not been solved mechanically.   The student is not a good judge of his own pronunciation, intonation, etc.

More Complex Machines   More complex machines are available or under development.   Among these are machines with complex response

[5] B. F. Skinner, "The Science of Learning and the Art of Teaching."   Reprinted from the *Harvard Educational Review*, vol. 24, no. 2, 1954, in Lumsdaine and Glaser, *op. cit.*, p. 110.

panels or even a typewriter keyboard. Some have film-strip projection as the display mechanism. The following is a brief description of an experimental machine using an electronic computer and slide projector.

Computer-based teaching machine An elaborate teaching machine used experimentally in 1960 consists of three major parts: (1) a digital computer, (2) a slide projector, and (3) an electric typewriter. The computer controls the operation of the machine, determines what materials are to be presented to the student depending on his previous responses, and analyzes the students' responses. The information for the computer is contained in rolls of paper tape in interchangeable magazines. The slide projector holds a large number of 35 mm slides and receives instructions from the computer to select and project slides in the sequence determined by the students' responses.

The student records his answers in multiple-choice form on the electric typewriter, which also prints messages from the computer telling the student how successful his responses have been. This machine permits flexible branching within programs on the basis of responses analyzed.

General Characteristics Although teaching machines show great variety of design and complexity, certain features set them apart from ordinary audio-visual aids. (1) Teaching machines provide individualized drill rather than group or classroom drill. (2) They require active responses by the students. (3) They provide correct answers for self-correction after each response, and (4) they do not permit the student to change his response once the correct answer appears.

Essentially all teaching machines (1) present problems to the student, (2) provide some means by which the students record their responses, and (3) immediately inform the student whether or not he has given the correct solution.

Evaluation It is a mistake to think of teaching machines as a way to overcome the teacher shortage. The teacher is still needed to control the students, require them to study, approve their good work, and disapprove their lack of it. The possible increase in numbers of students that can be taught by each teacher is offset by the expense and problems of handling the machines and programmed lessons.

Poor materials are not made good merely by putting them into program form. Poor programs remain poor teaching materials even if used through a teaching machine. The following items [6] from a Latin program are poor whether used in a teaching machine or by a live teacher.

[6] Examples as quoted by J. W. Rigney and E. B. Fry, "Current Teaching-Machine Programs and Programming Techniques." *Audio Visual Communication Review,* vol. 9, no. 3, supplement 3, pp. 58–59, May–June, 1961.

They deal with technical terms for a few grammatical items and substitute a translation for language practice.

Ablative absolute refers to a clause, attendant upon the main clause.
Having made this speech, he dismissed the meeting
(Translate into Latin)

Hac oratione habita, concilium dimisit.

Some verbs are conjugated only in the active but have passive meanings. These verbs are called *deponent* verbs.

Conor (try)   Conari is the _____
                Conatus sum is the _____
                infinitive   perfect indicative

A drill device for homework Under proper conditions, students having access to well-programmed teaching machines may drill routine material efficiently with the aid of such expensive materials. It may be possible, for example, for mature students learning to read a foreign language for the Ph.D. to do a good deal of practice drill by themselves if proper programmed material is available.

The programmed textbook The programmed textbook contains items of the same type as those used in teaching machines. To achieve the same effect as with the machines, the text appears on one page and the correct response is given on the next. Thus the student reads the text and writes his response on a separate piece of paper. He then turns the page to check his answer with that provided by the book. (This is equivalent to turning the knob on the machine.) On the page on which he checks his answer, the next item appears; its correct response appears on the following page. At the end of a number of items, the next answer is given at the beginning of the unit or chapter under the first item. The student proceeds to follow the items, one to a page until the end of the sequence, returns again to the beginning of the chapter, and goes through it again until the bottom of the pages of the chapter are reached. The process is circular, continuing to the end of the unit or chapter.

An example [7] will clarify the arrangement:

Lead: | 1. A stimulus which follows a response is called a(n) _____ if the rate at which similar responses are emitted is observed to increase.

---

[7] James Holland and B. F. Skinner, *The Analysis of Behavior.* McGraw-Hill Book Company, Inc., New York: 1961, pp. 51–54.

[next page]

| Response to 1:

 reinforcer
 (reinforcing <br> stimulus) | 2. A hungry pigeon pecks a key and is immediately given food. The (1) _____ of the pecking response will increase, since presenting food (2) ***** [8] a reinforcement. |

[next page]

| Response to 2:

 (1) rate
 (frequency)
 (2) is (con-
 stitutes, acts <br> as) | 3. If, instead of presenting food after the pigeon pecks the key, a loud noise is turned *on*, the rate of pecking will *not* increase. Presenting a loud noise ***** a reinforcement. |

[next page]

| Response to 3:

 is not | 4. . . . |

Scrambled textbook. The scrambled textbook presents each unit of information in a short text followed by a multi-choice item. Each of the choices of the item has a different page reference. If the student selects the right choice, he turns to the page indicated and is confirmed in his choice. He then proceeds to a new information unit. If his choice is wrong, he reads a brief explanation of the error and is sent back to the original unit to try again.

Programmed Learning Many of the features associated with programmed learning are not exclusive with it since they can also be observed in good materials not arranged as a program. The following combination of features, however, sets programmed material apart from other teaching aids.

1. The material is graded into small easy steps that can be taken one at a time with a minimum of error by the student. This is not an exclusive feature of programmed learning, since good materials of any kind are carefully graded, as are, for example, good readers.

2. The program requires the student to be active by responding to

[8] Asterisks stand for any number of words; blanks require one word per blank.

every new item. This is not exclusive with programmed learning either; it is found in audio-lingual language materials in which the student repeats or transforms every new sentence.

3. The program is to be used by each student individually, and this, too, is not exclusive with programmed learning. Individual tutoring, the oldest form of teaching, and language laboratories, one of the newest, are individualized, also.

4. Programmed learning provides for immediate reinforcement by supplying the correct answer after each response. This is also used in choral recitation in audio-lingual practice in which the teacher gives the right answer following the attempt by the class or hears and detects, like an orchestra leader, the error made by the individual student.

5. Perhaps the most distinctive feature of programmed learning is the merging of teaching and testing into one single process. In non-programmed teaching, there is a period of teaching and then a period of testing to determine if the students have learned what has been taught. In programmed learning there are no separate teaching and testing periods. Most items teach and test. The items may test something presumably learned through previous items, or they may teach and test something inferable by analogy, logic, or linguistic patterning from its own lead material.

Strengths and weaknesses A strength of programmed learning is that it couples the learning of the student with the teaching matter supplied to him. This has been interpreted as adaptation to individual differences, but it is only partly this. It adapts to individual differences by permitting the student to advance at his own pace through the program, but single-track programs force all students to go through every step, even if some students are capable of skipping many items. For example, a Spanish language program taken by a person who already knows Spanish will force him to go through every step just as the student who does not know Spanish. If the criterion of mastery is two successful attempts on each item, the student who knows the language has to go through every item twice. Multiple-track programs alleviate this weakness but do not eliminate it altogether.

To use an analogy, a man who wants to climb to a second floor will be helped by a stairway on which he may climb step by step. If, however, the steps are made only an inch high and he is forced to go through every step, he will feel frustrated, since he could manage a foot-high step and, if in a hurry, even a two-foot step at a time.

Preparation of programs Programmed material is not prepared by merely breaking up the content logically into its components and presenting it one item at a time. Significantly, all sources coincide in emphasizing that programming is an art.

What happens is that students can often grasp several steps simultaneously in some matters, while in others, a single step has to be repeated many times. In other words, some items of skill or knowledge are harder than others.

In second language learning, we have seen that difficulty can be determined in large measure by comparing the second language structure with the first. Scientific teaching takes this fact into account. Programmed material must do likewise. One may enjoy the luxury of ignoring this fact at his own peril, but may he do so at the expense of the effort and learning of the students?

Glossary of Useful Terms

Allophone. Each of various similar sounds that function as a single phoneme in a language. The *k* of *kill* and that of *skill* are allophones of the phoneme /k/ in English. (See PHONE.)

Alphabet. A set of letters or other graphic symbols that represent the phonemes of a language more or less accurately. English, French, Spanish, Italian, etc., use the Latin alphabet in their writing systems. Russian uses the Cyrillic alphabet. In ordinary spelling, these alphabets do not represent the phonemes of these languages consistently. An alphabet that consistently represents each phoneme of a language with the same letter is a PHONEMIC ALPHABET. An alphabet that represents speech sounds on the basis of their articulation without regard for their phonemic status is a PHONETIC ALPHABET. The most widely used phonetic alphabet is that of the International Phonetic Association and often referred to as the IPA. Phonemic alphabets are usually adaptations of the IPA to the phonemes of a particular language.

Alphabetic writing. A writing system that uses an alphabet, i.e., that represents the phonemes of the language more or less consistently. SYLLABIC WRITING represents the syllables of a language. LOGO-GRAPHIC WRITING represents the words or morphemes of a language.

Analogy. The creation of a word or construction on the pattern of another.

Train : Where is the train? = ship : *Where is the ship?*
Work : worked = go : *goed*

Goed is an unacceptable form often created by analogy by children.

Articulatory description. Statement giving the position and action of the vocal apparatus (tongue, lips, vocal chords, etc.) in producing the sounds of a language.

Association. Tie between two elements in the experience of a person so that when one is perceived, the other is elicited also. There is an association between the meaning of "cat" which can be experienced by seeing a real cat, remembering a cat, etc., and the English word *cat* for those who know English. When the word *cat* is experienced, it elicits the meaning "cat" by association.

ASTP. Army Specialized Training Program, established in more than 50 colleges and universities of the United States during the Second World War. The ASTP provided intensive courses in various languages, emphasizing the ability to speak the language and understand it when spoken by native speakers.

Attention and awareness. Capacity to perceive some things more clearly than others in a field. The number of things or groups of things that can be under attention simultaneously is limited to six or seven.

Attention pointer. A phrase or sentence directing the attention of the students to the problem being taught. Examples: "Notice the difference in the vowels." "Observe the first consonant." "Notice the position of the verb." The attention pointer is followed immediately by an example or a pair or series of examples illustrating the problem.

Audio-lingual. Approach to language teaching that considers listening and speaking the first and central task in learning a language, and reading and writing as skills that follow speaking and listening. Also AURAL-ORAL or ORAL.

Audio-visual. Teaching through the ear and the eye. Usually associated with the use of motion pictures, slides, and film strips, as visual stimuli and the sound track of the film, a record or tape with narration, or the voice of the teacher as the audio stimulus. AUDIO-LINGUAL and AUDIO-VISUAL are very different terms. Audio-lingual refers to listening and speaking, the two central skills in learning a language, while audio-visual refers only to one of these skills, the more passive one of listening. Visual refers to getting ideas through pictures, etc., whereas lingual refers to speaking.

Basic sentences. Useful sentences that illustrate the typical constructions or patterns of the target language. The basic sentences are overlearned by mimicry-memorization and then changed by substitution of different words and other pattern practices to establish the patterns of the target language as habits. The basic sentences are best presented in dialogues to provide context, but the chief value of the sentences is to serve as models for the establishment of the patterns.

Bilingualism. Popularly the ability to speak two languages equally or almost equally well, it is used technically to refer to any degree of knowledge of two languages by the same person. Bilingual areas are those in which two languages exist simultaneously. The roles of the two languages may vary; for example, one may be used as the language of the home and the other as the official language. Bilingual and multi-lingual areas are much more common than is usually thought.

Clichés (false clichés). Oversimplified and incorrect notions held by the people of one culture about another. These false notions may depict all the people of the other culture as gay, happy, romantic, and irresponsible, when, of course, they are not; or they may depict them all as greedy, somber, and cruel when they are not. People acquire these notions in the process of enculturation in their own culture. These notions have in the past found their way into the textbooks which then defeat one of the chief values that can result from the teaching of a foreign language, i.e., increased understanding of the target culture and of the student's own.

Consonant clusters. Sequences of consonants in close transition, i.e., constituting the onset or close of a syllable. /str–/ is an initial cluster in *street* in English. /–kt/ is a final cluster in *picked*. Each language restricts the consonants that may constitute initial or final clusters, and the permitted clusters differ for each language. /–kt/ is common in English but not permitted in Spanish.

Content. Meaning—insofar as it is systematically associated with lexical forms and grammatical structures in a language. Just as the forms and structure differ for each language within the over-all spectrum of human language, so the meaning content of various languages differs for each language and culture within the over-all spectrum of meaning as grasped by man.

Contrastive linguistics. The comparison of any two languages to discover and describe the problems that the speakers of one of the languages will have in learning the other. These comparisons are also applicable to the preparation of language tests, machine translation, and language variations in bilingual areas.

Cultural anthropology. That branch of anthropology that describes the structure of the customs, beliefs, and traditions of human societies. From these customs and beliefs come the specific meanings of the words of a language.

Culture. The ways of a people, including their music, art, customs, beliefs, traditions, literature, etc.

Dialect. Languages show variations geographically, socially, historically, etc. Each distinct form or variety of a language associated with a geographic area or social group is a dialect. The United States shows three major dialect areas: northern, midland, and southern. Within these areas are social dialects, such as cultivated speech and folk speech. Parallel distinctions occur in the English of the British Isles, in the Spanish of Spain and of Latin America, in the French of France and of Canada, etc.

Direct method. An approach to the teaching of a foreign language characterized by emphasis on presenting words and sentences to the students in ways that will show their meaning without translation or grammatical analysis. Historically, it developed at the beginning of this century as a reaction against a grammar-translation method which reduced language learning to rote memorization of rules and deciphering of texts through dictionary thumbing without practice in speaking or reading as such. There are many varieties of the direct method, or many direct methods. The scientific approach presented in this book uses a variety of direct-method techniques but differs from the direct methods in that it uses scientific linguistic and psychological information to grade and organize the teaching and justifies techniques on the basis of observable outcomes rather than on the basis of preconceived and closed notions about what manner of presentation is best.

Expression. The speech part of language as opposed to the content or system of meanings associated with expression.

Facial diagram. Section of a face showing the position of the organs of speech. Simplified facial diagrams are effective in showing the articulation of the consonants and vowels of a language.

Facilitation. Ease in learning a sound, word, or construction in a second language as a result of its similarity with the native language of the student. The opposite of INTERFERENCE, which refers to added difficulty in learning a sound, word, or construction in a second language as a result of differences from the habits of the native language.

Facility. Ease in using a language unit or pattern. Facilities range from automatic habits for the phonemes of the native language at one end of a scale to the minimum facility resulting from a single experience in using a unit or pattern in a second language.

Fit. The relation between a writing system and the spoken language it represents. In alphabetic writing, a perfect fit would imply a distinct graphic symbol for each phoneme and always the same symbol for the same phoneme. No writing system in common use shows perfect fit because of language changes that are not reflected in writing changes and because of imperfect phonemic analyses in setting up the writing systems, and borrowings which keep their foreign spellings. English writing is especially inconsistent as to fit, hence the use of phonetic or phonemic alphabets to teach English pronunciation.

FLES. Foreign Language in the Elementary School. Refers to the special techniques that are appropriate to teach languages to elementary school children, taking advantage of their ability to imitate strange sounds and their motivation toward play and song. Also refers to the classes and programs of instruction.

Grammar-translation method. A degeneration of successful medieval practices in teaching Latin by abandoning the speaking and reading practice and keeping only the rote memorization of grammar rules and the analytical translation of selected texts. This grammar-translation method stripped of language and reading practice became an ineffective exercise and produced a reaction which resulted in the DIRECT METHOD.

Grapheme. A minimally distinctive graphic symbol used to represent a language unit in a writing system. The letters of an alphabet are graphemes when used to represent the phonemes of a language.

Habit. Facility to use the units and patterns of a language at conversational speed with attention on the message and not on the language units or patterns as such.

Head. In a modification structure such as that illustrated by the example *fresh fruit, fruit* is the center or *head,* and *fresh* serves as a modifier of *fruit.* This is partly confirmed by observing that *fruit* can stand for the phrase *fresh fruit* in larger constructions.

Historical linguistics. Branch of linguistics that describes the changes that a language undergoes over the centuries and traces back in time the relations among languages and their families.

Interference. Added difficulty in learning a sound, word, or construction in a second language as a result of differences with the habits of the native language.

Intonation. System of sentence and phrase melody or pitch of a language. The same words of a phrase or sentence may be said with different intonations to express different shades of meaning or different attitudes. Each language has a small number of contrasting differences in intonation. Pitch contrasts that serve to identify specific words, as in Chinese, rather than being part of sentences and phrases are called tones, not intonation. Chinese is a tone language. English, Spanish, French, German, and Russian are intonation languages.

Juncture. Transition between sounds or between sound and silence in speech. In English there are at least four phonemic junctures: internal open juncture as in *night rate* in contrast to *nitrate;* and three terminal junctures—sustain, rise, and fade out—as might be illustrated in the example,

Suddenly, [sustain] he jumped. [fade out]
Into the fire? [rise]

Lab materials. Exercises, tests, supplementary readings, etc. usually recorded on tape for use in the language laboratory. Publishers now provide sets of tapes to accompany their language texts. Teachers prepare supplementary lab materials of their own to meet the specific needs and interests of their classes.

Language. English, French, Spanish, German, Italian, and Russian are complex systems of communication that have evolved with the cultural experience of the peoples that speak them. They can be studied from a variety of scientific and artistic points of view.. From the point of view of the language teacher and that of the student interested in mastering one of them, they are structured systems of patterns and units of expression tied to patterns and units of content that are used to convey the experiences and needs of a people. The use of a language depends largely on habit.

Language lab. Language laboratory. A separate room where students may practice speaking and listening with the aid of tape recorders, earphones, microphones, and/or other sound equipment chiefly as an audio-lingual supplement to class work. The language lab supplements the work of the teacher.

Lexicography. The art and science of dictionary making.

Linguistics. Linguistic science. The science that describes and classifies languages.   The linguist identifies and describes the units and patterns of the sound system, the words and morphemes, and the phrases and sentences that constitute the structure of a language.   He observes speech and presents its structure as completely, accurately, and economically as possible.   Linguists also study language changes over the centuries and dialect variations over geographic areas.   Linguistic descriptions are the most dependable source of information for the language teacher with regard to the language he teaches and its similarities and differences with the language of the students.

Linguistic approach.   Language teaching methods developed by linguists during and after the Second World War.   Characterized by imitation and memorization of basic conversational sentences as spoken by native speakers; description of the distinctive elements of intonation, pronunciation, morphology, and syntax on the basis of the sentences memorized; and massive practice in speaking and listening rather than in translation.

Linguistic geography.   The description of the variations of a language over its geographic area.

Linguistic ontogeny.   The description of the development of language in the individual from childhood to maturity.

Literature.   The writings in a language that achieve distinction through the beauty of their expression or thought or both.   In earlier times the chief purpose in studying a foreign language was to gain access to its literature.

Logographic.   See ALPHABETIC.

MLA.   The Modern Language Association of America.

MLA qualifications.   Standards of preparation for secondary school teachers of modern foreign languages prepared by the Steering Committee of the Foreign Language Program of the Modern Language Association of America, and subsequently endorsed for publication by the MLA Executive Council, the Modern Language Committee of the Secondary Education Board, the Committee on the Language Program of the American Council of Learned Societies, and the executive boards or councils of fifteen national and regional organizations of language teachers.   See pages 230–232.

Monitor function.   The ability to notice errors in expression when attention is on the meaning at normal conversational speed.

Morpheme.   Smallest element in language that is associated with some content.   *Books* has two morphemes: *book* and *–s*.

Morphology.   Description of the morphemes of a language and the patterns of formation of words.

Norms.   The collected scores of groups of students whose characteristics are known.   Norms permit better interpretation of a particular score by comparison with the scores of the larger group.

Oral-aural methods.   Also AURAL-ORAL.   Another term for what is now more commonly called AUDIO-LINGUAL, indicating the primacy of speaking and listening in language teaching.

Overlearning. Memorization of basic sentences to a point where they can be spoken at conversational speed with near native accuracy and with attention on the meaning.

Pattern. Any recurring design or arrangement of sounds, morphemes, words, phrases, or sentences. Each language has its own characteristic patterns at each of these levels. The sentence patterns of English are designs or arrangements into which different words can be put to fit the lexical situation. The sentence patterns of French, Spanish, German, etc., are different from those of English not only in the words but in the essential elements of the design as well.

Pattern practice. Any exercise involving repetition of a pattern with variation of the elements. When the attention of the student is deliberately drawn away from the specific language problem being taught, we have pattern practice in a stricter sense. Such practice forces the operation of the mechanics of the language more and more on the basis of habits and thus frees the attention of the student to dwell properly on the message.

Perception. Hearing distinctly those words and utterances that show minimal contrast, i.e., that differ in only one phoneme, and identifying as same those that show normal subphonemic variation but are phonemically the same.

Phone. Each occurrence of a PHONEME. Within each phoneme the phones may show more than one variety, e.g., aspirated and unaspirated /p/ in English. Each variety is an ALLOPHONE.

Phoneme. The smallest segment of speech serving to identify and distinguish the morphemes of a language. Phonemes actually serve to identify the morphs, which are the individual occurrences of morphemes. Since different morphemes build different words, it can be said that phonemes are the smallest segments of speech that can identify and distinguish words in a language. Each language has its own inventory of phonemes and patterns of occurrence of these phonemes and their allophones.

Phonemic alphabet. An alphabet having one letter for each phoneme of a language and always representing the same phoneme by the same letter.

Phonetics. Scientific description of speech sounds. When the description is made in terms of the articulation of the sounds in the organs of speech, we have articulatory phonetics. When it is made in terms of the physical features of the sounds, we have acoustic phonetics.

Phonology. Description of the phonemes of a language, their subphonemic variants (allophones), and their patterns of occurrence in sequences.

Phrase. Two or more words in a grammatical construction that function as a unit in a sentence.

Problem features. A phoneme in the target language that does not have a close phonological counterpart in the native language constitutes a learning problem. Such problems usually do not involve the entire phoneme but only some feature or features, e.g., English /z/ as in *zoo* is a problem for Spanish speakers specifically with regard to the feature of voicing since Spanish has a voiceless sibilant /s/ as in the English *sue*.

Programmed learning. Learning by means of materials that break up the task into minimal steps, requiring an active response for each step, and providing an immediate check on the correctness of the responses.

Programming. Preparing materials in frames for programmed learning.

Props. Facial diagrams, articulatory descriptions, a mirror to let the student see the lip articulation of a sound, a teaching trick that helps the student produce a trilled *r* by imitating the sound of an airplane, a line frame on the board to box the parts of a phrase, etc., are PROPS. Props are devices that help the student produce or understand a unit or pattern. Props and PARTIALS are the chief tools used by the language teacher in planting new units and patterns as available responses. Partials result from splitting an utterance into smaller parts or rendering it more slowly so that the student may focus attention on the parts separately.

Psycholinguistics. Combined approach through psychology and linguistics for the study of language learning, language in use, language change, and related matters that are less accessible to either science separately.

Recall. To bring into use something after it has slipped out of attention or use. Knowing a language involves instantaneous recall of content when an expression (form) is observed and vice versa.

Reinforcement. Increase in facility which is assumed to result when a correct response is immediately confirmed as correct.

Reliability. Technical term used in tests to indicate how steady (free from arbitrary fluctuation) the scores obtained with a test are.

Rhythm. The regular repetition of units of stress in time. English is said to have stress-timed rhythm because the time between primary stresses tends to be uniform regardless of the number of intervening syllables. French, Spanish, and Japanese are said to have syllable-timed rhythm because the syllables tend to be uniform in time so that a seven-syllable phrase is much longer than a four-syllable one.

Scrambled textbook. A type of programmed book in which the various choices after each information unit refer the student to a different page. The pages given after the wrong choices explain the mistake involved and refer the student back to the item again. The page given after the right choice contains the next information item and question.

Sentence. The smallest unit of full expression. Each language has a restricted number of patterns of sentences. Sentences are made up of parts of sentences such as subject, predicate, objects, complements, sequence signals, etc.

Set. See SPEECH SET.

Shaping. Rewarding gradual approximations to the desired response until the end behavior is fully attained.

Speech set. A normal speak-listen attitude that lets one concentrate his attention on the message while handling the structure of the language through habits.

Stress. Greater prominence of some syllables or words over others in the stream of speech. This prominence is produced in English by greater length, slightly higher pitch, and some increase in energy. In Japanese the greater prominence is chiefly a function of pitch. In Spanish the prominence is probably primarily related to greater energy.

Structure. The system of units and patterns of a language. Each language has its own distinct structure. The system of sounds of a language constitutes its phonological structure; the system of morphemes and word formation is its morphological structure, and the patterns of phrases and sentences are its syntactical structure.

Structure of expression. The system of units and patterns of the forms of a language as distinguished from their meaning content.

Structure of language. See STRUCTURE.

Style. Any variety in language that is characteristic of particular types of utterances, such as letters, poetry, prose, dialogues, scientific reports, formal speeches, or even characteristic of an individual's manner of presentation. Thus we may say that Hemingway had a distinctive style.

Syllabic. Having to do with syllables. SYLLABIC WRITING represents each distinct syllable by a separate graphic symbol. The list of symbols or characters of a syllabic writing system is a SYLLABARY.

Syntax. The patterns of construction of morphemes and words into phrases and sentences in a language.

Tabula rasa. The memory and habit store of an infant before it is channeled by experience. The use of the term is metaphoric, based on the old wax writing tablets.

Target culture. The culture of the language being learned or taught.

Target language. The language being taught or learned. This term is sometimes preferable to FOREIGN LANGUAGE, because the language being taught or learned may not be a foreign one. It is sometimes less ambiguous than SECOND LANGUAGE because the target language may be the third or fourth language for a particular individual. A SECOND LANGUAGE may also refer to a nonnative language taught or learned for national communication.

Teaching machine. Mechanical device that presents the frames of a learning program one at a time, requires a response, and then shows the correct answer. There are many varieties of teaching machines ranging from simple boxes to computer-based devices.

Toneme. Smallest segment of pitch sequence whose function is to identify and distinguish the morphemes or words of a tone language.

The tonemes belong to the morpheme or word in the same sense as the consonant and vowel phonemes belong to the morpheme or word. INTONATION PHONEMES, on the other hand, are sections of pitch sequence which function in intonation phrases and not as part of words or morphemes.

Trace. Minimal facility which is assumed to result from each experience. The trace is not directly observable but can be inferred from the fact that repeated experiences in using an expression result in observable facility.

Transfer. The extension of a native language habit into the target language with or without the awareness of the learner. When the transferred habit is acceptable in the target language, we have FACILITATION. When the transferred habit is unacceptable in the target language, we have INTERFERENCE, and an extra learning burden is assumed.

Utterance. A stretch of speech by a single speaker preceded and followed by silence on his part. An utterance can be a short exclamation or a two-hour oration. The term UTTERANCE is convenient in linguistic description to refer to the first segment of speech that can be assumed to be a valid language sample.

Validity. Degree to which a test measures what it claims to measure. Test validity is specific, i.e., a test that is valid as a measure of pronunciation may be quite invalid as a measure of intelligence.

Word. The smallest free unit of expression, free in the sense that a word does not have to occur exclusively as part of other words. Words are easily recognized as separable units of language even by speakers whose language has never been written. The fact that there may be some inconsistencies in the isolation of words by speakers cannot eliminate the word as an important unit of expression.

Writing. Graphic representation of a language. Pictures or graphic symbols do not constitute writing unless they form a system representing the units of a language so that its patterns can be grasped by the reader.

Bibliography

1. LANGUAGE AND LANGUAGE LEARNING
2. LANGUAGE TEACHING
3. TECHNOLOGICAL AIDS
4. PERIODICALS

1. LANGUAGE AND LANGUAGE LEARNING

AGARD, FREDERICK B., AND HAROLD B. DUNKEL. *An Investigation of Second-Language Teaching.* Boston: Ginn and Company, 1948. 344 pp.

ANGIOLILLO, PAUL F. M. *Armed Forces Foreign Language Teaching.* New York: S. F. Vanni, 1947. 440 pp.

BENEDICT, RUTH. *Patterns of Culture.* Boston: Houghton Mifflin Company, 1934. 290 pp. Sentry Edition with a new Introduction by Margaret Meade, 1961. 290 pp.

BLOOMFIELD, LEONARD. *Language.* New York: Holt, Rinehart and Winston, Inc., 1933. 564 pp.

BROWN, ROGER W. *Words and Things.* New York: The Free Press of Glencoe, 1958. 398 pp.

CÁRDENAS, DANIEL NEGRETE. *Applied Linguistics: Spanish. A Guide for Teachers.* Boston: D. C. Heath and Company, 1961. 62 pp.

————. *Introducción a una comparación fonológica del español y del inglés.* Washington, D.C.: Center for Applied Linguistics, 1960. 63 pp.

CARROLL, JOHN B., AND STANLEY M. SAPON. *Modern Language Aptitude Test.* New York: Psychological Corp., 1959.

CARROLL, JOHN B. *The Study of Language: A Survey of Linguistics and Related Disciplines in America.* Cambridge, Mass.: Harvard University Press, 1953. 289 pp.

CENTER FOR APPLIED LINGUISTICS. *Contrastive Structure Series.* Charles A. Ferguson, General Editor. Chicago: The University of Chicago Press. A series of contrastive analyses of the phonology and grammatical structure of English and the following languages: French, German, Italian, Russian, Spanish. (For German see Kufner and Moulton.)

CENTER FOR APPLIED LINGUISTICS. *Study of the Role of Second Languages in Asia, Africa, and Latin America.* Frank A. Rice (ed.). Washington, D.C.: Center for Applied Linguistics, 1962. 123 pp.

CHERRY, COLIN. *On Human Communication.* New York: John Wiley & Sons, Inc., 1957. 333 pp.

COMENIUS, JOHN A. *The Great Didactic (1628–32).* Tr. by M. W. Keatinge. 2 vols. London: A. and C. Black, 1907. Part I, *Introduction,* 178 pp. Part II, *Text,* 320 pp.

DELATTRE, P. *Principes de phonétique française a l'usage des étudiants anglo-américains.* Middlebury, Vt.: The French School, 1946. 68 pp.

DUNKEL, HAROLD. *Second-Language Learning.* Boston: Ginn and Company, 1948. 218 pp.

FRENCH, F. G. *The Teaching of English Abroad.* 3 vols. London: Oxford University Press. *Part I: Aims and Methods,* 1948. 122 pp. *Part II: The Junior Course,* 1949. 174 pp. *Part III: The Three Senior Years,* 1950. 188 pp.

FRIES, C. C., AND A. A. TRAVER. *English Word Lists. A Study of Their Adaptability for Instruction.* (American Council on Education, 1940.) Ann Arbor, Mich.: George Wahr Publishing Company, 1950. 109 pp.

FRIES, CHARLES C. *The Structure of English. An Introduction to the Construction of English Sentences.* New York: Harcourt, Brace & World, Inc., 1952. 304 pp.

GAGE, WILLIAM W. *Contrastive Studies in Linguistics: A Bibliographical Checklist.* Washington, D.C.: Center for Applied Linguistics, 1960. 14 pp.

GESELL, ARNOLD, AND FRANCES L. ILG. *The Child from Five to Ten.* New York: Harper & Brothers, 1946. 475 pp.

GLEASON, H. A., JR. *An Introduction to Descriptive Linguistics.* Rev. edition. New York: Holt, Rinehart and Winston, Inc., 1961. 503 pp.

HALL, EDWARD T. *The Silent Language.* Garden City, N.Y.: Doubleday & Company, Inc., 1959. 240 pp.

HALL, ROBERT A., JR. *Linguistics and Your Language.* Garden City, N.Y.: Anchor Books, Doubleday & Company, Inc., 1960. 265 pp.

HILL, ARCHIBALD A. *Introduction to Linguistic Structures.* New York: Harcourt, Brace & World, Inc., 1958. 496 pp.

HOCKETT, CHARLES F. *A Course in Modern Linguistics.* New York: The Macmillan Company, 1958. 621 pp.

KÖHLER, WOLFGANG. *Gestalt Psychology.* New York: Liveright Publishing Corporation, 1929. 403 pp.

KROEBER, A. L. (ED.). *Anthropology Today.* Chicago: The University of Chicago Press, 1953. 966 pp.

KUFNER, HERBERT L. *The Grammatical Structures of English and German: A Contrastive Sketch.* Contrastive Structure Series. Chicago: The University of Chicago Press, 1962. 95 pp.

LADO, ROBERT. *Linguistics Across Cultures.* Ann Arbor: The University of Michigan Press, 1957. 141 pp.

LEOPOLD, WERNER F. *Bibliography of Child Language.* Evanston, Ill.: Northwestern University Press, 1952. 115 pp.

MC GEOCH, JOHN A. *The Psychology of Human Learning. An Introduction.* 2d ed. Rev. by A. L. Irion. New York: Longmans, Green & Co., Inc., 1952. 596 pp.

MODERN LANGUAGE ASSOCIATION OF AMERICA. *Qualifications for Secondary School Teachers of Modern Foreign Languages.* New York: Modern Language Association of America, 1955. 4 pp.
————. *Reports of Surveys and Studies in the Teaching of Modern Foreign Languages.* J. W. Childers, Donald D. Walsh, and G. Winchester Stone, Jr. (eds.). New York: Modern Language Association of America, 1961. 326 pp.

MOULTON, WILLIAM G. *The Sounds of English and German.* Contrastive Structure Series. Chicago: The University of Chicago Press, 1962. 145 pp.

OGDEN, C. K., AND I. A. RICHARDS. *The Meaning of Meaning.* New York: Harcourt, Brace & World, Inc., 1923. 544 pp.

OSGOOD, CHARLES E., AND THOMAS A. SEBEOK. *Psycholinguistics: A Survey of Theory and Research Problems.* Baltimore: Waverly Press, 1954. 203 pp.

PARKER, WILLIAM R. *The National Interest and Foreign Languages.* 3d ed. Washington, D.C.: U.S. Government Printing Office, 1961. 159 pp.

PEDERSEN, HOLGER. *The Discovery of Language. Linguistic Science in the 19th Century.* Tr. by John W. Spargo. Bloomington, Ind.: Indiana University Press, 1931. 360 pp. Midland Book edition, 1962.

PIAGET, JEAN. *Le langage et la pensée chez l'enfant.* 3d ed. Paris: Delachaux et Niestlé, 1948. English translation. Preface by E. Claparède. 3d ed. (Revised and enlarged. Tr. by Marjorie Gabain. New York: Humanities Press, 1959. 288 pp.)

PIKE, KENNETH L. *Language in Relation to a Unified Theory of the Structure of Human Behavior.* 3 vols. Glendale, Calif.: Summer Institute of Linguistics, 1954–1960. Part I, 170 pp. Part II, 85 pp. Part III, 146 pp. (For students of linguistics.)
————. *Phonemics.* Ann Arbor: The University of Michigan Press, 1947. 254 pp. (For students of linguistics.)

———. *Tone Languages.* Ann Arbor: The University of Michigan Press, 1948. 187 pp.

POLITZER, ROBERT L. *Teaching French: An Introduction to Applied Linguistics.* New York: Ginn and Company, 1960. 140 pp.

Principles of the International Phonetic Association, The. International Phonetic Association. London: University College, 1949. 53 pp.

SAPIR, EDWARD. *Language. An Introduction to the Study of Speech.* New York: Harvest Books, Harcourt, Brace & World, Inc., 1949. 242 pp.

SAPORTA, SOL (ED.). *Psycholinguistics. A Book of Readings.* New York: Holt, Rinehart and Winston, Inc., 1961. 551 pp.

STEVENS, STANLEY S. (ED.). *Handbook of Experimental Psychology.* New York: John Wiley & Sons, Inc., 1951. 1436 pp.

Teacher Exchange Opportunities. 1963–64. Annual. Washington, D.C.: U.S. Government Printing Office, 1962. 38 pp.

Theory and Practice in English as a Foreign Language. Selected articles from *Language Learning,* no. 2. Ann Arbor, Mich.: The Research Club in Language Learning, 1963. 258 pp.

THORPE, LOUIS P., AND ALLEN M. SCHMULLER. *Contemporary Theories of Learning.* New York: The Ronald Press Company, 1954. 480 pp.

UNDERWOOD, BENTON J., AND R. W. SCHULTZ. *Meaningfulness and Verbal Learning.* Philadelphia: J. B. Lippincott Company, 1960. 430 pp.

VALDMAN, A. *Applied Linguistics, French.* Boston: D. C. Heath and Company, 1961. 116 pp.

WEINREICH, URIEL. *Languages in Contact.* New York: Publications of the Linguistic Circle of New York, no. 1, 1953. 148 pp.

WEST, MICHAEL. *A General Service List of English Words.* London: Longmans, Green & Co., Ltd., 1953. 588 pp.

WISE, C. M. *Applied Phonetics.* Englewood Cliffs, N.J.: Prentice-Hall, Inc., 1957. 546 pp.

2. LANGUAGE TEACHING

ANDERSSON, THEODORE. *The Teaching of Foreign Languages in the Elementary School.* Boston: D. C. Heath and Company, 1953. 119 pp.

BLOOMFIELD, LEONARD. *Outline Guide for the Practical Study of Foreign Languages.* Baltimore: Linguistic Society of America, 1942. 16 pp.

BROOKS, NELSON. *Language and Language Learning. Theory and Practice.* 2d ed. New York: Harcourt, Brace & World, Inc., 1964. 300 pp.

BUROS, O. K. (ED.). *The Fifth Mental Measurements Yearbook.* Highland Park, N.J.: Gryphon Press, 1959. 1292 pp.

FRIEŞ, CHARLES C. *Teaching and Learning English as a Foreign Language.* Ann Arbor: The University of Michigan Press, 1945. 153 pp.

GAUNTLETT, J. O. *Teaching English as a Foreign Language.* London: Macmillan and Co., Ltd., 1957. 124 pp.

GOUIN, FRANÇOIS. *The Art of Teaching and Studying Languages.* New York: Charles Scribner's Sons, 1892. 407 pp.

GURREY, P. *Teaching English as a Foreign Language.* London: Longmans, Green & Co., Ltd., 1955. 199 pp.

JESPERSEN, OTTO. *How to Teach a Foreign Language.* London: George Allen & Unwin, Ltd., 1904. Reprinted 1956. 194 pp.

JOHNSTON, MARJORIE C. (ED.). *Modern Foreign Languages in the High School.* U.S. Office of Education Bulletin 1958, no. 16, 1958. 166 pp.

KEESEE, ELIZABETH. *Modern Foreign Languages in the Elementary School: Teaching Techniques.* U.S. Office of Education Bulletin 1960, no. 29, 1960. 65 pp.
———. *References on Foreign Languages in the Elementary School.* Circular no. 495. Rev. OE–27008A, 1960. Publication Distribution Unit, U.S. Office of Education, 1960.

LADO, ROBERT. *Language Testing. The Construction and Use of Foreign Language Tests.* 389 pp. New York: McGraw-Hill, Inc., 1964.

MODERN LANGUAGE ASSOCIATION OF AMERICA. *MLA Selective List of Materials for Use by Teachers of Modern Foreign Languages.* Mary J. Ollmann (ed.). New York: Modern Language Association of America, 1962. 162 pp.

NEWMARK, MAXIM (ED.). *Twentieth Century Modern Language Teaching.* New York: Philosophical Library, Inc., 1948. 723 pp.

O'CONNOR, PATRICIA. *Modern Foreign Languages in High School: Prereading Instruction.* U.S. Department of Health, Education, and Welfare, Office of Education Bulletin 1960, no. 9, 1960. 50 pp.

OGDEN, C. K. *Basic English.* London: Kegan Paul, Trench, Trubner & Co., Ltd., 1930. 100 pp.

OHANNESSIAN, SIRARPI. *Interim Bibliography on the Teaching of English to Speakers of Other Languages.* Washington, D.C.: Center for Applied Linguistics, 1960. 53 pp.
———. *30 Books for Teachers of English as a Foreign Language.* Washington, D.C.: Center for Applied Linguistics, 1963. 12 pp.

PALMER, HAROLD E. *The Oral Method of Teaching Languages.* Cambridge, England: W. Heffer & Sons., Ltd., 1921. 134 pp.

————. *The Principles of Language Study.* London: George G. Harrap & Co., Ltd., 1921. 185 pp.

PASSY, P. *La méthode directe dans l'enseignement des langues vivantes.* Paris: 1899.

RICHARDS, I. A. *Basic English and its Uses.* New York: W. W. Norton & Company, Inc., 1943. 127 pp.

STARR, WILMARTH, MARY P. THOMPSON, AND DONALD D. WALSH (EDS.). *Modern Foreign Languages and the Academically Talented Student.* New York: Modern Language Association of America, 1960. 89 pp.

UNESCO. *The Teaching of Modern Languages.* Problems in Education, no. 10. Paris: UNESCO, 1955. 295 pp. A volume of studies derived from the International Seminar organized by the Secretariat of UNESCO at Nuwara Eliya, Ceylon, in August, 1953.

VIËTOR, W. *Der Sprachunterricht muss umkehren!* Leipzig: O. R. Reisland, 1905. 52 pp.

3. TECHNOLOGICAL AIDS

COUNCIL OF CHIEF STATE SCHOOL OFFICERS, AND OTHERS. *Purchase Guide for Programs in Science, Mathematics, and Modern Foreign Languages; Supplement to Purchase Guide for Programs in Science, Mathematics, and Modern Foreign Languages.* Boston: Ginn and Company, 1959, 1961.

GALANTER, E. H. (ED.). *Automatic Teaching: The State of the Art.* New York: John Wiley & Sons, Inc., 1959. 198 pp.

HAYES, ALFRED S. *Technical Guide for the Selection, Purchase, Use, and Maintenance of Language Laboratory Facilities.* Prepared under a contract between the U.S. Office of Education and the Electronic Industries Association. U.S. Office of Education, Bulletin 1963, no. 37, 1963. 128 pp.

HUTCHINSON, JOSEPH C. *Modern Foreign Languages in High School: The Language Laboratory.* U.S. Office of Education Bulletin 1961, no. 23, 1961. 85 pp.

LEFRANC, R. *Les techniques audio-visuelles au service de l'enseignement.* Paris: Bourrelier, 1961. 223 pp.

LÉON, PIERRE R. *Laboratoire de langues et correction phonétique.* Publications du Centre de Linguistique Appliquée de Besançon. Paris: Didier, 1962. 275 pp.

LUMSDAINE, A. A., AND ROBERT GLASER. *Teaching Machines and Programmed Learning.* A source book. Washington, D.C.: Department of Audio-Visual Instruction, National Education Association, 1960. 724 pp.

NAJAM, EDWARD W. (ED.). *Materials and Techniques for the Language Laboratory.* Report of the Language Laboratory Conference Held at Purdue University, Mar. 23–25, 1961. Bloomington, Ind.: Publication 18 of the Indiana University Research Center in Anthropology, Folklore, and Linguistics, 1962. 218 pp.

OINAS, FELIX J. (ED.). *Language Teaching Today.* Report of the Language Laboratory Conference Held at Indiana University, Jan. 22–23, 1960. Bloomington, Ind.: Publication 14 of the Indiana University Research Center in Anthropology, Folklore, and Linguistics, 1960. 221 pp.

REID, J. RICHARD. "An Exploratory Survey of Foreign Language Teaching by Television in the United States." *Reports of Surveys and Studies in the Teaching of Modern Foreign Languages.* New York: Modern Language Association of America, 1961. 326 pp. (Bibliography)

STACK, EDWARD M. *The Language Laboratory and Modern Language Teaching.* Fair Lawn, N.J.: Oxford University Press, 1960. 149 pp.

STOLUROW, LAWRENCE M. *Teaching by Machine.* U.S. Office of Education. 1961. 173 pp.

4. PERIODICALS

English Language Teaching. London: Oxford University Press.

French Review, The. Journal of the American Association of Teachers of French. New York.

Georgetown University Institute of Languages and Linguistics. *Reports of the Annual Round Table on Linguistics and Language Teaching.* Washington, D.C.: Georgetown University, 1951–.

German Quarterly. Journal of the American Association of Teachers of German.

Hispania. Journal of the American Association of Teachers of Spanish and Portuguese.

International Journal of American Linguistics. Indiana University, Bloomington, Ind.

Language. Journal of the Linguistic Society of America.

Language Learning. A Journal of Applied Linguistics. Ann Arbor, Mich.

Linguistic Reporter, The. Newsletter of the Center for Applied Linguistics of the Modern Language Association. Washington, D.C.

MLabstracts. Fullerton, Calif.

Modern Language Journal, The. St. Louis, Mo.

Word. Journal of the Linguistic Circle of New York.

Modern Language Association

QUALIFICATIONS FOR SECONDARY SCHOOL TEACHERS OF MODERN LANGUAGES.[1]

(Prepared by the Steering Committee of the Foreign Language Program and endorsed by the executive boards or councils of 18 foreign language associations.)

	Superior	Good	Minimal
AURAL UNDERSTANDING	Ability to follow closely and with ease all types of standard speech, such as rapid or group conversation, plays, and movies.	Ability to understand conversation of average tempo, lectures, and news broadcasts.	Ability to get the sense of what an educated native says when he is enunciating carefully and speaking simply on a general subject.
SPEAKING	Ability to approximate native speech in vocabulary, intonation, and pronunciation (e.g., the	Ability to talk with a native without making glaring mistakes, and with a command of vocabulary	Ability to talk on prepared topics (e.g., for classroom situations) without obvious faltering,

	and to use the common expressions needed for getting around in the foreign country, speaking with a pronunciation readily understandable to a native.	and syntax sufficient to express one's thoughts in sustained conversation. This implies speech at a normal speed with good pronunciation and intonation.	ability to exchange ideas and to be at ease in social situations).
READING	Ability to grasp directly (i.e., without translating) the meaning of simple, nontechnical prose, except for an occasional word.	Ability to read with immediate comprehension prose and verse of average difficulty and mature content.	Ability to read, almost as easily as in English, material of considerable difficulty, such as essays and literary criticism.
WRITING	Ability to write correctly sentences or paragraphs such as would be developed orally for classroom situations, and to write a short simple letter.	Ability to write a simple "free composition" with clarity and correctness in vocabulary, idiom, and syntax.	Ability to write on a variety of subjects with idiomatic naturalness, ease of expression, and some feeling for the style of the language.
LANGUAGE ANALYSIS	A working command of the sound patterns and grammar patterns of the foreign language, and a knowledge of its main differences from English.	A basic knowledge of the historical development and present characteristics of the language, and an awareness of the difference between the language as spoken and as written.	Ability to apply knowledge of descriptive comparative and historical linguistics to the language-teaching situation.

¹ *PMLA*, vol. 70, no. 4, part 2, pp. 46–49, September, 1955.

	Superior	Good	Minimal
CULTURE	An enlightened understanding of the foreign people and their culture, achieved through personal contact, preferably by travel and residence abroad, through study of systematic descriptions of the foreign culture, and through study of literature and the arts.	Firsthand knowledge of some literary masterpieces, an understanding of the principal ways in which the foreign culture resembles and differs from our own, and possession of an organized body of information on the foreign people and their civilization.	An awareness of language as an essential element among the learned and shared experiences that combine to form a particular culture, and a rudimentary knowledge of the geography, history, literature, art, social customs, and the contemporary civilization of the foreign people.
PROFESSIONAL PREPARATION	A mastery of the recognized teaching methods, and the ability to experiment with and evaluate new methods and techniques.	The ability to apply knowledge of methods and techniques to the teaching situation (e.g., audio-visual techniques) and to relate one's teaching of the language to other areas of the curriculum.	Some knowledge of effective methods and techniques of language teaching.

Index

Cultural anthropology, 24–25, 215
Cultural content, in dialogues,
    68–69
  objectives, 150–151
  of picture exercises, 195–196
  stages, 31
  through target language, 30
  teaching of, 152–154
Culture, 215
  behavior patterns, 24
  and customs, 28
  EMU (elementary meaning
    units), 28
  and ethics, 30
  literature, teaching of, 26–27
  target, 214–215
  variations within, 29

Description, articulatory, 66, 87,
    213
  of intonation feature, 80
Diagram, facial, 87–88, 216
Dialect, 17, 215
  boundary, 22
  which to teach, 74
Dialogue, 61–69, 198, 214
  how long, 62–64
  memorization with use of charts,
    198–199
  teaching of, 64–69
  value of, 62
Dictation, 197
Dictionaries, 21, 115
Direct method, 4–6, 215–216

Ebbinghaus, H., 36
Elementary meaning units
    (EMU), 28, 151–152
Exceptions, teaching of, 136
Exercises, pattern practice, 84,
    103–113
  types of, addition, 101
    completion, 101
    composition, 102
    listening, 95
    multiple substitution, 98–99
    oral repetition, 96
    pictures, 195–196
    question and answer, 101–102
    simple substitution, 83–84,
      96–97
      in variable position, 97

Exercises, types of, substitutions
    that force a change, 97–98
    synthesis, 101–102
    transformation, 99–100
Experience, learning through, 39
  partial, 82–83
  total and partial, 40–41
Experimental research on learning,
    35–36
Experiments, suggested, 44
Expression, 16, 216
  learning of, 38
  as substructure, 12, 221

Facial diagram, 87–88, 216
Facilitation, 40, 216, 222
Facility, 39, 216
  necessary for use, 34
Film strips, 200
Fit, 135–136, 216
  teaching the regularities of,
    135–136
Flash cards, 197–198
FLES (Foreign Language in Ele-
    mentary School), 113, 216
Fluency, 34
Foreign language, 221
  (See also Target language)
Foreign-language learning (see
    Language learning)
Free selection, 113
Fries, C. C., 6n., 94, 114n., 149n.
Fry, E. B., 207n.

Gestalt theory, 35
Grammar-translation method, 4,
    92, 216
Grammatical patterns, definition,
    90–91
  teaching of, 92–102
Grapheme, 134–135, 216
  associating graphemes and
    language, 135
  teaching graphemes by contrast,
    135
  (See also Graphic symbols)
Graphic symbols, 18

Habit, 39, 105, 216
Hayes, Alfred S., 187n.

Linguistic atlas, 22
Linguistic geography, 22, 218
Linguistic ontogeny, 22, 218
Linguistic science (*see* Linguistics)
Linguistics, 18–22, 217–218
  contrastive, 215
  definition and function, 18–19
  historical, 21–22, 217
Lips, 213
Listening, process of, 33–34
Literature, 141–142, 154–157
  abuse of, 141–142
  background for, 156–157
  definition of, 218
  proper use of, 141
  purpose of, 154–155
  selection versus simplification, 155–156
Logographic writing, 18, 213

Machine (*see* Teaching machine)
Material (*see* Language laboratory; Programmed textbook; specific materials)
Matthew, R. J., 214
Meaning, associated with intonation in target language, 82–83
  as cultural abstraction, 12
  as cultural content, 12
  elicitation by drawings, 194–195
  EMUs (elementary meaning units), 27–29
  of phonemes (*see* Phoneme)
Memorization, 45, 68, 197–198
  with use of charts, 198–199
Memory, interference with, 73
  span, 34, 42–43
    in second language, 34
  store, 33
Message (*see* Meaning)
Method, direct, 4–6, 215
  grammar-translation, 4, 216
  linguistic, 6
  scientific, 7–8
Mimicry-memorization, 92–93, 214
Mirror, use in pronunciation, 87
MLA (Modern Language Association) qualifications, 10, 218, 230–232
Mnemonic devices, 194–195
  (*See also* Memorization)
Models, for perception, props and partials, 80–83

Models, in teaching sounds, 89
  in teaching vocabulary, 123–124
Monitor function, 34, 42–43, 218
Morpheme, 13, 18, 213, 218
  definition, 20–21
  representation, 20
Morphology, 20–21, 218
Motion pictures, 201–202
Motivation, 34, 42
Motor learning, 36
Multilingual areas, 214

Native patterns in teaching pronunciation, 87–89
Noise, 72
Norms, 218

Ogden, C. K., 116*n.*
Ontogeny, linguistic, 22, 218
Opposites in vocabulary teaching, 122–123
Oral approach, 214
Oral-aural method, 214, 218
  (*See also* Aural-oral approach)
Overhead projector, 200–201
Overlearning, 93, 219

Palmer, H. E., 4–5
Partial experience, 40–41
Partials, 65
  in teaching pronunciation, 86–88
Parts of speech, 13
Pattern practice, 84, 219
  definition of, 105–106, 219
  exercises, 84, 103–113
  and FLES, 113
  method, 93–102
  place of, 112–113
  types of, 106–112
Patterns, 219
  native, in teaching pronunciation, 87–89
  problem, 84
  teaching problems in, 136
Pavlov, I. P., 36
Perception, 80–82, 219
  in learning sounds, 85–86
  models for, 80–82
Phone, 219
Phoneme, 13–14, 213, 219

Recall, 34, 43, 220
  practicing, 68
Recall time, 43
Recitation, choral, 66, 83, 197
Reid, J. Richard, 203n.
Reinforcement, 55, 220
Reliability of tests, 169, 220
Response, availability of, 43
Rhythm, 79–84, 220
Richards, I. A., 116n.
Rigney, J. W., 207n.
Ruger, H. A., 36n.

St. Cyril, 132
St. Teresa of Avila, 154
Sandburg, Carl, 155–157
Sapir, Edward, 114n.
Scrambled textbook, 209, 220
Seashore, R., 117n.
Second language, 221
  (*See also* Target language)
Second language learning (*see* Language learning)
Selection, 84
Sentence, 12, 220
  basic, 62, 214
  use in vocabulary teaching, 126
Sentence patterns, 13
Sequences of sounds, 88–89
Set (*see* Speech set)
Shakespeare, William, 154
Shaping of response, 55, 221
Skills, order of, 43–44
Skinner, B. F., 55, 206, 208n.
  teaching machines, 206
Slide projector, 199–200
Slides, 199
Sound system, 14–16, 70–71, 79–80
  order of presentation, 76
Sounds, features of, 79
  functioning as single phonemes, 213
  nonlanguage features of, 79
  teaching of, 85–89
Speaking, process of, 32–34
Speech set, 33–34, 40, 221
Stress, 80, 221
Structural distinctions, 14–16
Structure, 221
  content as substructure, 12
  of expression, 12, 221
    expression as substructure, 12
  morphological, 221
  phonological, 221

Structure, syntactical, 221
Style, 221
  conventions, 147
Syllabic, definition of, 221
Syllabic writing, 18, 213, 221
Synonyms, in vocabulary teaching, 123
Syntax, 21, 221

Tabula rasa, 221
Target culture, 30–31, 221
Target language, 30–31, 221
Teachers, MLA qualifications for, 10, 230–232
  professional qualifications of, 8–10
Teaching, exceptions, 136
  graphemes by contrast, 135
  problems in patterns, 136
  regularities of fit, 135–136
Teaching machine, 221
  audio models, 206
  computer based, 207
  constructed response, 206
  evaluation of, 207–211
  general characteristics, 207
  more complex, 206–207
  Pressey, 204–205
  Skinner, 206
  written answer, 206
Television, 202–203
Test, automatically given and scored, 204–205
Testing, common practices, common sense, 161
  dictation, 161
  grammatical analysis, 159
  listening, 162
  objective tests, 160–161
  reading, 162
  speaking, 161–162
  translation, 158–159
  usage and correctness, 161
  words in isolation, 159–160
  written composition, 162–163
  new approach, native language factor, 165
  problems in language, 165
  situation versus language, 163–164
  structural understanding of problems, 164–165
  norms, 169–170
  reliability, 169